MEET
DAVE LASSAM,
THE MAN FOR THE JOB

MEET
DAVE LASSAM,
THE MAN FOR THE JOB

My 39 Years Service in the
Royal Australian Navy

DAVE LASSAM

Rev. date: 07/19/2022

To order additional copies of this book, contact:
Xlibris
AU TFN: 1 800 844 927 (Toll Free inside Australia)
AU Local: (02) 8310 8187 (+61 2 8310 8187 from outside Australia)
www.Xlibris.com.au
Orders@Xlibris.com.au
841549

Why Did I Join the Royal Australian Navy?

I suppose the best place to start is at the beginning – funny about that.

On Christmas Day 1959, in the small town of Rosebery on the west coast of Tasmania, my mum gave birth to a very good-looking baby: me. Rosebery is quite small and had a bush hospital where I was born, but we were not destined to stay there for too long. My dad was studying geology at university, but he needed to go to where the work was, so my family upped sticks and moved to Newcastle, New South Wales, when I was 12 months old.

We moved into a housing commission house in Waratah West, where we lived for about nine years. Now Dad wasn't known for his style back then, which is why he painted the house mauve with matching dark purple gutters. Yes, I was scarred for life!

In the early 1960s, I started school and quickly earned a reputation when I was 5 years old to be quite accident prone. On the second day of school, I fell down our front steps and fractured my skull; I was playing in the school yard and was climbing up a tree stump, slipped, and ripped open my left inner knee area on a rusty nail, and I fell off my cubby house roof playing Batman with my mate from next door. By 1968, we were moving again, this time to Brisbane in Queensland.

This was a big move mainly because my nearest relatives were back in Newcastle, and by this stage, I had two brothers and a sister. We moved into a Baptist church manse in the suburb of Sunnybank, a southern suburb of Brisbane. I suppose we had a pretty normal upbringing in a working-class area, but this would change after a serious car accident. As I recall, on Friday, 13 April 1969, Dad decided we should go back to

Newcastle for a holiday over Easter. We had an old EB Holden sedan, with the three elder kids being in the back and my little brother in what was, I remember, one of the first child restraint seats which just hooked over the middle of the bench seat.

My dad was never what you would call a good driver, and he could be very single-minded when he was trying to keep to a schedule. 'Impatient' is the word. So we headed off to Newcastle via the New England Highway; remember that this was the late 1960s and the roads were pretty ordinary. I recall at one point in the trip, the three of us in the back seat were fighting about something, and we were warned that if we didn't stop, we would be turfed out and made to walk! Yeah, right —but that's exactly what happened. As the eldest, I was removed from the back seat on the side of a major highway and left there, being told that they would meet me in a mile up the road. Then off they went. I eventually caught up with them after walking the mile or so down the road. Needless to say I was somewhat quieter for the rest of the trip.

Unfortunately, the trip did not end as one would have hoped. Near the town of Tenterfield, there is a bridge over quite a long drop to a river below. We had been behind a bus for some time, and as I noted before, my dad was not a very patient man. As we came onto the bridge, which was only two lanes wide, he decided to overtake the bus. Unfortunately, the car coming the other way could not stop in time, and we had nowhere to go. The result of the head-on collision left my mum with lots of injuries, and Dad had head injuries. However, we all survived, but it was to be the end of my parents' marriage within about fiveyears.

After they split, my brother Peter and I stayed with Dad, while my sister, Denise, and little brother, Ross, went with Mum. As is quite common in these situations, both my parents found new partners in due course. Without going into too much detail, I did not get along with my new stepsister, and the result was I was bundled off to boarding school. This was quite devastating for me as I was sent there in Term Three of my Year 10. There was no way this was going to end prettily.

Brisbane Boys' College (boarding school) was particularly nasty for a new boy who had no idea of how this system worked. I was bullied, assaulted, and given an all-around hard time. However, it did build my resilience to such things, and when I finished Year 10, I was allowed to go and visit my mum, who had, by now, moved to Launceston in Tasmania. I was told by my dad that if I came back, I would be sent back to boarding school. Needless to say, I stayed in Tasmania and started at a brand-new school for the rest of my education.

I started college in 1976, and in 1977, I was completing my Year 12 matriculation at Alanvale College in Launceston, Tasmania. Midway through that year, if you had asked me what I was going to do at the end of school, I would have said I was going to be a forest ranger with the hope that I might emigrate to Canada to work in Alberta as that had been a childhood dream. However, this was not to be.

I had applied through Forestry Tasmania for a position where I could advance and make a difference in the environment, which, in Tasmania, was a high priority. As you can probably guess, this did not happen. The Forestry Commission in Tasmania had, during this time, a lengthy period where they did not recruit any new members. So with that in mind, I was a little dismayed but continued my studies at Alanvale.

After our final exams, a few of my mates decided that they were going to join the navy as they wanted to be fighter pilots. After some discussion, I thought I would tag along and see what they were on about, and we all ended up at the recruiting office in Launceston, which was located at an army reserve base in the city.

There were six of us who attended that first day, and after chatting with the recruiters, we were given appointments to return and undergo the initial testing for joining. I had been counselled, and the best option for me at that time was to become a medic. All my mates undertook the same preliminary exams but had an extra area to cover for prospective pilots. I was the only one who passed! Little did I know then that I was about to embark on a most amazing career for which I am ever thankful.

After I completed my schooling, I was at a bit of a loose end until my call-up to the navy. So after a week at home, I went to a nearby chicken farm and asked for a job. The interview was short and sweet. The boss asked if I had a pair of gumboots, which I did. He said to go home and get them –'You are working this afternoon!'

After a fairly short wait of about two months, I received word via the local police that the navy wanted to talk to me. I was living outside a small town near Launceston called Longford at the time and had taken the job at the local chicken farm while I waited for call-up. On this particular day, I was at work, and the navy had to call the police to try to find me. I was informed by the police to contact recruiting, where I was told that I would be joining on 7 February 1978, a week and a half away. I immediately quit my job at the chicken farm and prepared for the next part of my life. It was an exciting time. Could I do it? What was it going to be like? How long would I last? All were questions that would be answered over the next thirty-nine years.

Recruit School and Medical School

On 7 February 1978, I signed on the dotted line at the Hobart recruiting office along with two other new recruits as we enlisted in the Royal Australian Navy. Little did we know – as most recruits don't, to start with – where this would take us. For me, it was the start of a career that would last nearly four decades where I travelled all over the world and was part of an incredible team–but let's not get too carried away just yet.

When you joined, you had the option to sign on for either nine or twelve years. Now at 18, I had no idea how I would go, let alone possibly last twelve years in the navy, so I signed on for nine years in the first instance as a medical sailor. You may ask why I chose to become a medic. After discussions at the initial recruiting interviews, it was suggested to me that I should consider being a medic. This was based on my mum's current employment, where she worked at the Launceston General Hospital, and her father's job during World War II as a member of the St Johns Ambulance in Wales, UK.

Following another interview with the recruiting officer and a full medical examination, I was deemed fit to serve and was offered a place in the 7 February 1978 recruit intake, which I was thrilled to accept. The day came when I was to travel to Hobart and be sworn in as a recruit medic. I still remember it vividly to this day, the three of us standing in front of the recruiting officer, raising one hand, the other on a Bible, pledging allegiance to Queen and country. After signing away our lives, we were taken to Hobart Airport to fly to Melbourne –no dramas so far. It was a bit foggy, but our flight took off on time, as I remember, and we arrived in Melbourne an hour or so later.

The recruiters in Tasmania had told us to take the SkyBus into the city, where we would be met by a sailor who would take us to our next stop, HMAS *Lonsdale*. This navy establishment was located near what is now

Docklands and was an administrative base mainly in support of the naval reserves in Victoria. The reason we were taken here was that we had to wait until the next day to get the bus to HMAS *Cerberus* because the recruits from Western Australia would not get to Melbourne until that morning. So we were to overnight at HMAS *Lonsdale*.

Now way back in the 1970s, it was a little different to how recruits are looked after. We were met by a sailor who loaded us and our gear into a light-blue-and-white naval car, and I remember being still quite excited about this next stage of my life. Now back in the day, all navy vehicles were painted a light blue with a white roof —no radio and no carpet. I did find out some years later that the cars actually had the carpet replaced with rubber mats, and even the radios were removed. Apparently, the higher-ups didn't trust the lowly sailors with having a radio in the car. This actually cost more as the factory models came with all the whizz-bang bits, but we were not allowed to have even the radio. Anyway, we were off, and after a short drive, we pulled up at the gangway at HMAS *Lonsdale*.

The driver told us we had arrived when he said, 'Go to the gangway, see the duty killick, and he will sort you out.'

Having no idea what he had just said, we stood and watched the car disappear down the road. Right at that moment, I was not feeling necessarily happy and wondered what the hell I had got into, but with no other option, we did as we had been instructed.

The entry point for every naval vessel and establishment is called a gangway. The seagoing vessels have the typical sloping walkway, and the establishments have security access for vehicles and personnel. So we three brand-new recruits nervously headed to the gangway of HMAS *Lonsdale*, where we were greeted by a duty sailor who promptly advised us to go to the SCRAN hall and ask for the duty victualler, and 'he will sort you out'. To say we were a little confused was an understatement, but we eventually found the duty victualler, who advised us that SCRAN was off, and he then sorted us out for bedding for the night. We were issued two blankets and a pillow –no sheets or pillow case, and were then advised to go to the accommodation block, pick any donger, and that was where we were to stay until the morning. SCRAN was on at 0600. Now what is SCRAN, you ask? It is 'shit cooked by the Royal Australian Navy', and it isn't as bad as it sounds; sometimes it's worse! Well, not really, but again, we were a bit underwhelmed by our first day in the navy. However, as new recruits, we just had to obey the orders.

The next morning, we managed to make it to SCRAN and were then picked up by the bus from HMAS *Cerberus*. It was driven by Petty Officer Weapons Mechanic Tom Lawton, who would be my squad's instructor. A rather loud, bearded man, he was to become our leading light. He had been in the navy for some time – I think about fifteen years – and he had seen it all, and despite his gruff exterior, he was a great bloke.

As you might imagine, we all had feelings of excitement, trepidation, and expectations about joining. The navy bus went via the SkyBus depot in the city and picked up the interstate recruits, and off we headed for HMAS *Cerberus*, the navy's premier training establishment. HMAS *Cerberus* is located adjacent to the small town of Crib Point in Victoria. In the days when I joined, it was about a two-to-three-hour drive from Melbourne as the M1 had not been built then.

On arrival, we were grouped off into our squads, given a 'welcome to the navy speech' by the officer-in-charge (OIC), LCDR Ochriemenko, and sorted out with accommodation. We were billeted four to a room with lino floors and no airconditioning, but it wasn't too bad –and so it began. We had been allocated our personal numbers or PNs after we had signed our enlistment papers. I did learn later on in my career that if your name was Bond (yes, it's true), they would do everything to make sure that your PN ended in 007. This would then be a lifetime joke as when we were paid on payday, we were given a paypacket, but to receive it, we waited in alphabetic order, and as your name was called, you called 'Sir!', took a step forward with your identity card in your left hand, held it up for the officer to view, saluted with your right hand, and called out the last three digits of your PN. So if there was a Bond, he would step forward, salute, and go'007, sir!', much to the amusement of all present.

This ritual had been occurring for many, many years, and it wasn't until sometime after I joined that they changed it to directly pay into your bank account. This solved a couple of problems. First, it reduced the risk of theft as we had a large number of personnel in one place with a huge amount of cash on the base which could be a target for armed gunmen. This did occur once – an inside job, as you would expect – but after this happened, every payday at the undercover parade ground, each point had an armed gunnery jack (seamanship/gunnery sailor) in attendance, and as *Cerberus* had two choke points for entry, known as the main gate and the back gate, at the start of each payday, buses were driven across the roads to prevent robbers driving out. This definitely solved the problem, and as far as I am aware, this only ever happened once.

The other thing that the automation of pay into bank accounts solved was that the amount of time taken to conduct a payday went to zero. Usually, the payday would start at 0730 until 0900. Then we had to return to our squads and march halfway around the base to reach our training school, and with all the usual phaffing around, we most likely spent two and a half hours doing not much, waiting for our training day to start. Remember, this was the 1970s, and it was how things were done. As technology came to the fore, this streamlined many processes throughout the navy. To this day, when someone calls my name when I'm out, mainly at a dog show, my immediate response is '563, sir!' Most of my friends know what I'm on about, but I still get some looks every now and then.

Before we got that first pay, we had to wait two weeks from when we joined, but the pay, although good, was not even a blip on my radar right then. A whole new world was opening up for me, and every moment of every day was new, often challenging but also character building. Now I don't mean here that we picked on others, but we were under pressure to perform – scholastically, physically, and mentally. This last point was very important as it inculcated the need for teamwork, and that credo is used to this day. 'The team works.'

So the next twelve weeks were spent changing us from civilians into sailors. We started by being placed into our squads, so immediately, we had a bond, and these guys would help one another do their best. We were allocated a cabin with four to a room; we each had a locker for our uniforms and a single bunk bed each. Once we had worked that out, we were taken outside, placed in our squads, and then the fun started. We had to attend the base clothing store, where we would be issued all our uniforms, but first, we had to march the five metres or so from recruit school to the issue centre. We took a fair while to get the hang of marching in step together, but the excitement of that day still rings loud and true for me. I was embarking, along with my new best friends, on an exciting journey; everything was new and had to be understood, and we, in turn, had a responsibility to add as much as possible to the effort to create this team.

Once issued with uniforms, we returned to recruit school and were immediately given instruction on how to iron our rigs (uniforms). Sounds easy, but you had to get this stuff right because if you didn't, you would get into trouble not only for yourself but also for the other members of your squad. Sounds archaic, and today you probably could not get away with it. However, it certainly sharpened the mind when you knew that there were always consequences to your actions. Still, I thrived; it was exactly what I needed. The training includes many things, as you might expect – how to make your bed properly, how to iron your uniform correctly, how to spit-polish your boots, first aid, survival at sea training, a swimming test, weapons training, naval history and lore, and keeping duties, to name but a few. With only twelve weeks to convert a civilian to a sailor, it is a very hectic program.

One of my favourite modules was firefighting. HMAS *Cerberus*, had its own fire ground to the western side of the establishment. Today there is a modern state-of-the-art facility which has a gas-fired ship's superstructure for firefighting, and a ship's section tilted over that floods with cold water to imitate a sinking ship. In later years, as the OIC of the medical school, I would supervise medics rescuing patients under flooding conditions; to say the least, the facilities are now awesome.

However, back in 1978, it was a bit different. Environmental considerations, whilst known, were not top of the list when it came to training. We had a job to do. So imagine, if you will, an Olympic-sized swimming pool area, not deep but nevertheless filled with furnace fuel oil, a huge oil pit that was set alight, and we had to extinguish it with water. Now we know that this is probably contradictive to what you might expect, using water on an oil fire. However, at sea, all you have is sea water and usually plenty of it, so we had to know how to put it out. We were suited up with appropriate safety gear, which was basically our working uniform wearing anti-flash protection. Trousers rolled into your socks and head and hand protection –it was and is still a major part of every sailor's kit when going to sea. The heat from this fire was very intense, and although we worked in a controlled manner, it was still a huge adrenalin rush for all us young blokes.

I would just like to point out here that we did have females in the navy, but they were trained separately from the sailors (I wonder why?)in a separate recruit school. Their initial training was a few weeks less than the men, and we only ever got to see them at SCRAN. This would change in the future, where all recruits were trained exactly the same way after the decision was taken in the late 1980s to send females to sea.

The twelve weeks went by very quickly and was completed by a 'passing out' ceremony. This involved the graduating class being the guard of honour, often attended by the senior naval officer of Victoria or even the chief of navy (CN). These ceremonies are seen as very important as sailors move through their careers. It marks the finish of one part and the commencement of another. When we had completed the day's ceremony, we had to move from recruit school to one of the ship's accommodation buildings in preparation for the next part of my naval career, the medical training school.

We were a rabble when we started, but by the time we had finished the recruit training, we had been molded into sailors. We lost a few guys on the way – figuratively speaking, that is. Not everyone who gets into recruit school manages to get through. It can be quite tough and rightly so. Some people just can't handle the discipline, or they get homesick, but mostly, we get through.

Medical Training School

Sometimes in the training environment, especially at a large training base like HMAS *Cerberus*, you don't get to start your next course for any number of reasons. So it was for me and the others who were to train to be medics in 1978. We had a two-week wait, and the navy had some novel ways to keep us occupied during these. One was the old 'paint the rocks white' scenario, which is exactly what it seems. *Cerberus* is a very large base, and to keep it looking good, the grounds and environs are meticulously maintained. So I spent that two weeks painting the gutters and rocks placed around the base. It wasn't too bad, but autumn was upon us when we were ready to start our medical training.

The medical training school or MTS was located directly behind the old hospital at HMAS *Cerberus* in what was the 'old' F Ward. This ward was used during World War II for sailors injured during this conflict. When I arrived at the MTS, I was placed in a class of around ten other new sailors, including females, who would undertake the nine-month training course to provide the navy with another cohort of medical personnel.

You will note here I deliberately stated above that we had females on our course. In the 1970s, not every branch or category in the navy – or, for that matter, the army or RAAF – allowed females to work. In the navy, the branches that did were medical, dental, driver, writer and steward. It was to be some years into the future that females were to serve at sea, so at that time, there was no need to train them in other seagoing categories. This sounds sexist, and it was. Since the introduction of enabling females to serve at sea, this has changed dramatically and rightly so. Of course, there were always going to be 'old salts' who grumbled about this in the beginning, but I am pleased to say the navy now caters for both male and female personnel in all categories, including clearance diver, which is a frontline category.

My medic course started in late April 1978 and went for almost nine months. This involved, as you might expect, some pretty heavy subject matters, including anatomy and physiology, the treatment of all sorts of maladies, from the common cold to some of the less glamorous diseases such as syphilis and ingrown toenails. We had to be well versed in nursing procedures. Why, you say? Well, no matter what we were to treat in our future postings, especially at sea, once the initial treatment had occurred, a patient may well require certain procedures such as wound dressings, suturing, and other basic nursing skills.

At sea, the commanding officer (CO) has a ship to run in both peace and war. The fitness and health of every single member of the ship's company (crew) is vital to the smooth and efficient conduct of operations. To enable this to occur, we, the medics, must be competent to help achieve these outcomes.

As you would expect, this training was intense, but we also had some fun, and our teamwork was starting to really become apparent. Of course, as in any workplace, you will have those who tick you off or want to challenge the authority. Of course, these sort of people tend not to last too long. The navy has always been a hierarchical body, and if you don't fit into these parameters, you are not destined for a long career. I would say here too that as I had initially signed on for nine years instead of twelve as I wasn't sure how I would feel, I was quickly finding that I was loving the job, even at this early stage.

We studied many things, as you would think, from anatomy and physiology to making beds with hospital corners and preparing and administering medications. To add to this, we were required to undertake duties within the hospital. Everyone in the navy had to undertake duties depending on what your rate or branch is. Medics worked after hours in the hospital; engineers or seamen worked around the base doing security, fire party, and a myriad other duties. Usually, it was a roster of around one in four days. Trainee medics worked from 1600 to 2200 each duty under strict supervision by a duty senior medical sailor. So as you can guess, we didn't have much time to get into trouble.

Although it was a long course, we all graduated on time, and I was fortunate to top the course. I was thrilled, of course, and was even more chuffed when the OIC of the medical school took me aside and told me he was impressed, and he had been keeping an eye on me during my time at the school. One thing that we learn and is promoted quite heavily is everyone's duty to show leadership even at these early stages. The OIC said that I should consider transfer to the officer corps. I was, to say the least, very happy with his comments, and I did keep his words in mind, but first, I wanted to get out into the naval community and do my job as a medic, especially at sea. I eventually did apply for and was granted a commission as a naval officer, but this was about ten years away, and is another chapter in my career.

HMAS *Cerberus*

Over my career, I have spent many years serving at HMAS *Cerberus*. This establishment is the navy's largest training base and caters for anywhere up to three thousand personnel at any particular time. There are a number of faculties which oversee all the schools, including those schools that are tri-service. This means the subject taught in these particular schools is comparable with all three services: navy, army, and air force.

I have worked out that over my thirty-nine years, I was at *Cerberus* for approximately twenty years. I love the place. Many do not. It is a training base, so the rules tend to be stricter, especially for the trainees. This is for good reason. To mold a civilian into a member of defence takes a little longer than the initial recruit training of three months or so. As the member progresses through the training and completes it, more restrictions are removed, and this helps maintain the ideology, which, as I write this, seems absolutely relevant because the more people that get double-vaxxed during the COVID-19 pandemic, the more restrictions are eased.

My first time at HMAS *Cerberus* was, of course, recruit school. Back in the 1970s, it was a totally different place to what it is now. Males and females were trained in separate environments and were not allowed to mingle other than under supervision during meals. It was somewhat archaic, but it was the way things were done back then. We even had to go to church on Sundays up until we were granted first leave ashore, which did not occur until one month after we joined.

HMAS *Cerberus* used to have its own train line and red-rattler train that would take sailors from the base to Melbourne, with only one stop at Frankston to let sailors off, and then express to the city. It was pretty awesome, and the remains of the platform can be seen adjacent to the coxswain's office near what is now the back gate. This used to be the front gate, but this changed some years ago to better monitor access to the base following the terrorist attack on 9//11.

After recruit training, I had a couple of weeks' wait until the next medical course started, so we ended up in a squad of sailors painting rocks around the depot –somewhat of a letdown, really, but it did look good when we finished, and we had to be occupied while waiting for our training courses.

My nine-month medical training started in April 1978 at the MTS, and I did quite well, becoming dux of the class, before posting as a qualified medical sailor to the Royal Australian Naval Hospital Cerberusor RANHC. Up until this stage, I had been under training and so had not really added anything to the navy, but now that I was qualified, they let me loose on the unsuspecting crowds, which was a great yet somewhat daunting progression. Most of my first posting was pretty uneventful except for the incident with the cow, the West Head incident, and a few others.

Sailors who were qualified still had to complete further on-the-job training, moving around all the hospital departments to get a good feel for all things medical within the navy. We also had twelve months to complete a competency logbook before we were eligible to go to sea.

HMAS *Cerberus* —
West Head Gunnery Range

HMAS *Cerberus* was one of my favourite postings. I spent nearly twenty years there off and on, from recruit to seaman medical under training and seaman medical (qualified).

One of the areas as a young medic you could be seconded to was WestHead Gunnery Range (WHGR). This is located at Flinders, Victoria, right on a headland. Here, the navy has, as the title would suggest, a gunnery range. The range catered for, in the 1970s, the 4.5-inch guns used on the DDGs, the 40/60 Bofors anti-aircraft weapons, and the .50-calibre machineguns. All these guns pointed out to sea and covered an arc of Bass Strait.

Being sent to West Head as the medic was quite a pat on the head. You were seen to be trusted enough and skilled enough to handle any medical emergencies that may arise. However, you could not just sit there all day, waiting for something to happen. So the medic was also the telephone operator and the keeper of the dog. Back in the 1950s–1970s, many navy establishments had a depot dog, often of unknown parentage. We had a dog at West Head who didn't like loud noise. So on the days the big guns were firing, you would find him under the desk at the medic's station, which was at the front gate to the range.

I was the medic in 1978–1979 at WHGR. I recall that I had not had to do much medical work at all for the first couple of months. No sailor had injured themselves. However, on one particular day, everything went wrong.

I had asked if I could be involved in a shoot within the 4.5-inch gunmount. There are two main parts, the gunhouse (turret) and the gunbay underneath the turret, where the shells are loaded. On this particular day, I was given permission to go into the 4.5-inch gun to see how it all worked. First, I went into the turret. The gun is huge, but inside, it can be a bit cramped. I was able to feel and see all that went on. It was amazing. The smell of cordite (no, not napalm in the morning) and the pressure wave one feels as the gun fires is surreal. After a series of shots, I was told to leave the turret, and I descended into the gun bay beneath. Here, I was tasked to load the cordite onto the lift, which went up on rams into the turret before being fired. It was during this exercise that one of the gunners in the turret dropped a 4.5-inch shell and tried to catch it before it hit the deck. Unfortunately for him, this would not end well —not that the injury was severe, a crushed fingertip, but as I was the medic, I could not leave the gunbay until the serial had been completed. When I emerged, I found I had a patient; some ice and drilling through his fingernail with a twenty-five-gauge needle solved the problem. On the whole, I had had a great hour or so seeing and doing some awesome stuff, but more was to come.

On this particular day, the weather deteriorated during the afternoon. By 1500, storms in Bass Strait made for a choppy sea, and visibility was reduced, so the anti-aircraft shoot for the day was postponed. Sometime during the late afternoon, HMAS *Kimbla*, an anti-mine ship, was traversing from Melbourne enroute to Sydney. They had encountered the storm, and unfortunately, as one of the crew (a chief, I believe) went to relash some forty-four-gallon drums to the foredeck, a freak wave hit the drums, and they broke free, hitting the chief and carrying him away. To the best of my knowledge, his body was never found.

At that time, they also had a number of sailors injured, with some head injuries and broken limbs. The bus to take the day staff back to *Cerberus* usually departed at approximately 1530, so we headed back, knowing it would be some two hours before the *Kimbla* could dock at the Flinders wharf. The HMAS *Cerberus* hospital had been put on standby and the ambulance dispatched. It was at this time that I made a decision to assist. Technically, I was off watch, but the urge to help was quite strong and has become stronger over the years. So I jumped in my car and headed back to West Head. I'm glad I did.

The ambulance had arrived at the wharf, and the weather was getting worse. Finally, the *Kimbla* came into sight, but she was unable to dock as the waves would have smashed her into the wharf. From memory, *Cerberus* had launched a workboat to come out of Westernport Bay, heading west around the point, into Flinders. They rendezvoused with *Kimbla* and transferred the injured to the Flinders wharf. I was able to help the transfer from the wharf up to the ambulance under the guidance of Petty Officer Medical Pete Laidler. It was a pretty precarious situation, but we managed to get the injured safely ashore and to RANHC. Here, they were treated and kept in for observation.

Little did I know this was just the first of many incidents that I would be a part of over the next thirty-nine or so years.

The Cow

One might wonder as to why I called this next story 'The Cow'. It is a little involved, but as it is etched into my mind, here goes.

In 1978, after graduating from the RAN medical school as a seaman medical (SMNMED), I was posted to the hospital at HMAS *Cerberus*. HMAS *Cerberus* is located near Crib Point on the Mornington Peninsula in Victoria and is the Royal Australian Navy's largest training establishment. I should note here that all RAN ships and land bases or establishments have 'Her Majesty's Australian Ship' or HMAS as a prefix. The RANHC building was one of the oldest on the base circa 1913 and was in pretty good shape considering.

As I was a brand-new medic (one of many), I was put into different areas of the hospital to gain experience across a wide range of duties. One particular duty was that of medical storeman. There were two of us working in the medical store at this time: Petty Officer Craig MacGregor, my supervisor, and me. The job entailed the ordering, receipt, and issue of all medical and administrative supplies for the hospital. This encompassed a wide range of products, as one might expect for a hospital.

The ordering system was pre-computer in the late 1970s, so each department would submit a paper request for stores once a week or as necessary. We kept a small amount of stock for common items but had to send orders to the army medical store barracks in Broadmeadows, Melbourne, some two hours' drive away from HMAS *Cerberus*. On the particular day in question, we had already processed an order about two weeks prior from the operating theatre for six-inch plaster-of-Paris bandages to be used by the orthopaedic surgeon for personnel about to undergo surgery the following day. Unfortunately, their order had been delayed and not received by HMAS *Cerberus*. So we had to quickly come up with a plan to obtain the plaster, which comes in a box of seventy-two, from the army medical store. The only way we could do this was to drive the two hours to Broadmeadows, get the box, and return. The army medical store was contacted and advised of our urgent requirement. They promised to have the box of plaster waiting for us at the main gate to the establishment on our arrival.

We tried to requisition a navy vehicle for the trip; however, we were advised that there was nothing available at the time. This, of course, was causing some stress as we did not wish to cancel the operating list because of this reasonably minor but important problem. The ward master, who was second-in-command of the hospital, then directed me and Leading Seaman Ross McInnes to take Ross's personal vehicle to pick up the stores. This was unusual but not unheard of and, in this situation, was deemed appropriate. Leading Seaman McInnes was an operating theatre rating and would be involved in the next day's surgical list. The ward master advised that we were to wear service uniform for the trip, and we set off for Broadmeadows at approximately 1500 hours (3:00 p.m.).

The trip to Broadmeadows was fairly unremarkable, although it must be remembered that the freeway from the Mornington Peninsula did not exist in those days, and it was nearing peak hour. We arrived at the barracks a little after 1700 hours (5:00 p.m.) and retrieved a large box containing the plaster. So far, so good. Now for the trip home.

About halfway home, we decided to stop for something to eat and called in to a pub. We did tend to stand out a bit as we were in uniform but had a pleasant meal. I do not drink (yes, the only sailor in 1978 not to do so), and Ross had only one small beer. Shortly after we finished, we departed for HMAS *Cerberus* via the Dandenong–Hastings Road. This road is very dark, well into the country, and only one lane each way.

At around 2030, we were travelling to HMAS *Cerberus* and on a stretch of the Dandenong–Hastings Road that was on a slight downhill grade, doing about a hundred kilometres per hour. A car was approaching from the other direction and, about a hundred metres away, flashed his highbeam in warning. Unfortunately, he did not lower his lights, and it wasn't until he had passed that we saw the cow. It was, by this time, only twenty-five metres or so from us, walking away from the direction of our car, but right in the middle of our lane. Of course, being a good sailor, I let fly a few exceptionally good expletives as I ducked down. I remember a very hard thump and the sound of breaking glass; then we careered off the road on the wrong side, hit a slight embankment, and rolled onto the passenger side, where the car came to rest.

I was OK, and Ross was not too bad, but he could not release his seatbelt as his whole body weight was on the clip. I managed to stand up inside the car, with my feet on what was my passenger side door. I tried to open Ross's door, but this was obviously impossible, so I wound down his window and made it out of the car. Another car arrived at the scene, and I asked them to call the hospital at *Cerberus* and get the navy ambulance to come and pick us up. However, a civilian ambulance arrived shortly thereafter, and they had the tools to extricate Ross. He was placed on the trolley and wheeled towards the ambulance.

I suddenly remembered that the box of plaster for the operations the following day was still in the car. I ran over to the car, wrenched open the hatchback, which wasn't easy as the car was still on its side, and pulled out the box. Luckily, they allowed me to take it in the back of the ambulance, and after a short trip to Frankston Hospital, we were seen by the emergency department doctors. Ross had blood taken for an alcohol test, and I was quickly checked out for head injuries. I then rang the hospital at HMAS *Cerberus*. It was about 2300 hours by this stage. The petty officer medical on duty advised me he would send the navy ambulance to collect us.

Around midnight, our ambulance arrived. The driver, an able seaman aviation sailor, was new to HMAS *Cerberus* and did not really know his was around the peninsula roads. I directed him home to the base, but more excitement was to come. As we approached Crib Point from the Dromana direction, we came upon the main intersection of Disney Street and Stony Point Road. At this place, we were supposed to turn right at the 'give way' sign to head towards the main gate of the base. The able seaman approached this at some speed as he was unaware of this requirement. We took the corner at well above the safe turning speed and nearly rolled the ambulance as well as just miss an oncoming car. To say it was an eventful evening was an understatement.

The next day, the ramifications of this started to become apparent. The orthopaedic surgeries went ahead successfully. However, when Ross submitted his report and request for reimbursement for damages to his car, he hit a brick wall. It was made apparent that there had been transport available, so we had not been entitled to take his vehicle. Of course, this was not true, but we were only junior sailors. Four years later, Ross was finally reimbursed well after having repaired his car, which nowadays would have been totalled.

We had been very lucky that night. I later found out that the cow had been destroyed, but they never did find out where it had come from.

After about eighteen months, my second posting came out, this time to the Royal Australian Naval Hospital Albatross (RANHA), which was located on HMAS *Albatross* near Nowra, New South Wales, followed by postings to HMAS *Melbourne* (aircraft carrier), HMAS *Harman – ACT*, and HMAS *Huon* in Tasmania. It wasn't until 1986 that I returned to HMAS *Cerberus* as a petty officer to become one of the instructors at the medical school.

Being an instructor to new medics (or any new trainee, for that matter) is a great honour. You have been given the opportunity to help shape future members of your particular branch, and it behoves you to do the best job you can. I had been promoted to petty officer not long before I came back to the medical school and had to undertake the RAN instructor course before I could teach anyone. Of course, you had to start off a bit gently, and as most instructors do, I started with teaching first aid courses to the new recruits, but by the beginning of 1987, I was ready for my first class of baby medics.

Wow! What an eye opener! I had nine trainees on the course –one male and eight female! It was a real eye opener but, on the whole, a thoroughly enjoyable time. In those days, we would have up to three basic medical courses, one or two intermediate courses, and one advanced clinical course (ACC) at any one time in the medical school. The ACC was undertaken by petty officers to give them the skills to provide critical care at sea in a two-man sickbay. It is still done to this day and equates roughly to the training of a paramedic. This course was also done on selection, and luckily, I was chosen to start the next course shortly after I had finished training my first basic course(more about this shortly). During the basic course, the students learned all about anatomy and physiology, how to handle patients restricted to bed, how to administer medications, etc., everything you would imagine.

One module of the course that I enjoyed was the EXPED. This stands for the medical expedition. It was, if possible, conducted with the advanced medical courses and usually took place out in the bush in Central Victoria. Now, you say, why would navy medics go out into the bush? It's simple, really. When medics go to sea, it is usually as part of a two-man team depending on the size of the ship. When you are deployed and out in the middle of the ocean, it is quite a long way to the nearest hospital if something goes wrong from either an accident or illness which requires urgent treatment. To try to give the illusion of being distanced from help, we take them into an environment which puts them under stress and see how they respond. This module takes a week and is also a good break from theoretical and practical work in the classroom.

The Softball Game

Physical fitness in the Australian Defence Force (ADF), as you would imagine, is critical for not only our war-fighting capability but also the mental health of everyone. Apart from the requirements to attend organised physical training (PT) and organised sports afternoons, the CO of HMAS *Cerberus* required all personnel to attend certain carnivals for swimming and athletics, and on the odd occasion, he would host a 'CO versus executive officer (XO)' softball match. The CO at CERBERUS at this particular time was Commodore Carwardine, and he had chosen his team from around *Cerberus*, as did the XO. I was lucky enough to be picked for the XO's side, and the day of the game arrived with no practice or other preparation.

The match was underway. I was fielding at second base when the CO stepped up to bat. He walloped the ball, which sped over the ground to my left a fair distance. I backed up to second base, waiting for the throw from the outfield...and here thundered the CO, around first base and heading straight for me. Now the CO was a big bloke. He must be six-foot-four in the old money, and he had a fullhead of steam and was bearing down pretty quickly. The throw came in; I took it outstretched, foot on base, as the CO cleaned me up.

I raised my gloved hand with the ball in my grasp and asked the question 'Howzat?'

The umpire at the time, a PTI, raised her finger. 'You're out, sir.'

He was not happy, but he walked.

Now you will probably be asking why I am mentioning a softball game from the 1980s here. The reason is about eighteen months later, I had completed my officer training at HMAS *Creswell* and, as part of this, had to attend a meeting in Canberra at the directorate of naval officer's postings. I attended the meeting, and while I was waiting in a small room, along the corridor came a senior officer, none other than Commodore Carwardine. As he passed the door, he glanced in but continued towards his office. Then he stopped and came back to the doorway and stood there.

As is customary, I jumped up to attention and said, 'Good morning, sir.'

He looked at me and said, 'I remember you. You were a petty officer at *Cerberus*, and you played that game of softball and got me out!'

I was pretty stunned that he had remembered me from that, but he did. He seemed quite chuffed that he had, and we chatted for a minute or so before he left. It may seem a small thing to remember, but it has stuck in my mind for all these years.

One of the highlights of this posting to the medical school was that I was nominated for and was awarded the prestigious 'Legacy Instructor of the Year' award for 1987. I was extremely proud of this and mark it as a result of some of the great times I had at *Cerberus*.

It was also during 1987 that I decided I was going to apply to transfer to the 'dark side'. By this, I mean transfer to the officer corps as a medical administration officer (MAO). I deal with this in another chapter, but I mention it here to give the reader a feel for what I was doing at the time. I was instructing my basic medical course and then commencing my ACC, which is quite a difficult undertaking. At the same time, I was undertaking Year 12 English at Hastings High School, which is about ten kilometres from *Cerberus*. The reason for this was having English at Year 12 was compulsory to become an officer, and back in 1977, when I was in Year 12, I didn't like English, and we didn't have to do it, which is pretty weird when you think about it. However, I managed to pass this, and also, I passed the selection board.

The selection board was also conducted at HMAS *Cerberus* by a navy captain, a lieutenant commander, and a psychologist. It is a pretty daunting thing to experience, being asked all sorts of questions about why I wanted to change over, what I would do in this situation or that situation. One thing you need to know here is that when you are an officer, it doesn't matter what your branch is – i.e. in my case, medical, you are an officer first and foremost. We are expected to lead from the front, back, and sides. Sounds a bit strange, but you need to be a bit of a 'jack of all trades'. This was fine by me as I wanted to be able to help influence young people in their endeavours, which is one reason I eventually went back to recruiting, but I had to pass this board first.

Fortunately, I knew the psychologist from my previous posting to recruiting, so I was not so nervous with his questions –but(and yes, there is a 'but') the lieutenant commander was playing bad cop this day. I vividly remember his last question and my response. He asked me a question about being a divisional officer (DO). Now almost every junior officer will, at some stage, be a DO. This is a vital position within the navy and one where the officer looks after a group of sailors, all those entrusted to his or her care. We speak to them, keep them informed, try to help them with problems, whatever they may be, etc.

Now back to his question. He asked me, 'What would you immediately do if you were approached by a female member who stated she was pregnant?'

Now this has ramifications for the member, so you need to get it right. I sat there, getting the points right in my mind, but I didn't answer swiftly enough, apparently.

The lieutenant commander said to me, 'Are you slow or something, Petty Officer Lassam?'

To say I was a little affronted is an understatement! I took a breath and said, 'Sir, if you suddenly dropped dead on the floor from a heart attack, I would be over to you and commencing CPR in seconds. I am trained as a medic and would hopefully save your life because that's what I do. Now you have given me a situation that is not life-threatening and one which I am unfamiliar with and not trained for at this point, so I'm taking time to respond in the most appropriate manner.' I didn't hear from him again at the board.

I returned to the ACC and awaited the results. The board results are important, obviously, and even if you pass, your promotion to officer is not immediate. I was informed that I had passed the selection board (I got an A+), but I continued training, waiting for the end of the year, which was getting close, and I waited nervously for the results to come out, which they did on the Friday morning that we commenced Christmas leave. Talk about cutting it close. I was not required to finish the ACC, which was a shame, but at that time, it was not required for me to be a MAO. I was actually only a couple of months' clinical practice away from completing it, but they said no. So I was told I would become a sublieutenant on 15 January 1988 and would commence the special duties officer course in HMAS *Creswell*, Jervis Bay, ACT. I had gone to the 'dark side'.

I undertook the eleven-week course at HMAS *Creswell*. I was posted to the fleet medical administration office for three months, which was located at the Garden Island Dockyard near Potts Point in Sydney and then to the Campbell Park Offices and the directorate of navy health for about six months in Canberra. All this time, I had been away from home, with the odd weekend being able to travel to Melbourne. By the end of 1988, my first qualified MAO posting came out. I was to be the new administration support officer (ASO) at the RAN MTS back at HMAS *Cerberus*. I would spend the next four and a half years there, being part of the training hierarchy. I loved it.

After my posting as the administrator of the MTS, I was posted back to Tasmania as the senior naval recruiting officer (SNRO). This was very cool for me. I had been here as a leading seaman medical but was now back as the boss. However, my time here was fairly short, only six months or so, when I was moved back to Melbourne to the defence recruiting office in St Kilda. These postings are mentioned elsewhere in my book.

After this, I was sent back to HMAS *Cerberus* to undertake the post of the RANHC MAO. I am proud to say that I really enjoyed what was to be the final year of the old hospital. A new hospital was under construction at the other end of the base. The old hospital was over seventy-five years old and had served the navy well, especially during and after World War II. There were quite a few changes over the years, like moving the medical school into the old 'F Ward', which had been used for cancer patients.

When the building of the new hospital started, my old mate Steve Pullman, then a brand-new sublieutenant MAO, was posted in to assist with the finalisation of the building works and organise the move from the old hospital to the new. This allowed me to continue to manage the old hospital as we were still operational right up until the day we moved.

The new hospital was due to be opened in 1994, but with work not being as quick as hoped, the opening wasn't until April 1995. I was to be the last MAO of the old hospital and the first of the new hospital. Steve had done a great job with the organisation of the move, and early in 1995, we had moved in. That's when the trouble started.

Health Centre Cerberus

Whenever a new building is commissioned in defence, there is a requirement to report all defects so that the builders could rectify them before we officially accept the building. One problem we did have was that the old hospital was demolished on the week following our move to the new one, so there was no going back. Now why do I labour this point, you ask? Well, I spent the next two and a half years trying to get the building up to speed and running properly as a hospital should. The defect list we had made counted over two thousand items that needed to be repaired by the builder before final acceptance!

So began the next two and a half years of my life. As the MAO, I was responsible for the day-to-day management of the health centre for the OIC. This, at this time, included ensuring the defects were being sorted out. Now you may wonder why I mention these. Well, they were pretty horrendous. To make matters worse, the company that built the health centre went bankrupt, and for a time, there was no one to ensure things got done.

Some of these things ended up being very long term; others were picked up during the build, and we managed to get them fixed. It got to such a state that the minister for defence (MinDef) – at that time the Honourable Peter Reith, MP – visited HMAS *Cerberus* to review the situation. On that occasion, it fell to me and the chief dental rate to give him the guided tour and explain the difficulties we had. It was a pretty nerve-wracking time, but I knew the navy medical and dental personnel had done everything to make the place work. In addition, someone (not me) leaked the story to the press, which resulted in a banner headline –'HMAS *Shame*'. This did not impress me one bit, but I knew I had done everything I could to help make the hospital the best in the ADF.

Some of the problems, which I am sure will make the reader gasp, are as follows. First, the design of the central heads and showers was wrong. The ward area was different from the old hospital. In the old hospital, we had two wards, which were based on the old Florence Nightingale design: a long area with beds down either side and the ablutions at the end. The new hospital was a totally different design, with four bed wards with shared toilet/showers, a central nursing station, and a second ablutions area for use by patients who are wheelchair bound. These were the typical disabled toilets/showers, which were much larger to accommodate the wheelchairs and/or assistants to help the patient. However, in the central section, when a patient used the shower, the water drained straight under the door out onto the carpet in the corridor. The concrete had not been laid correctly, so the water did not go down the drain. This all had to be jack-hammered up and redone.

To add insult to injury, when Sub-Lieutenant Steve Pullman and I carried out inspections, we discovered that the glass in the doors of this area had not been frosted. So if a patient was using the toilet or shower, you could see in! The bedpan steriliser, which was mounted in the wall of the sluice room, failed the first time it was used. On investigation, it was found that whoever plumbed the system in had used a tile sealant to seal the hot water inlet. So when the steam heated it up, it blew the joint, and the not-so-nice water ran out onto the floor and into the corridor as well.

Many of the floor areas covered by linoleum were subject to water ingress from ground water. The concrete slab sat on a quite wet clay base, and after it rained, the water leached through the concrete up to the linoleum and dissolved the glue. This caused huge bubbles in the lino, which were big enough to trip over. Whilst the original builder was still responsible for around twelve months, as I recall, before they went under, the willingness to fix these problems was less than spectacular. One of the ideas to dry the concrete slab was tried in the dental school section to see if it would work. First, they pulled up all the linoleum in one of the dental assistant training bays; then they plumbed in several large gas-powered industrial heaters while, at the same time, using plastic sheeting to cut off that section from the rest of the health centre, which included turning off the airconditioners in that section. This will probably sound pretty unbelievable, but let me assure the reader that this happened.

One particular thing that really had me worried was that there did not appear to be a fire suppression system within the building. Now as a young medic, I had been trained in aspects of safety, and we watched a video called 'Hospitals Don't Burn!'– but they do. I discovered that in this brand-new building, they had not even put in firewalls in the ceiling space! I found this out when I was shown where and how the airconditioner system worked. This could only be reached by dropping a roof-space ladder from the ceiling and going into the roof itself. There were twelve large air-conditioning units here, with the heat exchangers on the flat roof outside.

In the summer of 1995, Melbourne had a heatwave that lasted a week, with temperatures rising over forty degrees Celsius every day. With the added stress on the airconditioners, the system failed, and the units would trip out. Now this building had no opening windows at all to try to alleviate the problem, but as I had been shown how to restart each unit, I spent a lot of time up on the roof resetting them. It again sounds unbelievable, but I can assure you, these things happened.

The physiotherapy department was state-of-the-art, as you would hope. It also fell foul of the leaching water from the ground water up through the slab. The really unfortunate and expensive part of the repairs for this was that the flooring was a special rubberised linoleum that had been imported from Italy! As it needed to be replaced, a new order was placed. After some months when it hadn't arrived, we were told that our order had been in a cargo container coming via ship, but the container had fallen overboard in the Indian Ocean! So we had to go back to square one! It was eventually fixed but about two years after we opened.

There were many problems with this building, as I have noted. A couple of the really big ones were not easy to quickly fix.

The building was very large and only one storey tall, overall about 6,500 square metres under roof. The entire water system was located within the roof space and spread out to all areas of the hospital. It was all copper pipe, and this led to this problem. After about six months or so, we would come to work after a weekend away to find that the water was bright blue in colour. This was obviously not good. It was immediately reported, and we stopped usage of the water and had large water coolers installed for drinking water. The problem got worse and was a concern for all the patients and staff. We had the water tested, and it came back with a thousand times the recommended amount of copper sulphate within the hospital system.

The original fix was quite original and did work for a while but was never going to be long term. The idea was to connect a high-pressure discharge valve that had to be manually operated first thing on a Monday morning by guess who? Yep, me. The valve was located about halfway around the water circuit inside the roof. Each Monday, when I got to work, I would go to the laboratory and the pharmacy and get those areas to turn on their taps full blast. I would then go into the roof and turn the valve on. This flushed the system through, and as I said, it did work for a while, but the water wastage was horrendous as we left the taps on for half an hour each time. I gather that later after the navy accepted the building into service, the water conduit had been replaced by PVC, and the problem went away.

Near to the end of my time as the MAO of the health centre, after two years of trying to get things done, a specialist company was appointed to review the entire building and report on what needed to be fixed as a matter of urgency. Their findings were pretty damning of the company that had built it. Not only were there the two thousand–odd faults, but also, they discovered some rippers that we were not aware of.

The hospital did have an emergency generator, as it should, and it was housed on the outside in a brick building. I was initially shown how to do practice runs on it to keep the fuel from going stale as it was diesel. The problem was although it was installed, it had not been connected to the hospital. So it would run really well but didn't actually do its job. In another area where the high voltage came into a transformer within the hospital electrical substation, there was a large orange box mounted on the wall. This was where the master controls for the air-conditioning units were located. They were supposed to synchronise the units, especially when the outside temperature was high. As I mentioned previously, we had had some problems with these, and when the building inspectors reviewed them, we found out why. The lovely orange box on the wall was just that –a large orange box that had not been connected to anything! When the company that built it was under pressure to complete the job, they just bolted it to the wall – no inlets, no outlets!

One last mention here was what was supposed to be a focal point within the building. Adjacent to the main entrance was a place where patients would gather and wait to be seen by the desk clerk. It was quite large and had an internally sloping roof which peaked with a large skylight, which allowed an abundance of natural light into the building. It was a large square-based steel structure with glass inserts. Unfortunately, the roof beams on which it rested were pine. Now Cerberus is quite well known for its shocking weather, especially as we are very close to the coast, so the southerly winds during winter can be quite nasty. The original problem became noticeable when it rained in high winds. As the wind would catch the skylight, it would move it as the pine supports were flexing under its weight. The corner of the skylight would lift, and the water would pour in, run down the angled roof, and drop onto the carpet. The hospital cleaner and I were very adept at getting the buckets out when this happened. The skylight was eventually removed as it was a WH&S hazard and has been replaced by a large backlit medical caduceus, which looks awesome.

I am very proud of the job I did while the MAO of the Cerberus Health Centre and also very proud of the staff who worked in her, especially in the early days. We had hoped for a great new 'adventure', I suppose, with a new hospital, but for the first few years, it was pretty much a nightmare. It is today a shining light among all of the ADF's health centres.

At the end of 1997, I was promoted to lieutenant commander, which, at that time, was the 'ceiling' rank for the MAO branch —that is, it was as high as you could go. I was very proud of this, and as a result of this promotion, I was given a posting which has the longest name of any billet I have ever heard of. I was to be *the officer-in-charge basic medical assistant training transition action group or OIC BMAT TAG.* This position was based at Bonegilla in the Albury–Wodonga military area.

Death Ball

This story sounds quite nasty but, at the time, was quite funny. I believe in leading by example, and I think those who know me would agree. This particular incident occurred at HMAS *Cerberus* back in the 1990s.

Physical fitness is an obvious requirement for all defence personnel. At the navy's premier training establishment, HMAS *Cerberus*, this was compulsory, especially in maintaining the fitness of the trainees. Recruit school would get everyone to a certain standard, and this has to be maintained throughout one's career. Each initial course curriculum had to have compulsory sport on a Wednesday afternoon and PT at least twice a week. This was usually with PT instructors (PTIs) at the *Cerberus* gym.

The medical school under my command at this time also had another day for PT, which was almost always some form of team game. This was held in the early hours on the main oval near 'A' Block. Games ranged from soccer to touch football and the all-time favourite – death ball.

To set the scene, as I noted above, I always tried to lead by example, so I would turn up for all the PT sessions, Wednesday sport, and our game day. At about 0630 (6:30 a.m.), we mustered at the playing field for a game of death ball. All staff and students were to attend unless medically unfit. The idea of the game is for two teams to use a large lightweight ball, one of the types that people used to sit on in their offices, so about four feet in diameter. The idea was throwing, kicking, or passing the ball between two posts to register a goal. 'Sounds like fun,' they said. 'No one ever gets hurt,' they said.

One little added rule is that you are allowed to run with the ball and bounce it every few metres and knock over anyone in the way. If you have ever played this game, you will know that if you get run into by someone with this ball, no matter how big you are, you will bounce off! It is a good game of rough and tumble for male and females to play in the spirit of fair play. However, as any sailor will know, when you are in sports rig, rank has no protection; officers are fair game (within reason).

So here we are – it's about 0645, and the game is well underway. It was still semi-dark at this time during winter, but there was enough light to see. I had the ball and was running towards my team's goal. Suddenly, I had an opposition player, a young seaman medical nicknamed 'Squirrel', right on my hammer, trying to rip the ball from my grasp. Now Squirrel was not a big guy; in fact, he was a slightly underweight young man who was an absolute demon when it came to this game. As he pushed past me, in the tangle of arms and legs and cheering, he accidentally elbowed me in the left jaw, dislocating the right side of the jaw, which thankfully popped right back. I saw stars, and I was out like a light for about two seconds.

It took me a little bit to properly regain my composure and make my way to the base hospital to get checked out. An X-ray showed I had no obvious damage, but I did have a very sore jaw and a thumping headache. It took the rest of the day for this to diminish enough for me to go back to work.

This story doesn't quite end here. The set-out of the medical school was within 'A' Block on the second floor, with my office on the top deck. The classrooms for the trainees were on the middle deck, and each classroom's door had a small window so I or my staff could look in to see how things were going without necessarily disrupting the class. I decided to have some fun with young Squirrel and walked down to his classroom. I knew he sat in the back of the room facing the door, so I peered in the window and just stared at him. Of course, he quickly noticed me and realised I was giving him the death stare. I kept this up for a few seconds and then left, only returning in about half an hour to do it again.

I entered the classroom this time and spoke to the whole group about some medical school business, all the time watching Squirrel intently. Then I spoke with him and let him know it was OK. The knock I had received was deemed in the spirit of the game, and he wasn't in trouble. This may all sound a bit weird to the reader, but such is the rank structure of the ADF; being someone who knocked out the boss, even accidentally, was a big deal.

To finish this story, at the end of the medical course, which was some nine months long, there is a presentation day. At this event, there are also presentations that are not so official. I personally made this one to Squirrel; he received the award for being the only person to knock out the boss and not be court-martialled! It was a very funny day – that last day, of course, but one I will remember for a long time.

Dog Show at *Cerberus*

Over my career, I spent a lot of time at HMAS *Cerberus*, as I have noted. Many people don't like *Cerberus* as it is in Southern Victoria and the weather can be pretty ordinary. Plus, it is also the navy's largest training base and includes the RAN Recruit School, the School of Ship's Survivability, and quite a few others and, during my time, the navy medical school where I was posted on more than one occasion. This story, however, deals with something you might not automatically think of, and that is a dog show.

Many who know me will remember that my hobby was dog showing. I bred bearded collies for over thirty-five years and was a keen exponent of the confirmation dog show and also dog obedience training. Back in the 1990s, I was at HMAS *Cerberus* again, this time as the ASO of the RAN MTS. Whenever we won ribbons at a dog show, I would bring them to work and hang them outside my office so all the troops would see. Now this was not an effort to big-note myself to all and sundry. It was, in fact, to show the junior trainees and also my staff that you could do many things outside of the navy which can enrich your life and also those of others. Might sound a bit wishy-washy, but nowadays, when mental health has become more important, being able to show ways of improving your own mental health can help others.

So I was then, I recall, the president of the Bearded Collie Club of Victoria as well as being a lieutenant in the navy. On HMAS *Cerberus*, we had a community hall for all members called Club Cerberus –nothing fancy but a building at the edge of one of the footy fields where we could have functions. Sadly, now this building has gone, but back then, I asked permission of the CO if we could have a fun-day dog show for my club and if we could use the facilities at Club Cerberus. The only stipulation, other than picking up after the dogs, was that we hold it on the Saturday immediately after the base closed for the Christmas break.

In the 1990s, to ensure as many as possible RAN members got a rest, especially the instructors of the many schools located at *Cerberus*, we had to take leave all at the same time for a month except for a skeleton crew to manage the infrastructure on the base while the remainder were away. So I was given permission to do this.

On the Saturday mentioned above, approximately twenty people and their bearded collies arrived at the base. It was a beautiful day, and we had a great time. We also managed a walk around the base, which is over 1,700 hectares, and have some great pics on the wharf in front of one of the patrol boats that was then attached to *Cerberus*. This was well before 9/11, and security was not as strong as it has become, but all the members of the Bearded Collie Club really enjoyed the day, and it allowed me to show them a little of the navy.

HMAS *Albatross*— 1979–1980

My second posting after the hospital at HMAS *Cerberus* was to the navy's air base, HMAS *Albatross*, near Nowra in New South Wales. This base is a working airport for military aircraft and also had space for small civilian twin-engine planes that bought passengers into Nowra, mainly from Sydney.

My initial workplace in the hospital was the ward. This was to increase and improve my skills at nursing as all the medics rotated through the ward at some stage for this purpose. You have to remember that when you go to sea, often as one member of a two-man team, you will still need to nurse patients as well as provide emergency treatment.

HMAS *Albatross* was – and still is, I might add – a very busy and somewhat dangerous place. Anywhere that has military aircraft working sometimes twenty-four hours a day is bound to be so. As I have noted, the medics all used to rotate through the internal departments of RANHA.

When I arrived to start work in October 1979, the only area not manned permanently was the 'crash ambulance'. This was a large 4WD Ford purpose-built ambulance fitted out with three stretchers, one slung from the inside roof. When the crash alarm sounded, whoever was closest to the front of the hospital would race to be first to get into the truck. This naturally looked and felt quite uncomfortable as medics pushed and shoved to get to be on the ambulance. Not long after I joined, the senior medical officer declared that a permanent 'crash team' was to be formed so that when the alarm was raised, a team of medical staff could attend the incident in the most orderly manner. I was given one of the positions on the crash team as I worked in the medical store at this stage, which was at the front of the hospital.

There were three major incidents that I was involved with in my short seven-month posting to HMAS *Albatross*.

First, early in my time at the air base, I was on duty and had to sleep in the ward. The night duty medic remained awake overnight and monitored all the in-patients and took any emergency phone calls. On this particular night, at about 0100, I was awoken and told that we (the navy) had been requested to attend the hospital at Moruya, on the south coast of New South Wales, approximately one hour's flying time from Nowra. There had been a car accident, and a young driver was in a critical condition; they wanted to transfer him to the Royal Canberra Hospital, and we had the only helicopter in the area available at that time.

I quickly changed into my uniform and collected a Paraguard collapsible stretcher and also the doctor's bag. Both the medical officer and I would transit to Moruya via a Wessex helicopter to attempt the transfer of the civilian patient. We deployed to the airfield and prepared to fly out. It was to be my first ever helicopter ride, and the weather was bad. It was pissing down with rain and blowing a gale! Of course, I was excited but also anxious; I didn't know what to expect. I checked and rechecked the stretcher; the medical officer was checking his bag but after that, all you could do was sit and wait.

After about an hour, we approached Moruya Base Hospital. Moruya is a small coastal town with the hospital set a little inland. It was difficult to see because of the weather even when we were almost on top of it. The weather was still really bad when we arrived, raining heavily and still very windy. The hospital building itself was only two storeys high, and the helicopter pad was to the rear of the accident and emergency department. As we landed, because of the combination of heavy weather, wind, rain, and rotor wash, where the wind generated by the turning blades causes a heavy downward airflow, many of the windows in the hospital blew open, curtains being sucked out the windowpanes and flapping against the walls. Once we landed, the aircrewman in the back checked all was safe to leave the aircraft, and the doctor and I disembarked and headed for the emergency department. I was busting for a piss at this stage, so with the Paraguard stretcher on my shoulder, I made a quick detour to the heads (toilet), while the navy doctor went to review the patient with the civilian doctor.

I joined him a couple of minutes later and started to prepare the stretcher to take the young man to the Wessex. He lay on the emergency trolley with his head level angled down below the feet. This is to help maintain blood pressure using gravity to push the blood from his extremities down into his body and towards his brain. After discussions with the attending doctor, we prepared to move him. I had already opened the Paraguard, and we placed this on a trolley next to the patient. The intention was to move him from the hospital emergency bed onto the Paraguard in the safest way possible. Unfortunately, as we moved him to the Paraguard, his blood pressure dropped severely, and he died. His body had taken an absolute beating when his car hit the telegraph pole. This was my first time dealing directly with death.

I remember the doctor saying, 'He's gone, Dave. Let's put him back on the trolley.'

We placed him back on the hospital trolley, and I packed up the stretcher and prepared to leave the hospital and fly back to HMAS *Albatross*. This was an unexpected and eerie end to the duty for me. I wondered what else we may have done to save this guy, but I knew that there was nothing. It took me about three days to get over this; the feeling of numbness and loss, even though I did not know this young man, was quite extraordinary. However, as we all do, I got on with the job.

For my entire posting at HMAS *Albatross* from October 1979 until June 1980, I lived on board in the single male accommodation. This wasn't too bad, but weekends could be deadly boring. On one such weekend, in particular on the Friday after work, my mate Able Seaman Medical Jim Pratt and I went to Nowra to do some washing. The laundromat in town was a tad better than what was available on the base. This particular day, we had finished around 1300 hours and planned to go ashore around 1400, do the washing, and maybe catch a movie. That was until 'it' happened.

We jumped in Jim's car and headed down the road towards town. The road out of the base was a bit of a problem sometimes, especially in the wet. It was a country road and had several large sweeping bends and trees close to the edge. Unfortunately, it was also quite dangerous and had taken the lives of more than a few young sailors. However, that is not what made this such a memorable trip.

As we approached Nowra, we came up to a small bridge which passes over a small creek. On the near side of the bridge was, at that time, bush and then the creek and then the first buildings of the outer edge of town. As is the norm, the road narrows on the bridge and widens on the other side. As we approached this bridge, Jim slowed to the signed speed limit, and we both saw, pretty much simultaneously, a couple of kids on pushbikes waiting to cross the road on the right far side of the bridge, adjacent to a small rise in the road. As we got closer, one of the kids made a dash for it and made it across the road. The other young fellow did not move, and so we thought we would be OK in continuing, although Jim was slowing.

Suddenly, this young boy bolted across the road. Jim jammed on the brakes, and I swore, as if in slow motion, the car's nose dug down, but we kept moving. The front of the bonnet hit the young lad dead centre, and I remember seeing him turn to look at us and go white; then he disappeared under the car. Fortunately, the car had only about two feet of momentum left when the car hit him.

I jumped out as Jim was glued to the wheel, as one would expect. I dreaded what I was going to see, but the young boy got up off the ground with only a very small area on his elbow that had lost a bit of skin. I quickly checked him over, but he was otherwise fine, shaken but

OK. His bike was jammed under the car, and it had bent the number plate.

At this stage, his mother was on the other side of the road and in some state of distress. I helped the young fellow over to her and retrieved his bike from under the car. The mother had seen it all and in no way blamed Jim for the incident. As she left, she was giving the young bloke an absolute tongue lashing and a swift clip round the ear. It ended well for us, perhaps not quite so well for the young fella, but it certainly shook us up.

As I stated before, HMAS *Albatross* is the naval air station (NAS)for the Royal Australian Navy. In 1979, there was an incident that is worthy of mention. I remember it as being around mid-morning when the crash alarm sounded. We had no idea what had happened; we just deployed our medical team by 4WD ambulance to the control tower. From here, we would be told in which direction we needed to proceed. Of course, the adrenalin was flowing as we waited to be advised about what had happened. We were then informed that a Skyhawk fighter plane that had been practicing for the annual air show had crashed. HMAS *Albatross*, at that time, was well out in the countryside, surrounded by farms. In case of aircraft accidents nearby, the base has many gates to be able to enter these farms to conduct rescue missions or secure downed aircraft.

We were directed to leave the establishment via one of the access gates and head onto farmland adjacent to one of the runways. As we proceeded, we were again informed that the pilot had ejected and had been picked up by one of the standby emergency helicopters. So we were told to return to the hospital. We returned as directed and found the pilot had survived the ejection with only minor injuries. However, as much as this situation was 'exciting', the strange part was yet to be told.

Per the standard operating procedures (SOPs) for this type of event, the crash site was guarded overnight so that aviation crash experts could review the site the following day. Guards were set as required and routines set for an overnight watch. When the crash review team arrived the next day, they commenced their investigation. It did not take too long to work out that there was a piece missing from the aircraft: the fuel injection/maintenance pod. This piece of equipment was a large metal box which we understood to be the main control for the fuel in the aircraft. It was a very large piece of the plane and was very heavy. However, it could not be located even after thorough searching of the crash radius.

Interestingly, several days later, the specific piece of equipment was found behind a barbeque at a local park in Nowra, a good many kilometres from the crash site. To this day, I am unaware of the outcome of the board of inquiry (BOI) that would have been conducted. This mystery did lead to a number of fairly obvious assumptions made against the maintainers of the aircraft, but I never heard any more about it. This was my first taste of an aircraft accident; little was I to know how many more I would be a part of during my career.

Air Day at HMAS *Albatross* was an annual event held at the base and was open to the public. It allowed people and families to come along and see their tax dollars at work, with an air show with jet fighters, helicopters, and training aircraft, tours, and events. On Air Day, all personnel were tasked with being 'on duty'. The day involved a number of aircraft flight displays and access for civilians to hangars and static displays. I arrived at work at the usual time but found out I was tasked with another job: patient transfers from HMAS *Albatross* to two different hospitals in Sydney –the Royal North Shore Hospital (RNSH) and the naval hospital at HMAS *Penguin*, located on Middle Head. I was given an update on the patients – one was quite physically ill, and the other had been involved in a car accident the day before and needed surgery at RNSH.

I obtained the appropriate paperwork for the transfers and was given final instructions from the duty nursing officer. In those days, we were lucky enough to have civilian ambulance drivers at most of our naval hospitals. The driver and I saw to the loading of the patients, ensured their comfort as best as possible, and we left.

It did not take long to realise that this was not going to be a normal patient transfer. As we approached Nowra, the driver had to stop for traffic lights. This caused the patient who had been in the car accident extreme pain as the ambulance jerked and moved about. The patient had been given strong pain relief, but this was not working, and both the driver and I discussed the best way forward. We decided to use the 'lights and sirens' as appropriate so as to allow us a smoother ride. This worked well for a while but would also cause some consternation with the civilian authorities. I had informed the local ambulance controllers what we were doing and why, and they were happy with this but advised caution. They were quite helpful regarding advice on how to proceed as I advised them that both my patients were deteriorating.

I was told that when we approached the toll gates on the tollway (this, of course, being in the 1970s, well before e-tags), we should bear to the left as they had moved the barriers to allow us through. Of course, as we approached the tollgates, we found that they had not done this at all, and we had to negotiate one of the tollbooths at speed. I don't know who got more of a fright, me or the toll booth operator. Our trip had caused some consternation, as I said, mainly on myself. I was extremely worried about both patients and wanted to get them to their destinations in the shortest, most pain-free way.

Within another hour, we had made it to RNSH sans further sirens, although I kept the lights running. We unloaded the car-accident patient and then proceeded to HMAS *Penguin*. When we arrived, I was pulled aside and told that I had to call HMAS *Albatross* and speak with the ward master (later to be known as the MAO). I did so and was told that the New South Wales ambulance controller had called the naval hospital to see why we had been on lights and sirens and that a lady had complained about being run off the road by a mad navy ambulance. I told my boss why we had run with lights and sirens and was told that I had done the right thing; my patients came first, and we did not do anything dangerous. I was relieved, to say the least, at this outcome and, of course, ended up being the talk of the hospital until the next emergency. I will say one last thing about this incident: you learn something new every day, and whatever the outcome, you will carry that lesson into the future.

During my posting to HMAS *Albatross*, we did have some strange callouts. I was duty on one weekend, and I was called up to the 'patch' to attend to the wife of a serving member. The 'patch' is the name given to the housing on the base for married members of the RAN. We normally do not treat civilians; however, we can apply life-saving assistance while we wait for a civilian ambulance to arrive. This particular case was interesting as it was also the start of my 'collection' – venomous and non-venomous spiders.

I arrived at the house in the patch by our ambulance and was taken inside to look after the wife of one of the petty officers posted to HMAS *Albatross*. She was a Māori lady and was feeling quite unwell. The only thing that she complained of, other than feeling very unwell, was that she had a red raised lump which was very sore on her lower leg. After the usual checks on pulse and respirations, I checked her all over and found the site of her discomfort. I ensured that a civilian ambulance had been called and continued to check her for a possible cause. She had been in bed earlier that morning when she advised that she had felt a bit of a sting on her leg. She had not worried about it, but when she started to become ill shortly afterwards, her husband called us.

I discovered that she had been bitten by a spider, which I found dead near where her feet had been in the bed. It looked like a redback. I immediately carried out the first aid for a redback bite, applying a cold compress, and awaited the arrival of the civilian ambulance. They took her to Nowra Hospital and administered the appropriate anti-venom. This incident gave rise to my collecting, whenever I could, spiders and scorpions from the local area to use as a form of database in the future if spider bites occurred. I had quite a few specimens in formalin in my office area, including the ever-present funnel web spiders.

Nearing the end of my posting to HMAS *Albatross*, I was involved in something that was quite distressing to a junior sailor who had only been in the navy for two years: the court martial of a senior officer. Just a quick sidenote: a junior sailor, as the name implies, is a person of lower rank, anywhere from seaman and able seaman to leading seaman. Then there are the senior sailors, ranging from petty officer and chief petty officer to warrant officer. Then there is the officer corps. Junior officers are midshipmen and sub-lieutenants to lieutenants. Senior officers are usually lieutenant commanders, commanders, and captains. Those higher in rank than this are called flag officers and are entitled to show flags on their command flagstaffs or vehicles in which they travel.

Now back to the story. Up until the mid-1990s, it was still 'illegal' to be gay in the ADF. Later in my career, as a recruiting officer, we had to ask the question of any prospective candidate 'Are you gay?' So needless to say, in the 1970s, being gay in the navy was a no-no. However, one of our senior doctors was, and he had been accused of using his position to attempt to coerce a young sailor under his care to undertake a homosexual relationship. There had been some disquiet and rumours floating around about this situation, and I was unfortunately dragged into it. On another weekend duty, I was called into the duty doctor's office and spoken to by the above mentioned officer. He asked me to take a sealed envelope to the onboard cabin of a sailor who had been recently in our hospital. I was told the room number and the block in which this sailor lived and proceeded to deliver the letter. However, the member was not in, and I returned the envelope to the officer. This act got me an invite to the senior officer's court martial!

When charges were laid against him some several weeks later, I was advised I had to make a deposition at the judge advocate general's office in Sydney. I was the only sailor required to do so and was escorted there by two senior nursing officers who were also giving evidence. It was a most upsetting and worrying time for me. I had only been in the navy for a short time, and here I was, about to give evidence against a senior officer. I returned to work and was advised that I would have to wait until the official trial began. Fortunately for me, in the end, I was not required to attend the court martial. Remembering that in those days, it was 'illegal' to be gay in the Royal Australian Navy, the punishment meted by the court when they found him guilty was always going to include discharge from the service.

Shortly after this time, I was posted out to my first sea posting: HMAS *Melbourne*, the RAN's flagship and only aircraft carrier.

The Ghosts

Not everyone believes in ghosts. I don't think I did until after I had joined the navy. This is particularly relevant to navy medics as all the ghosts I have felt were in our naval hospitals or in areas that had once been navy hospitals.

The three navy hospitals that I have been posted to over the years are HMAS *Cerberus* in Victoria, HMAS *Albatross* in New South Wales near Nowra, and HMAS *Penguin*, which is lodged on Middle Head in Sydney, New South Wales. The HMAS *Cerberus* hospital had seen many transitions over the years. The first building erected at HMAS *Cerberus* back in 1913 was to be the front office of the hospital, which stood near the wardroom for almost seventy-five years. There were several wards and laboratories, mainly used during World War II. Later, these wards became the medical school, where I was posted several times during my career.

My first 'encounter' occurred in early 1979. By that stage, I had graduated as a medic and had been posted to RANHC. I was on duty this particular day/night as a member of the emergency party. We had our own ambulances and were required to stay the night in the duty quarters. This was a small office-like room which held two sets of bunk beds. It was located on the walkway between the medical ward and the X-ray department. The walkway had a covered veranda that connected most areas of the hospital. It was also the route that the night duty medic would take from the duty station in the surgical ward to the duty quarters if we were required to go out in the ambulance. When we were called out, which was quite often, I would wake at the slightest sound of running/fast walking feet on the boards of the walkway as the medic made their way to wake us up and go to the emergency.

On the night in question, at about 0230 hours, I heard footsteps coming up the walkway and immediately jumped out of bed and started to get ready to deploy in the ambulance. However, the footsteps, which were quite loud, kept going past the door. This was quite strange, so I went to the door, opened it, and stuck my head out to see what was happening. To my utter surprise, there was no one there, *but* the footsteps continued down the walkway towards the front officer area.

Needless to say, the phoofer valve clenched rather quickly, and I pulled my head in and slammed the door. It was one of those moments where 'fight or flight' was about to kick in. I told the other members of the team what had happened as they had heard the steps too. It was a very fitful night's sleep after that!

My other 'encounter' at RANHC occurred many years later in the old F Ward, which had become the medical school. At the time, in 1990, I was the ASO, having been promoted to lieutenant in that year. It was one of those jobs that was high demand, so I would sometimes come in to work on the weekends to prepare for the upcoming week. Also, at this time in my career, I was quite into dog showing. We had two bearded collies at the time, my old boy Zac and a younger bitch, Bonnie.

On the Saturday evening, I decided to go to work for a couple of hours, and I took Zac with me. He had been to the medical school before, and it had not concerned him. As I opened the side door to the medical school, which was the old 'F Ward', I got the classic chilled feeling, but (note it was winter) I wasn't too concerned. Zac, on the other hand, was having none of it. He refused to come in the door and carried on so much, I took him back to the car. I decided to grab the paperwork and take it home to the married quarters, so I returned to the building.

The F Ward corridor is quite long and had been a cancer ward many years earlier. Several older sailors had passed away in the building, and there were always the tales of ghosts. I now wholeheartedly believe in them. The moment I walked in, I felt the temperature drop, and I had a really bad feeling I was being watched. Now there will be those among you reading this who will think I'm full of it for suggesting this, *but* this feeling of being watched was so powerful and disconcerting that I quickly left. After this experience, I never went back into the building at night. Other sailors had told me of similar feelings and even apparitions over the years, especially when the building was a cancer ward.

I did have another fright during my posting to HMAS *Albatross* in 1979. HMAS *Albatross* is the home of the fleet air arm, as I have noted earlier. In those days, when we had an aircraft carrier, all fixed-wing aircraft and helicopter squadrons were based at HMAS *Albatross*, but when the *Melbourne* deployed, she would embark several squadrons, including Skyhawk fighters, Grumman tracker antisubmarine (folding wing) aircraft, Seaking helicopters, and Wessex helicopters. There were many days and nights of flying at the base, and we had to have twenty-four-hour medical cover for flying but also to cover the operating theatre and general sickbay duties. It was on one of my night duty weeks that this next incident occurred.

The layout of the hospital was fairly simple. It consisted of a single-storey building with two entrances: one for the ambulance and the main doors. There was a corridor which ran from the front entrance right through to the rear of the hospital. The initial area was for outpatients, with a pharmacy, laboratory, and administration office all towards the front. As you walked down the main corridor, another corridor went off to the left at about a reverse sixty-degree angle. This, in turn, went to the operating theatre and also the WRANS ward. At this time, females were enlisted into the navy as members of the Women's Royal Australian Navy. As such, as was done at the time, they had separate quarters onboard and also a separate ward in the hospital if they were admitted to RANHA. Further down the corridor was the main ward on the left, and the recreation room (basically a covered veranda) was at the rear. On this particular evening, I had arrived for duty and had been given a handover from the evening staff. There were only a few patients in the main ward, no females in the WRANS ward, and there was no night flying. So all and all, a pretty quiet night was expected.

As part of the night duty, I had to undertake rounds every hour or so. This included checking all entrances were locked and windows shut if required. There was no wind that night. Now this is an important fact. It was a still night, no storms or breeze of any kind. At around 0230, as I remember, I was conducting a set of rounds and was walking down the main corridor. Only a few internal lights were on. I had just passed the corridor to the operating theatre when every window along that section suddenly slammed shut, not altogether but as if someone was running their fingers over piano keys. To say I crapped myself was an understatement. The bangs were intensified by the fact that it was so quiet within the hospital walls. I did, nervously, torch in hand, go down the theatre corridor to see if I could work out what had happened. There was no other explanation other than a ghost of sailors past had been having a go at me. I still get goosebumps just thinking about it. I did report this to my workmates the next morning. They did, of course, take the piss out of me and said I was a goose, but to this day, I swear that this happened.

HMAS *Melbourne*: CVS 21 –
Aircraft Carrier— 1980–1982

My first seaposting was not what I had originally requested. Once every year, we would have a report raised on us which covered all sorts of things, including competency, adherence to naval traditions, dress, bearing, and leadership qualities, to name a few. At the same time, we were required to submit a form with preferred postings out as far as five or ten years. I had filled in my preference card (note that at that time, I was single and had yet to go to sea), but I was somewhat dismayed to find out where I was going next.

I joined the aircraft carrier HMAS *Melbourne* on Friday, 13 June 1980. The ship was in dry dock at the Garden Island Dockyard in Sydney at the time, and back in those days, if you were not married, you lived onboard the ship, even in drydock. The trouble with this was that you had to step ashore to use the heads (toilet) or have a tubs (shower) as, at that time, when at sea, all grey water was pumped straight over the side, which is not a good thing in a dry dock.

I must admit that the *Melbourne* was not my first choice for sea posting. I would rather have gone to one of the destroyer guided missiles (DDGs) or destroyer escorts (DEs). However, with a posting to HMAS *Albatross* prior to this, I guess the writing was on the bulkhead (wall). HMAS *Melbourne* had a bit of a bad reputation; some say she was jinxed. This came about from the two collisions she was involved in, one in 1964 and the other in 1968. As well, in 1980, she was quite old, being a World War II design, having been built in 1955. However, as I was to find out, she wasn't a jinx at all. She was one of the best ships in the fleet as far as I was concerned and was a great start to my seagoing career.

The first thing I recall about the sickbay on the *Melbourne* was that in the ward, there were eleven beds, including the resuscitation bed, one toilet, and a bath/shower. The only other bath on the ship was in the admiral's cabin.

I lived in 3 Delta Starboard Mess. The nomenclature means we were three decks down from the flight deck, 4 Bulkheads, back from the pointy end, and on the righthand side of the ship. All of our warships at that time were of British design and used this form of mapping within the ship. It did take a little while to get the hang of it, but it became second nature quite quickly. Later warships of U.S. design had a different nomenclature, but I won't detail it here. Needless to say, living in a mess which was about ten metres long and three or four wide was quite a shock as there were thirty or so men in this compartment. So we were woken at 0600, as I recall, to the sound of 'Wakey, Wakey', which was by bugle call. Then we left the ship via the gangway to the demountable showers, returned on completion of ablutions for SCRAN, and went into the sickbay for work.

I was initially involved in the medical store as I had had some experience of this at HMAS *Cerberus* and HMAS *Albatross*. My workspace was literally like the inside of a wardrobe, approximately six feet long and four feet wide. It was very tight and extremely noisy when we were underway. However, I really enjoyed this part of my job, but as you would expect, all the medics rotated through a few of the areas within the sickbay and even to other areas of the ship. During my posting to the *Melbourne*, I did get to 'drive' the ship by doing some time on the helm. It was a bit different back then, with a large wheel of the type you see in old movies; nowadays, it is a very small dial on the panel which is on the bridge. On the *Melbourne*, the helm was on 2 Deck, below the flight deck, and had no access to any windows! All you had to look at was a giant linear compass on the bulkhead directly in front of the wheel. It was something definitely different, and as I learned throughout my career, even though some say never to do it, I volunteered to undertake many different experiences which actually gave me a better feel for life in the ADF.

After she was released from the drydock, we had to prepare to go to sea for what was known as workups. These are a number of exercises and drills carried out while underway to test the seagoing integrity of the ship and crew. On the first day we sailed for workups, I was quite nervous. I hoped that I would not get seasick, but even on a ship the size of the *Melbourne*, this was possible. The head of the medical department was Surgeon Commander John T. Clift, RAN. Unfortunately, he had a bit of a different sense of humour when it came to his staff, and he would often try to make one of us suffer. On that first day, it was me.

CMDR Clift directed that I paint the heads (toilet) as soon as we were underway. Now I don't know if any of you have been put in a small room the size of a toilet cubicle, no windows or air, have had the door shut, and have had to paint the floor and walls – as well as being on a ship that started to roll. Yes, I know it was an aircraft carrier, but it did roll a bit when we passed through Sydney Heads out into the Pacific Ocean. I was OK for a while, but the smell of the paint and the motion and the fact that the water in the bottom of the toilet moved up and down as well with each pitch and yaw as we moved through a wave –needless to say, I did not last too long before I was driving the 'porcelain bus', not an auspicious start, but I guess it was to be.

As sailors past and present know, it's not all piña coladas and getting a tan, being at sea. We do actually work. We also train –a lot. The type of training and specifics may have changed in some areas, but in the main, everyone must undertake proficiency training especially designed to keep us current at sea. This includes first aid, damage control, firefighting, collision-at-sea drills, man-overboard drills, abandon-ship drills, and (especially being on an aircraft carrier) crash-on-deck drills. This one would benefit me greatly on the *Melbourne* but also for future sea postings, in particular HMAS *Kanimbla*.

One of the training evolutions that really stuck in my mind occurred in 1980, as I remember. HMAS *Melbourne* was deployed to Jervis Bay on the New South Wales south coast and was tasked with protecting HMAS *Creswell* from attack from 'enemy' forces which had been building up on the western side of this naval base. HMAS *Creswell* is the RAN's officer training establishment, and even though I didn't know it at the time of this exercise, I would be returning some eight years in the future to undertake officer conversion training. More of that later.

The exercise would commence at around 1600, and crew from the *Melbourne*, which was moored in Jervis Bay, were to land via boat and helicopter and establish a headquarters within the base. I was chosen to be one of the junior medics that were to transfer to the base by helicopter. I had been on a Wessex helicopter before, and I still remember the exhilaration of this short journey. We landed on the main playing fields and made our way – carrying medical equipment, including army stretchers – to the headquarters and set up a small sickbay to triage and treat 'wounded' sailors. So far, so good. Not much happened for the first hour or so, not that we had much feedback; the old 'hurry up and wait' routine was the order of the day, but this was to change pretty quickly.

We were waiting for the word to go and render assistance when the door of the headquarters burst open and a young sailor who looked like he had seen a ghost staggered through the door. He was pretty upset, and it took a couple of seconds for him to make sense. Now a small divergence. We had been told that the opposition would actually be members of the SAS. Those of us that carried weapons were not issued ammunition but were told that when you contact the enemy, you shouted, 'Shot fired! Shot fired!' It was then up to umpires to designate who was alive/dead or wounded –simple enough, but the SAS had a slight advantage over us. They had been issued with heaps of blank ammunition which was near its expiry date and so had to be used or later destroyed!

Now back to the young sailor. Apparently, during the exercise, he had decided to sneak a smoke behind a tree, which, as you may guess, wasn't really the sensible thing to do. He was puffing away happily and gave his position away. The SAS soldiers snuck up behind him and, at the right moment, fired a round into the air. He had no idea what had happened, but he screamed in fright and bolted for the HQ. By all accounts, the SAS guys had a great laugh at his expense.

So now we were aware that the opposition had a distinct advantage, but it was all part of the realism of training back then. Shortly after the sailor had told us about the blank rounds, the first call came out for a medic. I went with a couple of 'armed' sailors to pick up a wounded enemy combatant. We made our way to where we had been told the casualty was, and I carried out first aid on a bullet wound to his leg. Now it was dark; visibility was OK, but the enemy decided I was too slow. So suddenly, they started firing from the bush about thirty metres away. This spurred us to move quicker, and we placed the patient on the stretcher and headed off. As we started to get closer to the headquarters, we again came under fire. I immediately stopped our run and took cover for a few minutes to see if we could lose the enemy.

Shortly, I resumed the return of the patient to the headquarters, and the doctor took over his treatment, and the naval police took him into custody. This is when it all went to poo. I had just finished my handover when the door opened and a naval commander walked in, sporting an umpire's armband. He walked up to the enemy patient and got him to take off his shirt – he had three sticks of dynamite strapped to his body! I couldn't find a hole to crawl in quick enough. I thought I may have stuffed up very badly and the headquarters had been blown up. However, because I had stopped on my return with the patient, he designated that the bomb had gone off well before we entered the HQ. It is a lesson I have never forgotten, and the naval police also got their knuckles rapped as they had frisk-searched him and had not found the dynamite.

All in all, many valuable lessons were learned and one I've never forgotten, especially in later years. We were perhaps not attuned as we should have been to 'terror'-type events back then, but that, as we know, all changed in 2001.

Deploying to the Indian Ocean

The Indian Ocean deployments were quite common many years ago, but as time went on, they diminished as our role in the area changed, particularly after 9/11. However, they were conducted for a reason, both politically and militarily. On the last Indian Ocean trip, the trouble started even before we left Australia.

We had conducted our workups along the south coast of New South Wales and had been designated fit to sail. Unfortunately, there were some in the civilian community, in particular the dock workers, who were anti-military, and on the day we were supposed to leave, the union called a strike of waterfront workers, including tugboats and wharfies, who let go the lines for us to leave port.

On this occasion, we were at Procedure Alpha, where all sailors not required below decks were to be in the appropriate uniform for that time of year, muster on the flight deck in an orderly fashion. This does look quite spectacular, as the reader may attest to when seeing Australian or foreign warships entering or leaving harbour.

So we are all on deck, waiting for the ship to depart. Because of the aforementioned strike action, sailors from other ships not deploying were required to take over the jobs of handling the lines from on shore and removing the gangway, which required a crane. However, how were we to actually make our way out to sea without a tugboat to ease us out from the wharf and turn us into Sydney Harbour? The answer was quite simple and had been used many times long ago to do this but had not been used for many years.

The ship was obviously under power, but we needed to get the bow to move away from the wharf first and then apply power to drive the ship forward. Just a quick interlude here: the *Melbourne* always docked starboard side to. This means that when we came back to Sydney, she backed into the wharf space, which was then known as the fitting-out wharf. This allowed the island or superstructure to be on the correct side next to the wharf when we departed.

So to get started on my first overseas trip with the grey funnel line (an affectionate name for RAN ships), the captain lowered the port-side anchor or pick, as it's called. Once it had reached the bottom of the harbour, he ordered the pick to be weighed, and as it dug in before it came up, this forced the bow to move towards the port side or the left.

I recall he only had to do this twice to get the bow heading into the safest area before applying forward power. It was an awesome move and really stuck it to the wharfies, who thought they had stopped us from going. I was never sure of the real reasons they were against the trip, but I was only an able seaman at the time, and that particular political information was of little concern to me. I was just glad we were underway.

Many of my memories of serving on the *Melbourne* are of the daily things we did which were often a bit dull and boring, just like any other job. Still, some incidents were very quick to develop, and if you weren't what we now call 'situationally aware', things could come back to bite you. It wasn't all bad by any means, and we did actually have some fun on board.

At night time, when things were usually quiet, the off-watch medics would gather in the sickbay where there was a little more room to play mah-jong. This is an ancient Chinese game similar to cards/dominoes but with a naval flair. It was a great way to de-stress after a particularly long day or one filled with a bit more action than may have been expected.

On the odd occasion, we were not able to fly aircraft through another nation's airspace. In 1980, we were traversing to Singapore and making our way through Indonesian waters. As we weren't flying, a wire guard rail was placed at the front of the flightdeck. After one particularly long eighteen-hour day, ABMED Grant 'Bungy' Williams and I decided to see if we could sneak up to the flight deck for a look. It was about 2330 or so and very dark when we climbed up and over the starboard Bofors gun sponson and quickly made our way forward. At night, with no aircraft or lights on, and on this night no moon, the front of the flight deck was in darkness, so we couldn't be seen from the bridge. We sat, legs dangling over the front of the carrier, watching the stars, the fluorescing water under the bow, and dolphins swimming alongside the ship. It really was an awesome time. We only managed it once, and I don't know if anyone else tried it, but in the warm, tropical night air, everything else just faded, and we could relax.

My first ever foreign port visit was Djakarta in Indonesia. To say the least, it sure was an eye opener. Of course, sailors tend to congregate in the somewhat less salubrious areas of town on their off-watch hours. However, we also went to the usual places that tourists frequent. On this particular day, I happened to be one of the duty medics aboard the *Melbourne*. It was on a weekend, as I recall, and several sailors had ventured to the local swimming pool, which had a huge water slide. This slide was straight down from about seventy high, with three 'bumps' on the way down. At the bottom was a pool of around two feet deep. Many Indonesian youngsters frequented the pool and were very adept at getting the most out of the slide. This, they did by standing rather than sitting and 'surfing' down the slide into the pool. Now, of course, when a Jack Tar (sailor) sees this, he wants to be able to say that he did it too, and so several sailors attempted this trick. Unfortunately, for one sailor, his life was about to change.

An able seaman launched himself down the slide and fell over, landing on his bum as he hit the first speed hump. This caused him to become airborne, and he came down on the slide on his head, dislocating the C6–C7 vertebrae in his neck. He then slid into the pool at the bottom, which as mentioned was only two feet deep. Many people had been watching the Australian sailors trying to match the local kids, and rescuers rushed to help the young bloke. Fortunately for him, the first person to reach him was a petty officer steward (POSTD) from HMAS *Melbourne*.

Now stewards are not only trained in their main job of working in the wardroom for the officers but also cross-trained in advanced first aid so that during a conflict, they can assist the medics. The POSTD took charge of the situation with the young sailor and would not let anyone else touch him. He supported the sailor's head and neck and called for an ambulance. The ambulance took him to the local hospital, but this story does not quite end here.

HMAS *Melbourne* was due to sail in a couple of days, and it was decided that the patient would be transported to Singapore via the ship, our next stop, for ongoing support prior to his medical evacuation (medevac) to Australia. So he was transported to the ship and carefully placed on the trauma bed in the middle of the sickbay. His head and neck were supported by sandbags, and he was made as comfortable as possible. Notwithstanding his medical condition, once the ship sailed, the command had to be able to return to full active duty – that is, begin to fly again. To ensure the patient was not jeopardised by any of the vibration and jolts caused by the steam catapult, which was housed directly above the sickbay, we had to do a gradual steam workup. This entailed the following.

I was on the telephone from the sickbay to the catapult operator on the flight deck. He started by firing the mechanism with no aircraft attached at a low pressure, and each time, the doctors would ask the patient if the shock of the firing caused him pain. Each time he said no, they cranked up the catapult, relaying messages via me back and forward. This continued until they reached the correct pressure to launch an A4 Skyhawk or Grumman tracker aircraft. The patient was comfortable with this, so we were able to return to flying stations enroute to Singapore. Once in Singapore, he was landed and transported back to Australia for more definitive care. I cannot remember the sailor's name, but I believe he made a very miraculous recovery that took some time. The last I heard, he was walking again.

In 1980, HMAS *Melbourne* deployed on what was to be her last Indian Ocean deployment, as I have mentioned. This deployment included a stop in Colombo, Sri Lanka. I remember this destination quite vividly because of several incidents that occurred. Our arrival was conducted, as usual, with Procedure Alpha. This is where all personnel other than those required to keep the ship safe and underway dressed in the appropriate uniform (rig) and mustered along the flight deck. One had to be quick and early to get the prime position up forward, right in the middle of the flight deck. On this particular day, I managed, with a few of the other medics, to get this prime position. It was very hot, and we did all get sunburned, but it was a pretty amazing view of the harbour entry.

After the visit to Colombo, we departed as usual, again with Procedure Alpha, and this time, things got a little exciting. I had managed along with a couple of the other medics to get prime position again. As we started to get underway, quite slowly, of course, within the harbour, we could see a large dhow coming through the harbour entrance. A dhow is a fishing vessel of distinct design and varying sizes. The main point of interest is that it has an angled yardarm for the huge sail it carries. This particular vessel was very large, and the mast was taller than the *Melbourne*'s flight deck. This entrance consisted of, I recall, two large rock barriers to keep out the heavy seas that would come through to the land in the event of heavy weather. As we stood there, the large dhow started to come closer to the *Melbourne*, and we realised it was on a collision course. As time seemed to move slowly, the dhow kept coming, and we could feel our engines start reversing as there was no manoeuvring room. The dhow kept coming, and it was obvious that they could not change course because of the lack of wind. The *Melbourne*, at this time, was in full reverse power and really shuddering. The dhow came so close that it almost disappeared beneath our bow, and I could have almost touched its mast, but the CO's skill ensured we did not hit it. However, a few of their crew jumped overboard as they believed they would be sunk. It was a very close call, but no one was injured and no vessel damaged.

After we left Colombo, we were to continue in a westerly direction as part of the deployment. We hit some rough weather a day or so out of Colombo – nothing too bad, but this was the start of another drama. We started to get some pretty sick sailors coming to the sickbay, suffering from severe vomiting and diarrhoea. It soon became – pardon the pun – a bit of a flood. Notably, all the ill personnel were junior sailors, i.e. from the lower decks, and importantly, all ate at the junior sailors café. No senior personnel became ill. This immediately raised the suspicions that the cause of the 'outbreak' was something from this area.

I recall that we had some very sick young sailors; we filled the sickbay with them, all on intravenous drips and requiring constant care. We also had to empty one of the starboard messes (where sailors sleep) and turn it into a makeshift sickbay. I was given the job of running this sickbay under the supervision of one of our senior sailors. We saw over fifty patients who were suffering quite badly from the aforementioned symptoms. Blood tests and faecal tests were done, and a diagnosis of bacillary dysentery was made. As one might imagine, apart from this being not at all fun for the patients, we medics had a pretty dismal time of it too. In fact, we co-opted several sailors to assist with the basic care of the patients as we needed to have some rest ourselves.

The outbreak lasted about four days, and most sailors were back to work within that time limit. However, their absence from the workplace did make it quite difficult for the rest of the crew to maintain the same level of battle readiness that we required. Most people initially thought that the outbreak was caused by some food that had been embarked from Colombo. However, the investigation proved otherwise.

Back in those days, all grey water from the ship's galleys (kitchens) went straight overboard using a series of pipes. The downside of this, apart from the ecological damage that we are now very aware of, was that when you hit rough weather, if the waves were big enough, they could backwash through the pipes. On the particular day out of Colombo, a series of events would coincide in a rare occurrence which nonetheless caused this nasty problem. First, the main dishwasher broke down, so the dirty plates had to be washed by hand. This was done in water that was not necessarily hot enough to kill the bacteria. Then the investigation found that during a particularly rough section, the water in the pipes had blown back into the sink, but the water had not been changed. Therefore, years of sludge and the attendant bacterial growth in the pipes were dumped into the washing-up water, which was a perfect breeding ground. The plates were washed in this water and hand-dried before being used at the next meal, only by junior sailors.

After this discovery, the routines for cleaning were immediately amended so that this would not happen again. It was a hard lesson to learn for a lot of the crew, and happily, I would say that this would not happen today as grey water is not pumped over the side but has to be removed by licensed contractors in each port that a Royal Australian Navy ship visits. To coin a phrase, it was a shitty experience, but all affected personnel recovered I would like to thank all those non-medical sailors who assisted the medics; we could not have done as good a job without you.

Crash on Deck

There were two crash-on-deck events that occurred while I was serving on the *Melbourne*. For one, I was asleep as I was the night duty medic but was still required to attend once the alarm had sounded. My recollection of this incident was that the pilot had successfully launched from the *Melbourne* but had only reached about three or four hundred metres in front of the ship when the engine failed and he ditched into the sea. The pilot was safe and returned to the sickbay for observation.

The second occasion, I was more closely involved with as I was the duty flight deck medic for that week. So whenever we were at flying-stations, a medic was required to be on the flight deck, watching every take-off and landing, and if we were doing twenty-fours (twenty-four hours straight of flying operations), the duty flight deck medic was there. This was required so that if there was an incident, the medic could see exactly what happened, and this would assist with the immediate assessment of possible injuries. For instance, if a pilot ejected before the plane stopped, there could well be spinal and/or neck injuries.

This particular day, we had been at flying-stations since about 0600 hours, local time. We had many launches and recoveries during the day, and as the medics are to watch each one, it can become a little mundane, but you can quickly see if something occurs 'out-of-order' which could lead to disaster. As I stood just outside the island (the sticky-up bit on a carrier), I leaned on the front tyre of 'the Beast'. This is an articulated mobile crane that can drive anywhere on the flight deck to move crashed aircraft. This is a particularly important piece of equipment during warfare to ensure the ship can remain able to fight at sea by maintaining a clear flightdeck if an incident should occur.

So there I was, leaning on the front tyre, watching the launch of an A4 Skyhawk jet fighter. The aircraft moved slowly forward to the launch position where a wire cable is hooked onto the under-surface of the jet, just in front of the nose wheel. The other end forms a loop around the catapult slide, which, when released or fired, flings the aircraft forward, under full throttle, to gain enough speed to get it into the air. The jet-wash barrier is raised to protect those of us to the rear of the aircraft from the blast of the jet as it gains full power. Then the pilot, under the advice of the flight deck officer, while keeping the wheel brakes on, pushes forward on the throttles to gain thrust, and at a command from the flight deck officer, the catapult is fired, and off she goes.

As I watched, all the sequences were occurring as they had done so many times that day. However – and yes, there was always going to be an 'however' – just before the pilot was given permission to go full throttle, while the aircraft engine was idling, the catapult failed and fired at about 30 per cent power, to my untrained eye. The pilot could not possibly get the engine up to speed in time, so he was standing on the brakes, but the catapult was too strong and was dragging the plane forward with nowhere near enough momentum to launch. As the nose wheel reached the end of the flight deck, there was a loud explosion and then a huge cloud of yellow smoke. This was followed by another loud bang and a splash, and of course, the crash-on-deck claxon was screaming to advise all on board that we had had an accident. This all happened within the time it has taken you to read the first line of this paragraph!

The jet had been pulled off the flight deck; the first bang was the pilot ejecting, with the second bang being the canopy falling back down and landing on the flight deck, just missing a flightdeck crewman, followed by the large splash. As the aircraft front wheel dropped over the front of the ship, the aircraft rolled to the port (left) side and crashed into the sea and was floating upside down. The pilot's parachute deployed, and he landed in the sea, but his chute became entangled in the undercarriage of his jet, threatening to drag him under.

I will just pause here to explain one of the safety measures also employed by aircraft carriers – and as such did the *Melbourne* – when launching fixed-wing aircraft. Before we start the launch series of fixed-wing aircraft, a Wessex helicopter is launched and flies beside the ship off the port side stern – that is, on the left side towards the rear. It sits there, moving at an equal speed to the ship, and is used to rescue aircrew from ditched or downed aircraft. This flight on the *Melbourne* was always called PEDRO. As well as pilot, co-pilot, and aircrew, a ship's diver, in full wetsuit, sits in the open doorway so that he could be deployed the instant that an emergency occurs.

On this occasion, everything from a safety point of view went well. The diver jumped from the helicopter, helped cut the pilot from his parachute, and assisted in winching him into the aircraft. This then flew the few hundred metres onto the flight deck, where I was waiting with a Stokes litter stretcher. He was quickly placed in the stretcher, and after a very quick check to ensure he wasn't bleeding badly, we moved him to the forward lift. On the *Melbourne*, we had two lifts, one forward and one aft. These giant lifts bring aircraft from the hangar three decks below up onto the flight deck to begin operations. Here, we placed the patient onto the lift, which descended to the hangar.

When we touched bottom, a hatch in the forward bulkhead was opened, and we stepped into the corridor right next to the sickbay, an obviously clever design for just such emergencies. It was a matter of twenty or so steps to get the stretcher into the sickbay, onto the resuscitation bed, where the senior medical officer and other medics were prepared to treat his injuries. Once I had handed over the patient with a quick brief on what I had seen, I was sent back to the flight deck. Notwithstanding the fact that the catapult would be out of commission for a while, we still had aircraft in the air that had to be retrieved.

The memories of this event are very strongly embedded, and as usual, people see things differently, and time appears to slow. However, from the time the pilot ejected until the time he was in the sickbay under treatment, it was no more than four minutes!

Training at Sea

Whilst underway at sea, every naval vessel undertakes different levels and types of training. This is to prove to the CO that his ship is ready for action, whatever that may be, and also to ensure the ship is safe within itself in case of fire, flood, crashes ondeck, aircraft down (in the sea), battle damage, or myriad other problems.

This particular day, we were in the Indian Ocean, out in the middle of nowhere. The captain called for a 'helo down' exercise. This comprised deploying a large floating cylinder made of concrete with a large steel pole running through it. At the end of the pole was a lifting point. This whole rig was painted white with bright orange stripes. The exercise was to test and time the response to a ditching at sea. Usually, the initial response was for the bridge to turn immediately, on being made aware of the incident, helm hard over towards the side closest to where the aircraft had ditched. This had two outcomes. First, by immediately going hard over on the helm, the ship would move in that direction, which meant the screws would move away from where the aircraft was in the water, thus avoiding a further nasty incident. To make that clearer to the reader, if the helm went hard to starboard, the rear of the ship and thus the propeller would move to port, away from the downed aircraft. Second, this manoeuvre would prepare the ship for what is known as a 'Williamson Turn'.

Imagine, if you will, driving your car, turning to the right and then to the left to complete a 180-degree turn. You would now be heading back in the direction you have come from, along the same line. At sea, as a ship makes headway, it leaves a wake, a line of disturbed water. This stays visible for some time. So in the event of a man-overboard, an aircraft incident, or other emergency where the ship needs to find someone/thing, you can follow the line of the wake to make finding the person or object easier.

As I said above, this was the usual response to this exercise: complete a 'Williamson Turn' and hopefully successfully retrieve the object or personnel. As one might imagine, a ship as large as an aircraft carrier has a pretty long and large turning circle, and this may mean the difference between life and death for any personnel in the water. On this occasion, I was lucky enough to be the flight deck medic again, and to say I was astonished but impressed with the captain's seamanship is an understatement.

As soon as the alarm was raised, the bridge immediately called for emergency stop all engines. Even on the flight deck – or roof, as I called it – you could feel the ship shudder as we started to slow. However, we did not start the turn as I was expecting. It took about a kilometre for the ship to stop, and then amazingly, the bridge called for reverse engines. The ship slowly started to reverse along the wakeline left by the ship! I moved to the starboard rail outside the 'island' and watched as we slowly made way in reverse, right up to the target. By this time, another helicopter had launched with divers onboard. On arriving at the target buoy, the divers had immediately entered the water and attached the lifting strops. When the ship came alongside the buoy, the ship's crane, which sat aft of the island, was used to haul it onto the flight deck. It should be noted that all naval helicopters are fitted with floatation devices which automatically deploy when the aircraft ditches in water. My understanding was later that it was one of the fastest ever retrievals during an exercise.

The Royal Jahore Polo Club

Now what am I going on about here, you may well ask? In 1981, HMAS *Melbourne* visited Singapore for the third time in just over twelve months. Having already partaken in a large number of adventures in Singapore, I was ready for something new. Enter ABMED Grant 'Bungy' Williams – again. Bungy had volunteered for and completed the underwater medicine course at HMAS *Penguin* in Australia before joining the ship. During this course, he had to undertake SCUBA diving and learn all the problems that divers can have during these quite dangerous missions.

The course also attracts international students from other navies. When Bungy was under training, one of these students was a member of the Singaporean Navy, named Iskandar (Esky). He and Bungy became quite good friends and stayed in touch after the underwater medicine course. Esky was posted to a naval base in Singapore, but he lived in married quarters in Malaysia, over the causeway from Singapore. Bungy invited me to go and visit the naval base with him, and we met Esky and his team. At some point that day, we made arrangements to cross the border and go and watch a polo match the next day.

I also found out that Esky was the godson of the King of Jahore Province! We met with Esky, and he drove us to Malaysia and out to the polo field. Imagine an area within site of Singapore Island, about the size of half a dozen footy fields. To one side sat a two-storey building that looked like a palace. This was the actual Royal Jahore Polo Club building. We watched a game of polo in which Esky playcd, and as the afternoon started to wane, the clubhouse was lit up by a series of golden lights. It looked pretty awesome. As the last match was completed, Bungy and I were asked to go to the clubhouse.

We entered this magnificent building to find a huge area with a bar and chandeliers, all brightly lit. We went up to the bar and were met by the King himself. Now to say we were shocked is a bit of an understatement. Here we were in a foreign country being shouted beers by the King himself, and for two able-seamen, I would think this was unprecedented. As one would expect, he was an absolute gentleman, and we discussed all sorts of things, including the carrier. He was very interested in how much it would cost to get one. Not being that high up the food-chain, we could not answer that.

A short time later, the King's son, the Crown Prince, arrived. He is an American car fanatic, and he came in a gold-coloured Pontiac ('Yank tank', as we called them). The Prince was a very nice chap as well and agreed to have photos taken with us. Noting here for all you millennials, we did not have cameras in our mobile phones; in fact, we did not have mobile phones either. They were some way off in the future. We had to use the trusty Instamatic camera with actual film that had to be developed once we got back to Australia.

After a little while, we had to leave, but before we did, the King invited me and Bungy to the Prince's coronation ceremony, which was to be held later that year. This was an absolute honour to be asked, but unfortunately, we were not allowed to go. Not only would we still be at sea, but also, I have a sneaky feeling the hierarchy would not have been happy with two ABMEDs attending such an auspicious event. Ah, such is life, but both Bungy and I had an awesome time – and one we remember well.

Cockies

One of the unfortunate travellers on a warship, especially older vessels, are cockroaches. The *Melbourne* had a few, let me tell you. Ordinarily, you would think, *No big deal, just a few cockies*. However, these ones were buggers. The main type was the American cockroach. These are relatively small, about two to two and a half centimetres long, and light brown in colour. They, like all cockroaches, are not happy to be in lighted areas, so they were out and about when the lights were switched off in a compartment. One of our favourite pastimes was to go into a compartment, turn the lights off, wait a few minutes, turn the lights back on, and see how many you could kill by stamping on them! When the new style of sandal was brought into the seagoing uniform – they were plastic with a knobby tread – they were seen as giving the cockies a fair go during our stomp nights. OK, I know, small things amuse small minds, but it was fun.

The navy did try to fumigate for them, and when the ship was in drydock, just before being released for sea, they would shut the ship up tight, with all personnel ashore, and pump what I was told was poisonous gas throughout the ship to kill them, but they are hardy little buggers. This worked for a while, but we found out that as they were dying, they were laying eggs, which were impervious to the gas, and once it had cleared, they hatched. So there was no way to really rid the place of them.

I do remember a few occasions though when the cockroaches caused a problem. I have seen many sailors, including myself, who had small bite marks on their bodies when we had been at sea for a time. They could not have been mosquito bites, so the only thing we could think was cockroach bites –not a nice thought, but that's what we lived with. On two occasions when I was working in the outpatients section, I had sailors come to see us with ear problems. The first sailor had a heap of wax in his ears, so he asked to get it syringed out –no problems. I conducted the washout and found a large lump of wax was washed into the kidney dish, but it looked strange. It had thick hair-like structures sticking out of it. I broke up the mass using tweezers to find a dead cockroach! It had crawled into the sailor's ear when he was asleep and got stuck and died, and the wax did its job and surrounded it like any foreign body –a little bit gruesome but one of those things.

The second one was a sailor who presented to the sickbay complaining of a continuous loud noise in his ear –a sort of ringing, scratchy sound – and it was really annoying him. I did the usual checks and noticed when I looked into his ear canal that there was something in there, moving! I gently washed the ear out, and bingo! There was the culprit –a live cockroach! It had crawled into his ear and had been tap-dancing on his ear drum, causing the loud, scratchy noise. It was pretty gross and does not reflect on the sailor or his cleanliness. Cockies were just a part of life at sea back then, and he was just unfortunate to get one in his ear while he slept.

Now sailors are well known for their hijinks when in foreign ports. Some sailors get pissed and others misbehave in the red light areas of the ports where the ship visited. One particular case that arrived in the sickbay on a Monday morning was, to say the least, very itchy. As usual, I was on sickparade duty this particular morning. We were in Djakarta, Indonesia, and most of the crew had been able to take some extended leave. As usual, the line-up for attention was quite long. I called the next patient into the treatment room, and I asked him what the problem was.

He said, 'I think I've got crabs!'

Now for those of you unaware of crabs, they are small insects that are transmitted usually by close sexual contact, and they live in the person's pubic hair. Under magnification, they actually look like tiny crabs, thus the name. At the mere mention of the word 'crabs', I get an itchy sensation – really! So I immediately got the sailor to move back to the wall and asked him to drop his overalls so I could check. Now again, crabs are quite small, but they are visible to the naked eye, so usually, you have to get close to see them. This guy, who 'thought' he had crabs, was obviously deluded. I could see a seething mass of the little critters from ten feet away! I immediately told him to carefully pull his overalls back up, and I left the room. Unfortunately for his mess mates, anyone who gets this type of thing has to undergo a special regimen of daily chemical application and also daily changing of bunk linen – not only his but the whole mess! It can be a lengthy process to make sure it does not spread in the close environment of a naval warship's living quarters. He survived!

On returning to Australia, HMAS *Melbourne* returned via the west coast and crossed the Great Australian Bight from Perth to Melbourne. In comparison to the trip against the Roaring Forties earlier that year, this journey was like a millpond. However, we were to receive the wrath of the dockyard workers union again.

HMAS *Melbourne* was to make port in Melbourne in December 1980. Those sailors who were Victorian or Tasmanian were to take leave and go on Christmas break. This was a common practice as it reduced the cost of travel. If we had to return all the way to Sydney and then fly to Victoria or Tasmania, it would obviously cost more, but first, we actually had to dock in Melbourne, and the local waterside worker's union had decided to black-ban us again and would not provide tugboats or wharf labourers to tie us up when we came alongside. The way we did it was quite ingenious, and as I learned later, this method of bringing aircraft carriers alongside anywhere without using tugboats had been developed during World War II.

First, the captain requested sailors from nearby HMAS *Lonsdale*, a naval establishment located nearby to the wharf area, to attend the wharf to assist with manning the lines for coming alongside. Once this had been done, the captain conducted an amazing evolution (or event). We were not going to undertake a Procedure Alpha, so most sailors were restricted to below decks; however, I was lucky enough to be the flight deck medic on this occasion.

At this time, as I recall, HMAS *Melbourne* had a complement of six Grumman tracker anti-submarine aircraft on board. These planes had twin propellers and were able to fold their wings to reduce the space required to stow the planes below in the hangar deck. The CO ordered five aircraft, as I remember, onto the flight deck, two forward of the island, three aft. All planes were to face to the starboard side and were lashed securely to the flight deck.

As we made our way through the heads and were within about a kilometre of the wharf, all the aircraft were started and warmed up. The noise was deafening, as it usually is, but it made an impressive sight. As we drew closer, the ship slowed but maintained a small amount of headway. Then the captain ordered the forward planes to go full throttle, and amazingly, the bow started to move sideways towards the wharf. He then ordered them to idle and ordered the aft planes to full throttle, which, in turn, moved the stern sideways towards the wharf. He alternated this and basically wiggled the aircraft carrier safely alongside the wharf, where the sailors from *Lonsdale* received the hawsers and lashed her to the wharf.

It was an amazing feat of seamanship and one I shan't forget. A crowd had formed on the wharf to greet the ship, and when the ropes were sent across, they broke out into applause and cheered, and – I will admit – so did I. It really was brilliant, and I don't think the wharfies were too thrilled, but I'm betting they secretly admired that evolution.

I went on leave later that day and returned to the ship in early January back in Sydney. This year, 1981, would be the ship's last deployment, and preparation had to start some time beforehand. This naturally was a time of some easing of pressure within the sickbay as all afterhours work required was conducted at the ashore sickbay at HMAS *Kuttabul*, which is located within the Garden Island Dockyard. One incident occurred though which is worthy of mention because it enlightens the reader into not only how dangerous being on a warship can be but also what can happen when human error occurs.

After a weekend off where I had stayed ashore, I was returning to the ship around 0630 on the Monday morning. Now when you return from 'short leave' after a weekend, you expect to find your ship as you left it: at her normal berth and in the same condition as you left her. This was not to be this particular day. She was where I left her, but there was something wrong, and it took a couple of seconds to realise what the problem was. As I made my way around the corner of a building, she came into sight but was listing to starboard, quite alarmingly. I had no idea as to what had caused this but quickly made my way up the gangway and asked the duty quartermaster what was going on. He wasn't sure, but apparently, the 'shit had hit the fan' down aft. I went to my mess, 3D STBD, changed into uniform, and went to the sickbay.

It was soon made apparent that a serious error had been made with a duty sentry not conducting his rounds correctly over the weekend. On the *Melbourne*, we had vast freshwater tanks low down inside the hull on both the port and starboard sides. To maintain trim or keep the ship weighted correctly so she floats properly, when water is used from one tank, water from the other tank can be pumped across to keep us level. This was normally done automatically by the pumping system, and on the Sunday night, one of the pumps started to pump across the tanks, but it never stopped running. This caused a huge amount of water to transfer to the starboard tanks, and the weight of this water caused the ship to list or heel over to quite a degree by flooding certain compartments which are not supposed to be full of water!

One of the reasons this was allowed to go on undetected during the night was that the sailor whose duty it was to check the lower spaces during his rounds in the early hours didn't. When the ship is in Condition Yankee, which is required during the silent hours, certain hatches in the lower part of the ship must be shut and dogged down. This basically means just like in war movies where they shut the hatch and spin the wheel and the door locks. This is done to protect the ship and personnel if something happens at night, such as fire or, as in this case, flood. The duty sailor failed to conduct his rounds correctly. In each hatch is a screw-down brass plug, and this allows visual access to the compartment for checking purposes without endangering the sailor or the ship. So unfortunately, the sailor made a decision to 'radar' the rounds – that is, record it as checked and OK without actually checking it. If he had done so by removing the brass bung and listened, he would have heard the water rushing in and felt the draught as the air was expelled. It was to prove a costly mistake on his behalf.

Why was I involved in this, you may ask? One of my more permanent jobs was as the medical storeman. I ordered all the drugs and medical stores we needed for the deployment. These were stored in a separate area from the sickbay. Well, the area that was flooded was the 6 Sierra compartment –that is, six decks down into the lower part of the ship towards the stern. This is where all the war stock for the sickbay is stored Thousands of heavy-duty bandages, intravenous fluids, and a myriad other medical supplies were located in this area. I lost the lot to the flood and, at that time, was costed around $250,000. One point of interest was that all the bandages were made during World War II, and once we had removed everything from the store to clean it out, the bandages, which were still in their original packaging, were taken away and gamma-irradiated and eventually returned to the ship. Whatever the reason the sailor didn't complete his duties correctly, the outcome was very serious for him and could well have been disastrous for the ship. Lesson learned.

Another incident that comes to mind is when we first left drydock. I had joined the *Melbourne* while she was in the dock at Garden Island, and in those days, we still lived onboard the ship, and being in drydock made things a little difficult. As the *Melbourne* didn't have storage facilities for grey or black water – that is, we pumped sewage and shower water directly over the side when at sea – this obviously could not be done whilst we were 'on chocks' in drydock. So to have your morning shower and other ablution requirements, you would have to leave the ship via the gangway and make your way to the portable shower and toilet blocks on the caisson. This was but a small inconvenience, but if you had to get up in the night to go to the loo and you were in a hurry, things could go awry.

However, once the maintenance work on the ship had been completed, we left drydock and made way to the fitting-out wharf, which is directly opposite what is now the Wooloomooloo apartment complex, but in the 1980s, it was the fleet gymnasium. Our next move was for sea trials to make sure all the work had been completed and the ship was working correctly, and here is where a major mistake had been made. The fire suppression system throughout the ship used seawater pumped directly from the ocean —no real surprise there —but a few days before we went to sea, we found out what that mistake was.

Not only the fire suppression system used seawater but all the heads (toilets) too. Now I can't recollect exactly when we found out, but I flushed the sickbay heads, and unfortunately, what came out into the toilet bowl was not water but FFO or furnace fuel oil! This stuff is used to keep the boilers going to make the steam to drive the ship, and here it was in the toilet, and as you might expect, it was black. This, of course, was reported straight away and caused great consternation because the firefighting system used the same lines, so if there had been a fire and we had tried to put it out, we would have poured FFO directly onto it, which is not a good thing! This had been caused by the maintenance engineers not following procedure and by reconnecting the pipes the wrong way. It could have been a disaster, as you might imagine, but luck was with us that day.

The Bank

As I write this, we are at Stage 4 lockdown here in Melbourne during the COVID-19 pandemic of 2020. Why I am mentioning this is we were told today of the businesses that are allowed to remain open, including supermarkets, pharmacies, and banks.

Back in the 1980s, when we were at sea – before the days of debit cards, EFT, etc. – the supply officer on board was also the representative of the Commonwealth Bank. So when you got paid, you put your money into your account manually, and if you needed money to go on a run ashore in a foreign port, you would get foreign currency through him as well.

I had had a Commonwealth Bank account since my early days at school. It came with a little metal money box shaped like a bank building. So I thought, *No dramas. I will use this at sea. No problems.* However, the problem came when I went home on leave on return from the Indian Ocean deployment in 1980. Once we arrived in Melbourne, Victorians and Tasmanians went on leave, as I mentioned before. I flew home to Launceston for a couple of weeks off for Christmas. When there, I needed some money, so I went to the Commonwealth Bank to get some(note that ATMs were a thing of the future at this stage).

So I trundled into the bank and presented my withdrawal form to the teller, only to be told I could not have my money. When I asked them why, I was advised that as the account was started when I was a little tacker, my mother would have to sign a form for me to withdraw money! So I had to go to my mum's workplace with the appropriate form to get her to sign my account over to me. Talk about embarrassing! All her workmates thought it was hilarious. I was old enough to be in the navy and be ready to fight for my country, but Mum still had to sign for me to get some money out of my own bank account –and no, I'm not over it!

Melbourne Group 99 (MG99)

On my second trip, the last deployment for the *Melbourne*, we were to visit Hong Kong and Singapore and several other foreign ports. We spent sixteen days in Hong Kong, which was a 'good run ashore', as we liked to call it. We left Hong Kong a day early, as I recall, as there was a typhoon heading that way, and the captain decided we should outrun it rather than get caught in port. So we left and headed for Singapore. Little did any of us know that this part of the journey was going to be quite special and affect so many people's lives well into the future.

On 21 June 1981, while transiting to Singapore, one of the *Melbourne's* Grumman tracker anti-submarine aircraft (Number 851) sighted a thirty-three-foot vessel, the *Nghia Hung*, which was not looking very seaworthy. There were ninety-nine Vietnamese refugees on board; the boat was leaking, and they had run out of fuel. Both water and food had almost run out, and the refugees onboard had set a signal fire on the upper deck to attract attention. Luckily, the tracker saw the signal fire and immediately informed the *Melbourne*. The ship made best speed to the area, where we picked up the refugees, and their boat was later sunk by HMAS *Torrens*, as I recall, using her guns to make sure it would not be a danger to shipping. The group we saved were designated Melbourne Group 99 or MG99.

Now as luck would have it, I was on night duty again. So at the time of the rescue, I was in my rack. However, that didn't last long. I attended the sickbay and found that we had ninety-nine patients! The refugees were all placed on the foc'sle (pronounced 'fulk sell') or forecastle. This was at the front of the ship, one deck below the flight deck. At the time, the oldest person was a 87-year-old grandmother and the youngest a 6-month-old baby. Another note here: the Vietnam War had been over for about five years at this time, but many South Vietnamese people were still trying to escape the Communist North Vietnamese regime.

They would pay boat captains large amounts of cash to try to sail to a safe country like Australia. These were the 'original' boat people.

All the crew of *Melbourne* wanted to help these people. The stores people brought clothing and blankets and stretchers, the cooks did what they do, and the medics looked after their health. Many of the refugees were seasick, dehydrated, and hungry. After a couple of days, the number of patients in the sickbay had lessened other than the 6-month-old, her mum, and the older grandmother. By the time we reached Singapore, all were well, and it really did give us all a great feeling to have been involved in the rescue. When we arrived in Singapore, the refugees were taken ashore and placed in a refugee camp, which wasn't far from where we were docked. Although I did see a couple of them a few days later when I had walked past the camp, basically, that was the last time we saw or heard about them.

Epilogue. About a week ago, as I write this in April 2021, I was online in a group that was started for all navy personnel who had served on HMAS *Melbourne*. I have been able to chat with guys I served with back then, and that has been awesome. Anyway, as noted, about a week ago, I was scanning through the comments on the site when I noticed a name that caught my eye. It was a Vietnamese name, nothing really unusual, but you did not see many of those on this website.

The gentleman had been given access to the site as he had been one of the refugees we had rescued. He was keen to chat to anyone who had been there at that time. So I started to chat. He had been about 19 years old at the time and had nothing but praise for us. He did note that their boat had been seen by several other ships, but they had not stopped to help. Only the *Melbourne* did. He told me that he was looking at organising a reunion of refugees and members from the *Melbourne* on the fortieth anniversary of the rescue, which is on 21 June 2021. I did manage to have a phone conversation with this gentleman, Steven, and I have sent him as many photos of that day as I have. Nowadays, of course, there would be millions of pictures, but back then, of course, I only had the little Instamatic camera and had to have the film developed back in Australia, but the ship's photographers took many pictures of this event, and these were displayed at the reunion. Needless to say, I was thrilled to chat to him, and hopefully, COVID willing, I may be able to attend the reunion.

Further Epilogue: I was not able to make it to Sydney at the time as Victoria was in its fourth COVID lockdown!

Now you would think, among all the chaos that the above story entailed, that I was flat out during my night duty. I was, but something else happened the very next day that would also stay with me for life.

As I recall, about 1300 or so the next day, the ship received an SOS from a Korean cargo container ship that they had a severely injured crewman that needed help as they did not have a doctor on board. The *Melbourne* responded, and we launched a helicopter to pick up the patient and bring him to us. On arrival, he was placed on the emergency bed in the sickbay and was assessed. He was in a bad way. Apparently, he had been painting the small mast above the bridge on his ship and had slipped and fallen to the main deck, about 120 feet below. You would think that he should have been killed, but obviously, he had survived. He had a severely fractured skull, an open fracture of his left arm, and a suspected fractured tibia or lower leg.

He was unconscious, but he did come around several times, but his brain was swollen, and the internal pressures caused him to behave erratically. This was dangerous for him as well as the staff, so we had to use restraints. It was decided that he needed individual care, so as the night dutyman, I was given that task. To help with the refugees, ABMED Ron Cawthron was tasked with being the second night dutyman.

As with any patient who is severely brain injured, several nursing procedures need to be attended to, including catheterisation. This is where a catheter is passed into the bladder via the penis, in this case, to allow for the drainage of urine. This is just a part of usual care in these situations, and the medical officer performed this procedure, while I assisted.

Now as he did this, he said to me, 'Hey, Dave, look at this. Do you see those lumps?'

I did. On either side of his penis were two bead-like lumps. I was to find out that these were surgically implanted plastic beads to enhance sexual enjoyment, not something you see every day but apparently quite common in Asian men! I spent the rest of the evening keeping a close watch on him. Every now and then, he would rouse, and he did open his eyes, and I saw some semblance of recognition that we were looking after him.

The following day, as we were closer to Singapore, he was medevaced by helicopter to one of their main hospitals. We heard some time later that he had undergone some eight surgeries but unfortunately had succumbed to his injuries. I can't recall when we found this out, but it was saddening, and some time later, after we had returned to Australia, the CO received a letter from the shipping company that owned the cargo ship. They wanted to thank us all, especially the medical staff, for doing everything we could to save his life. That was a pretty sobering moment, I must admit.

My time on the *Melbourne* ended in January 1982, when I posted to HMAS *Harman* in Canberra. Although she could be a tough ship to be on, I remember my time on her with some pride, especially with all the things we as a medical department were a part of and, most significantly, the rescues of MG99.

The Cold War I

As you know, my first sea posting was to the aircraft carrier, HMAS *Melbourne*. Many will have heard of this ship, and it was often said to be a jinx ship, owing to the two collisions in which she was involved, the first in 1964, the second in 1968. Initially, I thought I was getting shafted, but as I thought about it then and reminisce now, it was a great start to my seagoing career. I have many stories from my time on the *Melbourne*, and this one starts shortly after I joined the ship at Garden Island Dockyard in Sydney on Friday,13 June 1980.

Prior to a ship deploying, many things have to happen, such as storing ship (that is, loading all the required food, fuel, spares, and other essentials), workups (becoming ready to deploy on operations), and training for various other things. One of the other important requirements is a security lecture to all the crew regarding the ports we were to visit on the upcoming deployment and also reminding us all of the possibility that even in Australia, we could be vulnerable to foreign operatives trying to get information about defence. Note that at this time, 1980, the Cold War was still underway; the lecture on security had a fair bit to do with how to handle people asking too many questions of you in a foreign port in regards to your service – for instance,'What ship you are on? How many others are there? What do you do?' As usual, sailors are required to undertake these lectures as a matter of necessary importance.

About two weeks after this lecture, as I recollect, I was stepping ashore with my mate Able Seaman Ron Cawthon. We were going to his mum's place in Western Sydney for the weekend. The plan was to catch a taxi outside the main gate at Sydney's Garden Island naval base and go to Central Station, where we would catch the train. However, this would be no ordinary taxi ride.

We went through the normal security checks at Garden Island and made our way to the taxi-stand that was just outside the gates. We got in the cab; I was in the front, and Ron sat in the back. We gave the driver our destination, Central Station, and we moved off.

Within a minute, the driver started asking us questions.'What ship are you off? How many men are onboard? What do you do in the navy?'

I looked back at Ron, and he nodded; we were in a possible situation that had been mentioned at the security briefing. I answered the driver's questions very vaguely (I am good at vague). I said we were on the aircraft carrier but did not know how many were on board. We were just medics and weren't told anything. The questions still came, but neither of us gave any answers that were not already in the public domain.

At the same time, I was memorising the taxi number, which was on the dashboard, and Ron was doing the same from the back seat. We finally arrived at the station, paid, and got out, noting the car registration number as well. We discussed what to do and went straight to a pay phone(for all the millennials reading this, a pay phone is a phone in a large box on the street where you put in coins to pay for a call; mobile phones had not been invented yet). We managed to get onto the naval police at Garden Island and gave a quick explanation of what had happened. We were directed to attend the naval police office at Garden Island first thing on Monday morning and were advised not to talk to anyone or each other about it. Once the call was finished, we made our way to the appropriate platform at Central Station and caught the train to Campbelltown.

As directed, we attended the naval police office at 0800 hours on Monday morning, where we were immediately separated and taken to separate interview rooms. Later, Ron and I discussed what had happened and found out that we had both been interrogated at length about the incident. 'What did the cab driver say? What sort of questions? Was he pushing you hard to answer? What did you tell him?' Both Ron and I answered as truthfully as we could and signed statements to that effect, but this was not the end.

Even though this had appeared to be quite exciting from our perspective, it quickly was forgotten as we prepared for and undertook our Indian Ocean deployment. After we returned to Australia some six months later and had been on leave, we returned to the ship. As I remember it, at some stage, we were called up to see the CO. This usually only occurs if you are deep in the poo, but this time, there was a nice surprise.

We were shown a letter from the Australian Security Intelligence Organisation (ASIO) that had been sent to the CN and that had then been forwarded to our CO. It was a letter of commendation for both Ron and I for reporting the incident and giving the investigators such good intelligence. The letter stated that they had investigated the taxi driver and found out that he was indeed a Russian (USSR) spy, although quite lowkey. He had been trying to get as much information off sailors who were going ashore for quite some time. However, when the ASIO operatives investigated him, they found enough evidence to have him deported.

We never saw this letter again. It may be on my file, but I am not sure. I spoke with Ron a little while ago in early 2017 to see if he remembered the incident; he did. It made quite an impression on both of us for the rest of our careers. In 2016, just before I retired, I went on a tour in Russia whilst attending the World Dog Show, which was held in Moscow. We also visited St Petersburg. I do clearly remember going through immigration when we were leaving the country and being scrutinised for some ten minutes. I must admit I felt a little nervous as it was known that I was still a serving member of the RAN at that time, but I obviously made it out of the country back to Australia. This incident brings back those memories I have spoken about but also reminds me of how the RAN and ADF, by their very nature, encourage lifelong friendships, even after service. Good onya, Ron.

The Cold War II

Even though the previous episode was somewhat forgotten by me during the Indian Ocean deployment, it would soon pass my mind again. The main thrust of deployments during the 1980s was to 'fly the flag', exercise with foreign navies, and keep a presence in the region.

HMAS *Melbourne* visited quite a few ports – including Djakarta in Indonesia, Singapore, and Cochin in India – as well as conducted long-range surveillance. To counter our efforts, the Russian Navy deployed quite a few spyships, which were badly disguised antennae ships, and also some large destroyer warships.

On this particular day, as usual, we would all be able to see what ships had been shadowing us over the past twenty-four hours. On a bulletin board in the main café, which is where all the junior sailors eat, pictures from the surveillance aircraft would show us the types of vessels.

I was off watch at the time when a call went out from the bridge that a large Russian warship was off the port quarter (lefthand side towards the rear) of the *Melbourne*. Of course, we all rushed to the weather decks to have a look. What surprised me was the size of this Russian ship. It was huge! It was sailing in the same direction as us, maintaining a similar heading and stationed about five hundred to six hundred metres away. This was pretty exciting but also a bit scary, especially with what occurred next.

As we stood watching this massive warship, we could see the signal lights flashing from its bridge towards our bridge. That was OK– until the 'action stations' alarm could be heard ringing out from the Russian vessel. This was somewhat disconcerting, as you could imagine. Here we were in the middle of the Indian Ocean without any support ships, fronting a heavily armed warship. As the claxon continued, the Russian ship started to load its missiles onto the forward missile ramps. Then they would retrieve them into the ship. This occurred a few times and was designed, I believe, to try to intimidate us. Well, it did me! However, the fleet commander was resilient, and we continued on course. As the *Melbourne* did not have any armament asides from some anti-aircraft guns, there was not much else we could do. The interesting thing – and what I thought was quite funny – was what a mate of mine told me later on. He was on the bridge at the time and was able to read signal lamps (the flashing lights you see on war movies). Apparently, the Russian captain had signalled us asking when we were going home. Our admiral signalled back, 'After the movie.' I am led to believe that this may well have upset the Russians, and they decided to carry out their missile drills.

Now some of you may think this is just crap. However, these are my recollections of the day, and I would not make this stuff up. It certainly brought the Cold War right up to our doorstep and was a reminder of what we were doing as a part of the global community at that time.

HMAS *Harman*— 1982–1984

After taking leave from HMAS *Melbourne* over Christmas of 1981, I was posted with promotion to HMAS *Harman*. This base is the main naval communications station and is located just inside the border of the ACT, adjacent to Queanbeyan, New South Wales. It is quite a large base, and it has several outstations, one being located in Belconnen, to the north of Canberra, where the six-hundred-foot radio communications masts are located.

I posted to the sickbay, naturally, where there were four permanent navy staff and a visiting civilian doctor. As one would expect in such an environment, the medics all had a cross-section of jobs to do. My main area was the pharmacy and medical stores, both of which I had done on the *Melbourne*. We also had a small ward, but it wasn't used as such but did get used as an X-ray room. The sickbay was quite old and had an ancient portable X-ray machine as well as a wet darkroom. I would eventually get some rudimentary training in its use to enable me to take X-rays of hands and feet.

Although small, HMAS Harman was the administration hub for all naval personnel posted to the Canberra area, including the Campbell Park Offices and Russell Offices.

ANZAC Day

As usually happens where service personnel are required or requested to attend ceremonial commitments such as ANZAC Day, it falls to the newly promoted members who have been 'volun-told' to attend specific roles. This happened to me for ANZAC Day 1982. My name was put forward to be the navy representative for the catafalque party, which would stand at the cenotaph in Canberra located to the front of the National War Memorial. I saw this not as only a duty but an honour. This position required some extra training, which was conducted at Duntroon Military College under the auspices of the regimental sergeant major (RSM). This was going to be interesting.

As well as the catafalque party, defence always allocates personnel for a ceremonial guard from each service –navy, army, and airforce. This was in the days before we had the Federation Guard, which is a tri-service unit, which means its members are provided by each service, and they get to travel the world (ANZAC Day in Turkey) and provide military guards for visiting dignitaries and so on. However, back in the early 1980s, we had three separate guards, one from each service, and a catafalque party.

About two weeks before ANZAC Day, our training commenced. The full guard practiced together, and the catafalque party practiced as a group but separate from the main guard as our role was distinctly different. At this time, the navy, army, and airforce all used the SLR 7.62 rifle as our weapons of choice, and all training was done with them. They are reasonably heavy and quite long, so when we were ordered to 'rest on arms, reversed', this required specially timed movements to take the rifle from the shoulder arms position, turning it upside down, and resting the barrel on the toe of your nicely polished boots. I can tell you from experience this does hurt after a while.

We trained each afternoon on the RMC parade ground and were hammered if we made an error, but this was why we trained – to get it right! The RSM is a very loud member of the Australian Army. He has usually been around forever and takes great delight in threatening you with his pace stick. The pace stick is carried by an RSM at all times and is around three feet long, shiny brass bits on the ends, and it folds in half. So when you are being trained on the length of a marching pace, he will whip out the pace stick, open it up so it's like a pyramid which also luckily happens to be the correct length of stride one must take, and proceed to show you how to do it. This sounds worse than it was, and it is a bit of a laugh nowadays (from navy, anyway).

So after all our training, the day was approaching. We had to ensure our uniforms were in excellent condition (specky) and guard belts and gaiters painted white. These really stand out, especially with the navy dark blue uniforms. The RSM gave us our final orders before we left as the next time we met would be on ANZAC Day.

He basically said, 'If any one of you faints on parade, you can bloody well stay there, and my pace stick will sort you out.'

I will note here that the right-hand marker (the tallest bloke) for the airforce was six feet and four inches in the old money, and he was one whom the RSM had been pretty hard on regarding fainting on parade –and you must remember this was the 1980s; things were said and done differently then.

So along comes the big day. The uniforms are winter dress, so they are a bit heavier than normal work dress and get decidedly warm fairly quickly. Of course, this ANZAC Day was very warm from the start, so we had to be on our toes. The commemoration started at 1000 hours, as I recall. We had arrived in good time, and finally, the parade fell in. It is after everyone else is settled that the catafalque party slow-marches onto the cenotaph and has to march in time up the stairs at the front to the catafalque itself. We each had a corner, were turned to our correct directions, and given the order to rest on arms, reversed. We did so, and so far, all was going well. Noting that the catafalque party was in this position for the next ninety minutes in the quite hot sunshine, you may be getting an idea what was about to happen.

Eerily, I was struggling a bit – pain through my foot from the rifle, hot, couldn't move *at all*, blurred vision from sweat – but I was not going to fail in my duty no matter what! I didn't, but somebody else did.

As the ceremony continued with the Prime Minister (PM) speaking and all the other speakers had almost finished, I was aware that the catafalque guard would shortly dismount the cenotaph and march off. Now before this happens, the main guard has to shoulder their weapons, right turn, and when the band starts, they march past the dais with a salute to the Governor General or whomever is his/her representative. So I'm wiggling my toes, flexing my leg muscles and arms to get ready for movement. We are called to 'attention' and prepare for a general salute while the national anthem is played. At the precise second the main guard came to attention and shouldered arms, there was an audible gasp from the crowd just after a loud thud.

Yes, the tall RAAF member had fainted just as he moved his weapon. As he fell, his bayonet sliced his palm, and he fell flat on his face. I could not see it from where I was, and I wasn't going to flinch, not that I could do anything from this distance, but he lay there, and no one moved to him for a good minute. Then apparently, an ambulance crew went to his aid and took him off the parade ground. I found out later that he had knocked a few teeth out and broken his jaw, but he did make a full recovery.

I felt extremely proud that I had been able to do my part in what is our National Day of Remembrance to remember those who have fought in all wars and not returned and also those who have served anywhere in the world for our country, Australia.

Rocks in the Head

Why, you may ask, have I called this part 'Rocks in the Head'? This goes way back to when I was a youngster and culminated here in HMAS *Harman*. On the first day of school back in 1964, I was keen to get going, but I fell down seven concrete steps at our house. I hit my head and had a lump on the right side of my forehead. I was taken to hospital, and they put a Band-Aid on it, and that was that – the usual 'Harden up, princess; drink a cup of concrete' days!

Now fast-forward to 1982, and I'm at HMAS *Harman*. I have been wearing the sailor's cap as required for four years, and the rim has been rubbing on the lump on my forehead that has been there since the fall. I happened to mention this to one of our visiting medical specialists. He had a look and said to attend his rooms at the Royal Canberra Hospital, and he would take a closer look after I'd had an X-ray.

I turned up after an X-ray and went into a minor surgery area near his office. He numbed the area with local anaesthetic and started to cut into the skin. Then I heard a crunching sound. I had no idea what was happening, but he told me to relax. When it was over and stitched up, he showed me what he had done. He had found several small pieces of concrete that had been enveloped by fibrous tissue. The 'rocks in my head' had been there since I was 5 years old as the hospital staff back then had not cleaned the wound properly. Additionally, the X-ray had shown that I had a healed hairline fracture of my skull. This wouldn't be any surprise to my shipmates.

My time at the sickbay at HMAS *Harman* gave me great grounding for my next posting to my own sickbay in HMAS *Huon* as well as recruiting duties in Tasmania. I had learned a great deal, including sickbay management, how to take an X-ray, and a plethora of other duties.

One last thing I will mention about my time at *Harman*: a job that was part of my remit was to maintain all the first aid boxes which were located in all our buildings around the base. This also included the aerial farm at Belconnen. As I have noted elsewhere, the radio towers at Belconnen are an essential communications link for the Royal Australian Navy and are located on the opposite side of the ACT to HMAS *Harman*. So once a month, I would go around all the first aid boxes and restock them. The one place that intrigued me was one of the buildings directly next to the aerials. When I entered the first time, I was quite surprised at what I found. In a corner under a stairwell was a fluorescent light bar that was turned on. The interesting thing was that it was not connected to the power! The reason it was on was due to the electromagnetic energy that was created by the huge transformers that kept power to the aerials –pretty amazing but also kept me on my toes. I didn't want to be there any longer than necessary!

The Bet

I was due to post out in early 1984 to HMAS *Huon* in Tasmania, but because of funding restrictions, no movement of personnel was allowed unless absolutely necessary, and there was a pay freeze as well. During the posting cycle, the navy tries to move the replacement into position so that the new incumbent can get a handover to best be able to perform the job pretty much straight away. Sounds good – doesn't always work, but in this instance, my relief arrived, and I could not deploy for a few months. No big deal –extra hand around the place, and it gave Craig Pullman extra time to get the hang of the job.

Now in 1984, we could still smoke inside, and I usually had a durrie burning while working at my desk in the pharmacy, obviously not the look nowadays, but even then, I was trying to quit. Craig was also a smoker, and we decided we would try to stop together, so we had a bet. We each bet $5 – yes,$5 – that we would stop smoking! Back then though, $5 was, I reckon, worth about $20 now. I gave up cold turkey, as did Craig.

My posting finally came, and I deployed to Tasmania, still without smoking. I learned a year or so later that Craig had unfortunately succumbed and had started smoking again. Well, a bet's a bet, right? So I tried contacting Craig, but these were the days before we all had computers, so I couldn't 'find' him through email or mobile phone. In 1987, as luck would have it, I met Craig's twin brother, Steve, who was also in the navy. He and I were on the same course, being the ACC at HMAS *Cerberus*. We have been friends ever since 1987, and of course, every time I saw him over the years, I asked Steve to speak to his brother for me, as one does. As quick as a flash, nothing happened.

Fast-forward to 1995. I had been an officer for some years at this time, and Steve had also been promoted to the officer corps. As a junior sub-lieutenant, Steve was posted to HMAS *Cerberus*, where I was at that time; he actually worked with me in the transfer to the new hospital that was being built then. I took this opportunity to ask if Steve could speak to his brother again. I was told to bugger off several times, and still, nothing happened.

In April 1996, after almost exactly thirteen years, I received in the mail a cheque from Craig Pullman for the princely sum of $5. I must admit I was shocked to receive it, but to further honour this monumental occasion, I wrote a small explanatory version of the paragraphs above and, along with the original cheque, framed them for posterity. Some years later, Craig did ask if I had cashed the cheque as he had been unable to balance his cheque account. I copied and framed a version and sent it to him. By the way, I've never smoked since the day of the bet!

HMAS *Huon*— 1984–1986

As a true-blue, dinky-die Taswegian, I had wanted to get a posting to Tasmania at some time in my career, and as luck would have it, I managed this feat twice during my service. At the naval base, HMAS *Huon*, located on the Derwent River, almost in the centre of Hobart, the medic has two roles. The first is as the base medic to run sick parades, medical filing, make specialist appointments as required, and be available for a medical officer's consultations and assist on 'rocky' nights. Rocky or reserve nights were held every Tuesday evening, so no matter what, the medic was required to be in attendance. The second part of the job is to be the medic for the recruiting office located on Davy Street in Hobart. This has now moved to Anglesea Barracks, which has an awesome view of Mount Wellington.

I was a fairly new leading seaman when I posted here the first time. It was a little bit daunting at first as I was the only fulltime medical cover at the base and also had the above mentioned recruiting job. Even so, I was keen to do well. I have many fond memories of this base, which unfortunately, in my opinion, no longer exists, and even with the requirement to support the naval reserves, the base was closed in the 1990s.

Before that occurred, I managed to have a great posting. One of my favourite recollections was serving onboard HMAS *Ardent*. This was an attack-class patrol boat which had been sent to Hobart to be used by the Royal Australian Naval Reserve (RANR) sailors and officers in support of the navy. The main role was to conduct Bass Strait oil rig surveys or BSORS. This involved sailing up the east or west coast of Tasmania and into Bass Strait for the security and protection of Australia's oil rigs. A small crew of around nineteen would take the boat out for this purpose once or twice a year. I, however, was never allowed to go as there was only one medic in Tasmania; my main job was in support of recruiting, and thus, I had to stay ashore.

However, I did have one day trip on *Ardent* which was great fun. The engineers at HMAS *Huon* were responsible for the maintenance of the engines of the boat. On this particular day, we were due to take *Ardent* out into Storm Bay, to the south of Hobart, to commence engine trials. As this was to take less than a day, I was allowed to go, not as the medic but as the kellick of the forecastle! This was a big deal for me as I was in charge of the lines and the 40/60 Bofors anti-aircraft gun –not that we were going to use it, but anytime you put a medic in charge of something that goes bang...I'm just saying!

We departed the wharf at HMAS *Huon* at around 1000 hours and made our way south down the Derwent River. As we approached Storm Bay, the engine trials began. These involved speeding up and slowing down, vigorous turns, and other engineering tests. It was a new experience for me, having only served at sea on HMAS *Melbourne*, the aircraft carrier, at this time in my career; the patrol boat was notably smaller. I would also note that it was winter –in Tassie! There was snow on the mountain, which is almost in the middle of the city. It was cold and even more so out on the water.

The skipper at that time was a lieutenant. He was a funny bloke, and I remember him wearing a Russian bearskin hat while he was on the bridge. He also decided that we were going to have lunch ashore before we returned to the wharf at HMAS *Huon*. Previous to our departure, he had contacted the local hotel at a town called Kettering, on the west bank of the Derwent. On our way back from the engine trials, we pulled into the wharf at Kettering to find the local school bus waiting to pick us up. Several members of the crew remained on board as security, and the rest of us hopped on the bus and headed up the hill, around two hundred metres, to the pub where we had lunch. To say it was awesome is a bit of an understatement. I had the best fisherman's basket one could imagine. There was no alcohol allowed, for obvious reasons, and after an hour, we headed back on board to resume our return to base. It was one of those times that sailors remember when we were allowed to have a bit of fun in what can be a very serious occupation.

Sometimes we have to conduct ceremonial duties throughout the RAN and ADF. HMAS *Huon* was no different. Two occasions of this nature have also stuck in my mind. The first was a visit to Hobart by the commander-in-chief Pacific fleet (CinCPACFLT), the USN's ranking officer in the Pacific. His home base is in Pearl Harbor in Hawaii. For the fortieth anniversary of the Battle of the Coral Sea, the admiral flew to Hobart in his dedicated Boeing 707 jet from Hawaii, where a commemoration was to be held at the cenotaph, located just outside of HMAS *Huon*, on a small hill.

Of course, as often happens, we were 'volun-told' of our duties on the specific day, and I was tasked to look after the flight crew of the aircraft. So apart from the commemoration service, I had to show the crew around. The two closest 'touristie' type places were Mount Wellington and the Cadbury Chocolate Factory. We ventured up the mountain, with me at the helm of the twenty-two-seater bus. For those who have not been to Hobart, the trip up Mount Wellington is a must-see-and-do experience. Following this, we went to the chocolate factory, some distance from Hobart, further along towards the head of the Derwent Valley. This was awesome, as one might expect, and the Cadbury staff made the U.S. personnel feel very welcome. Now these probably don't sound all that exciting, but as I have learned over my many years in the navy, making friendships and points of contact with Allied forces is especially helpful.

The crew had a great day, as I did, but I was in for a bit of a surprise. The CinCPACFLT admiral was due to leave Hobart the following day at around 1000 hours. I had to pick up the flight crew again from their hotel in the morning, and as we got to the aircraft, I was invited onboard for breakfast. This, to me, was a big deal. I was taken onboard and had a great breakfast of eggs, beans, bacon, hash browns, and juice.

For someone who had only been in the navy for a short while, I was absolutely thrilled to have been invited.

I recall that the winter of 1985 was the only time a RAN establishment was closed because of snow! It was a bitterly cold time, and on this particular day, snow fell down to sea level. At this time, I and most of the other guys lived in Kingston, which is down the highway to the southeast of Mount Wellington. It snowed so hard that the only major road was closed, and blizzard conditions lasted all day. After I eventually got through to the quartermaster at the main gate of HMAS *Huon*, he advised that the base was closed and I should not come in – not that I could, anyway. Still, it was an interesting moment in time.

Originally, my posting to HMAS *Huon* from HMAS *Harman* was postponed because of a situation with funding in around 1983. This also affected my next promotion to petty officer. How, you wonder? Let me explain. Back in the 1980s, when you wanted or were advised to prepare for promotion, you had to do a series of mini-courses called higher rates. These included first aid, firefighting, PT instruction, marching, and what is now called ship's survivability, where each person has to take charge of a party of men (no girls at sea at this time) and stop major flooding of a mock-up ship's compartment. This last part was conducted at HMAS *Penguin* in Sydney only a couple of times a year. Each candidate was to complete the training, including appropriate theory and practical exams. The practicals were for you to show your leadership skills in the above areas so you were capable of taking it to the next level. This could also only be undertaken after you have completed twelve months in your current rank. Sounds a bit complicated, and it has since changed, but back then, this was the requirement.

Now I had been promoted to leading seaman after I left HMAS *Melbourne* and arrived at HMAS *Harman*. So I was only eligible to apply for promotion to petty officer in around 1985. Again, this doesn't mean I was going to get promoted straight away; it was just a prerequisite before you were put on the promotions list.

In HMAS *Harman*, I was the first aid instructor anyway and still had to pass a test and was able to do all of the training except the ship's survivability as all funding for any training was stopped indefinitely because of a funding crisis in the whole of the navy, army, and air force. *So no problems*, I thought. We have the ability to request that this be waived for the actual promotion to the next rank when one is otherwise eligible but cannot complete a part because of no fault of their own.

As my posting was also delayed, I took the opportunity to write to the promotions section to request that this training requirement be set aside until later. To say I was a tad disappointed with the response from the 'higher-ups' was an understatement. I received a letter back stating I would not have this stood aside. That was that. I was pretty crushed by this as I had volunteered to go to the course at my own expense when I became aware it had been postponed but had been refused. Additionally, I was pretty down because once I posted to HMAS *Huon*, it would be nearly impossible to get leave to undertake the course in Sydney when I was the only medic in Tasmania, but life goes on.

I eventually posted to HMAS *Huon* in 1984 at that stage without any way of completing this necessary training. After about twelve months, as I recollect, I was chatting to the chief petty officer writer in the personnel section, which was located in the senior naval officer's office in a building down on the constitution dock. The chief spoke to me about the response I had received from promotions and said he would apply for a waiver for me. As he was the guru for this, I agreed, and off the letter went under the CO's signature.

The reply was received about a month later. It stated, and I quote, 'Leading Seaman Lassam should have known to complete this training before the funding crisis became apparent.'

Now, really, what was the bureaucracy thinking? I was supposed to be fully aware of what was coming and completed a course which I was ineligible to undertake as I had not completed twelve months in my present rank!

The CO and the chief were gobsmacked at the way I had been treated and suggested I undertake a redress of grievance (RoG). This is a system the navy uses where members can take issue with decisions that could be seen as being unjust. It is a big step, but the chief and the CO were confident I had a case. Because RoGs are taken very seriously, my letter requesting a review of this went straight to the top to the chief of naval personnel. Obviously a very wise and just man, he immediately quashed the previous statement and had my name placed on the promotions roster. I was very pleased, to say the least, and was extremely happy when my promotion was granted in 1986. This, however, would also mean I would have to move on again, but in the interim, I remained at HMAS *Huon* as a petty officer medical.

Life was pretty good while I was in Hobart, and I had another special event that I was involved in just before I left. During the navy's seventy-fifth anniversary celebrations in 1986, the USS *Missouri*, a USN battleship, had finished a refurbishment and was conducting a worldwide tour and was included in these celebrations. You may remember that the *Missouri* has a special place in world history. It was aboard her in 1945 that the Japanese nation signed their unconditional surrender to the Allied forces in the Pacific, thus ending the horrors of World War II. At the place on the ship where the signing took place, there is a brass plaque placed in the wooden deck detailing the event.

The year 1986 was also the seventy-fifth anniversary of the founding of the Royal Australian Navy, so to combine this within her world tour, the USS *Missouri* visited Australia, and one of her ports of call was Hobart. I was looking forward to her visit and had to prepare for it from a medical standpoint. Those who have been to Hobart will have noticed that there are a large number of one-way streets in the city. This can be somewhat confusing, especially if you are on a visiting warship from another nation. I had some street maps made up showing the quickest routes to the emergency department at the Royal Hobart Hospital, along with ambulance phone numbers and my number as a contact.

A point of note here: I had been posted back to HMAS *Cerberus* to start as an instructor in the medical school in late 1986. The *Missouri* arrived on the Wednesday, and my last day at work before I flew out was the following Friday. Anyway, I made my way to the wharf where she was berthed and saw the biggest warship I had ever laid eyes on. She was gorgeous! I made my way up the gangway and reported to the USN quartermaster and requested to see the chief medic. About five minutes later, a chief arrived, and I explained who I was and what I had done to make their visit easier. This is usually done for all visiting warships and helps strengthen ties between Australia and whatever nation's ships are in port.

I was taken below decks, and we made our way to the sickbay. The term 'That's not a sickbay; *this* is a sickbay' comes to mind. It was huge. They had all the mod cons of the time: X-ray, CATscan, labs, the whole thing. I was introduced to one of the doctors and left with the chief to discuss things. He was very pleased with my welcome package of information, and we spent a while going through things. Now as my replacement was already in place and I had technically been replaced at HMAS *Huon*, I was allowed to work with the *Missouri* medical crew for the next two days. Luckily, my then wife worked at the Royal Hobart Hospital, so if we needed to get sailors seen by specialists etc., this could be quickly organised.

I really enjoyed my few days on board, but on the Friday, I was due to leave and then fly to Melbourne on Saturday to take up my next posting. I said my farewells and headed home, feeling pretty good. I'd had a great time at *Huon* –served on the patrol boat; been awarded 'Sailor of the Year', which is given for showing exceptional efficiencies in my department; and now worked with the USS *Missouri* –but it was not over yet.

When I got home, my wife called me from the hospital and said to come in as there was a problem with one of the U.S. sailors. I went straight in and sorted out the problem, which was an administrative one. I returned to the ship to finalise the paperwork and was greeted by the chief medic. He was so appreciative of all I had done that he made me an honorary medic of USS *Missouri*. *How cool is that?* I stayed in touch with the chief for a few years, but as happens, you lose touch. Still, I remember this time like it was yesterday.

As an addendum, in 2017, after I had retired, my partner and I went to Hawaii with friends for a holiday. Of course, there were only two things on my mind for the whole trip: first, go to Pearl Harbor, and second, go on *Missouri*. Anything else was extra. On the day we went, I remember going up the permanent gangway as the USS *Missouri* is now a national treasure and is permanently located in the Pearl Harbor precinct. Volunteers take tours of the ship every day. When we visited, after our tour, I had a chat with our tour leader, a lovely lady. I told her my story and also gave her a Royal Australian Navy lapel pin. She was thrilled with that and also thanked me for my service. I was very humbled by this, and I intend to go back one day.

Bass— The Depot Dog

There has been a tradition in the past for naval establishments to have a 'depot dog'. Not all had one, but they were a part of the ship's company, held a rank, and could basically do what they wanted. During my early career, there were two dogs of note; one was at WHGR, whose name I cannot remember, and at HMAS *Huon*, there was Bass. He was a brown Labrador, quite fat, and didn't have much coat. His greatest attribute was his ability to walk into a room, fart, and walk away. He was brilliant at clearing the room. He was good company though and would sleep in the quartermaster's office at the main gate with whomever was duty overnight. In winter, he was almost always in there next to the heater, but his farting ability was twice as deadly.

One of the funniest things I had seen in my then nine years of service was the day the CN, an admiral, came to inspect the base. This has been a tradition for many years across all fleet units and establishments. Every two years, the admiral's rounds were conducted, where the CN would do a tour, inspect personnel and the ship/establishment, and give a pep talk to the troops. In 1986, as I recall, Rear Admiral (RADM) Mike Hudson was due to inspect HMAS *Huon*. As previously noted, *Huon* was only a small depot and consisted of the main buildings at the top of the hill and then stretched down to a single tennis court, which was high set, and then down to the water's edge of the Derwent River.

Divisions, also known as the troop's inspection, would be held on the tennis court. The court was bitumen, surrounded by a high mesh fence, and had had the net removed. A dais was moved into place so the admiral could stand high and look down upon us and give us the good goss (gossip). That day, divisions was at 1000 hours or 10:00 a.m. – no problems. The sun would be high, but we were in the shade. All was set. The admiral's car came in the main gate and stopped, the doors were opened for him by a sailor, and the admiral alighted, and he mounted the stairs of the dais to review and speak to the ship's company of HMAS *Huon*.

However – yep, you knew it was coming – Bass made his entrance. At that time, Bass held the rank of leading seaman, and he had his own identity card for that purpose. Imagine, if you will, a fairly serene setting, a sunny day in Hobart (no, I'm not making that up), everyone fallen in, ready for inspection, and the big boss arrives and takes his place to review us. Then suddenly, Bass ambles around the corner of the building as he did, surveying his dogdom, when he sees some funny bloke he doesn't know standing up on a dais.

Bass immediately goes into security mode. He rushes towards the admiral, barking like crazy and looking like Cujo. Of course, one of the boys left the squad and had to restrain Bass and take him back to the main gate and put him in with the quartermaster while the admiral's parade continued. Needless to say, the incident was one well remembered by those who were there that day, but Bass, for his indiscretion, was busted back in rank to able seaman. After I left HMAS *Huon* in 2006, he had been promoted a couple of times, made petty officer and then lieutenant. He passed away a few years later, and I believe he is buried under some of the trees on the base.

Although HMAS *Huon* was decommissioned in later years, it has a great place in my heart. It was my first sickbay where I was in charge, and even though we only had a small number of personnel, I learnt a great deal medically, in recruiting and also in leadership. I would return to Tasmania in the 1990s as a lieutenant in the position of senior naval officer – recruiting.

Promotion — Welcome to the Dark Side(1988)

In defence, in all three services, there has always been a bit of an 'us and them' mentality between the sailors and officers, soldiers and officers, and airmen/women and officers. There is good reason for this, the major one being chain of command. Orders are given at the higher level and passed down the chain, and when you know that in war, which is what we are trained for, you need to have that separation to ensure as best you can that emotions and friendships do not, as best as practicable, affect the 'machine'.

Of the three services, I would say the navy is a little more relaxed in this area as we tend to live in fairly confined spaces for lengthy amounts of time, and being a tad more relaxed does make life a little easier. Mind you, when a sailor – say, me, for instance – decides to apply for and is granted permission to transfer to the officer corps, sometimes known as 'the dark side', things can be a bit hairy for the first little while.

The medical branch in the navy has been one branch that has encouraged this transfer for a long time. To be eligible, you have to be the rank of petty officer medical and have held that rank for at least twelve months. When I transferred in 1988, you did not have to have the twelve-month-long ACC on your résumé, which you do now. I was three-quarters through that course when I was promoted, and for some reason that I still don't understand to this day, I was removed from the course to undertake the 'knives and forks' course(officer training) at HMAS *Creswell* at Jervis Bay, ACT. I was bitterly disappointed at not being able to finish the medical course as I had done very well on that course to date and only had three months' practical in a civilian hospital/ambulance environment to undertake. The previous nine months' training was wasted –well, not wasted. I have used all the clinical skills I had learned in my first ten years in the navy to help others (see chapter on 'shit magnet').

Back in those times, when you were promoted to officer from the ranks, you magically changed at 2359 hours on the specified date —no fanfare, no presentation of shoulder boards. You were just ...it, a sub-lieutenant MAO. On the night I changed over, I was even asked to move out of the senior sailor's accommodation before I had had breakfast. I had to get special permission to stay there in civilian clothes and was then to leave straight away. I was departing at 0900 the next day, so there was no point in moving to the wardroom (officer's mess) beforehand. I must admit this was a bit of a kick in the guts, but I knew I just had to suck it up if I was going to make it as an officer.

Officer training for the navy is conducted in one of two places. One is the Australian Defence Force Academy (ADFA) in Canberra; the other is HMAS *Creswell*, located in Jervis Bay on the New South Wales south coast. The ADFA was designed to train all three services' young officers straight from school, where they can earn a university degree from this campus (University of New South Wales) while being trained in various officer skills for their eventual role in their desired service.

The other, for the navy, is HMAS *Creswell*. Here, people who do not wish to get a degree or already have one can join and be trained as officer, and those who are transferring from the 'lower deck' to the officer corps are trained. You are taken from your previous posting and placed on a course which was eleven weeks long back then. Here, you are taught all sorts of things, such as how to eat properly, which fork to use and when, weapons training, marching(which we hopefully already knew), naval history, naval law, how to be a DO, and a myriad of others, including passing a boat driving test on a forty-foot workboat —remember, officer first before branch.

I will just touch on the DO here as it is really, very worthy of note. This system is pretty much a navy thing. From day one, a recruit, then sailor, will be assigned to a division within their posting, and each division has a DO. Now what I'm going to say here may be a bit contentious, but in the navy, sailors come first! We cannot be the team we are without them. So they need to be kept happy. This does not always happen (nor is it always possible), and there is an old adage that states,'If sailors aren't whinging, something is terribly wrong.'

To maintain the best environment for sailors, we need to have a senior person to look after them and to be their 'parent figure' somewhat. The DO keeps an eye on all the information that might be pertinent to them and ensures this is disseminated appropriately. Each sailor is interviewed regularly and attends regular group divisional meetings so that grievances may be heard or comments/ideas shared. I found it to be a very rewarding job, sometimes a bloody painful job, but in the long run, I believe I was able to help the majority of my people lead a productive and more harmonious path in their careers. I know it sounds a bit corny, but there aren't too many huge corporations that give that kind of support to their people.

So officer training commenced with the issue of extra uniforms, cabin allocations, duties, etc. As trainees, we had a DO as well. As we were senior people who had been around a while, this was not new to us, and as officers, we were expected to be proactive in looking after ourselves.

Australia Day 1988 — The Bicentennial

Special Duties Officer Course 07 was my transfer to the officer corps. We joined HMAS *Creswell* a week before Australia Day 1988, which, you may remember, was Australia's bicentennial. Those who do remember it will note that Sydney was the main setting for the celebrations, and they were going to be huge. One of the main attractions was to be the tall-ships and other naval vessels sailing past under the Sydney Harbour Bridge. The tall-ships were sailing ships from around the world that had been invited to join in on our special day.

I was very keen to get to Sydney to watch this but was advised that to get into the Garden Island Dockyard, which would give us the best vantage point on the harbour, we would need tickets. As a bolshy, young, good-looking officer – well, OK, just bolshy – I was a bit incensed that as a serving member, I had to get a ticket to go to my own naval dockyard. So I went to see my DO. I had a discussion with him, and he said he would look into it, so hopefully, I could drive up to Sydney from Jervis Bay on the Saturday morning and watch the event.

The next day...nothing. I hadn't heard from the DO. I was getting a bit antsy about it but had to wait. By Thursday, still with no news, I went back to my DO late in the afternoon to ask again about the tickets.

He took one look at me and said, 'Pack your sea bag. You join the German tall-ship at Garden Island tomorrow morning long with a supervising lieutenant and a class of midshipmen.'

Wow! My plan had worked. Even though I didn't have a plan, it worked. I was going to see the sail-past from the front row, on a tall-ship.

The plan was that we would drive by minibus to Garden Island on the Friday morning and join the ship alongside and spend the day on board, getting sleeping allocations (being a hammock) and learning the safety features of the vessel. There were ten million people on the wharf, all trying to get a look at and get on the ships when we arrived as there were a number of them for visitors to see, so actually getting to them was a bit of a struggle.

That afternoon, we were to move from alongside Garden Island to further up Sydney Harbour to drop anchor in preparation for the next day. I did speak a little German as I had taken this subject in high school, but luckily, all the crew were quite fluent in English, but the effort I made to speak in German was well received.

The ship was Segel-schul-schiff *Gorch Fock*. That is German for 'Sail Training Ship *Gorch Fock*'. As part of the Bundeswehr or German Defence Force, their naval officers under training have to complete a six-month posting to this ship, and this usually involves a trip around half of the globe. The *Gorch Fock* had come almost to the end of her first half of the trip, and we were sailing from Sydney to Melbourne, where there would be a crew changeover; the current crew would fly back to Germany, while the new crew flew out to Australia to then sail back to Germany.

That night, our supervising officer would not let us go ashore with the other five thousand sailors from around the world who were in Sydney for the celebrations. I can't think why not as the German crew had stepped ashore, but no matter – we survived that night. The next morning, we prepared for the sail-past. We, as the guests, were to stand amidships away from the gun-whales and wave to the crowds as we sailed down the harbour. The Germans would sail the ship. Our task was to be a part of this celebration and then continue out Sydney Heads and turn south for Melbourne.

The harbour that day was amazing. The sun was shining, with a light breeze and approximately four thousand small craft all out, waving the flag and having a great time. Of particular note was that almost every small boat on the harbour had at least one or two young ladies who thought it was appropriate to wear almost nothing – in fact, a lot of nothing. I no complain!

That day was very emotional as well – Australia had clocked up two hundred years since settlement –but we weren't going to hang around. The ship set all sails, and we headed south. It took us nearly a week to reach Port Phillip Bay. On the way, the Germans taught us how to sail her, and even though I am a tad intimidated by heights, I climbed the rigging on the main mast right to the top and moved out on the yardarms to the end to help drop and furl the sails. It really was a magical experience. By the end of the week, I was loving climbing the rigging and, along with other Australian officers, was having an awesome time.

On reaching Port Phillip Bay, we were required to wait outside the heads as there were some large container ships moving out, so we sailed back and forth. To our amazement, we were paced by a huge humpback whale and her calf. She was right up next to us and was surprisingly interested in the ship – a truly amazing experience.

Once we were given permission to enter harbour, we climbed the masts again to furl the sails. As you may imagine, this takes a bit of doing and especially teamwork. As I was bent over the yardarm, I felt a twinge in my guts. I had pulled a muscle or something. I had to immediately go down to the deck, and by that time, I was in agony. I couldn't believe how painful it was. I was taken to the doctor but had a hell of a time trying to get him to understand exactly what was wrong. So they decided to medevac me to... the hospital at HMAS *Cerberus*! I had only left the base a week or so ago, and now I was back! Of course, everyone took the piss out of me for being a sook, but they looked after me very well.

Apparently, I had diverticulitis, an inflammation of the small bowel, probably caused by constant leaning over the yardarms; I had scrunched it up a bit, and it wasn't happy. Luckily, I was only in hospital for a few days, and on the Friday, I was taken by navy bus back to HMAS *Creswell* to recommence my training. I still wasn't 100 per cent, and we had to go on expedition training that week, which was a bit of a strain, but I got through that pretty well. I had only been on the dark side for a month and already been in the wars, but the experiences I was part of had been well worth it.

The Fleet Medical Administration Office

After completing the eleven-week special duties officer course, my first posting was to the fleet MAO (FMAO) located on Garden Island in Sydney. Here, I was to understudy the fleet MAO for three months. Funnily enough, up until the late 1980s or so, there was no billet for MAOs or nursing officers at sea. This would change eventually for the better as what was the point of being in the navy if you didn't deploy?

So I joined the FMAO, and as the newbie, I was, of course, the 'shitty little jobs officer'. This was OK as I really didn't know much about being a MAO at this stage, and some may say I never did! It was a great start, actually, to understudy a senior MAO. Although it was a short stint, I did get to go to sea onboard HMAS *Brisbane* for their pre-deployment test, known as 'workups'.

Every ship in the fleet that is preparing to deploy anywhere outside Australia for an operation or to fly the flag undergoes a rigorous trial at sea. The CO puts the ship through many exercises, both internal, for example a fire or flooding drill or both, medical emergencies, power failure, external attack from a ship, submarine, or aircraft/missile, either all at the same time or parts thereof. So you can imagine it can be quite hectic. The ship will undergo these trials, called workups, before the fleet examination team comes on board. The names have changed over the years, but the premise is the same. Train until you get it right and be checked by fleet staff, and if you pass, the ship is fit to deploy. If not – and this sometimes happens – back to the drawing board.

So off we go for the HMAS *Brisbane* test. Now admittedly, at this time, I hadn't been to sea for a few years because of how my career path had changed –no biggie –but day one at sea was always going to be a bit iffy with the prospect of seasickness. We gathered in the wardroom to discuss plans for the day, and off I toddled with the FMAO. Then we hit the Heads, Sydney Heads. Brother, was it lumpy out there. The ship was all over the shop, or so it felt, but I was doing OK. One of the first tests they undertook was engine failure. Now that's all well and good, but in a fairly rough sea with no power to direct headway, it can be quite unnerving. Still, we got through that and continued with different exercises, as I noted before. Three of the most memorable ones for me over the next two days kept me on my toes.

The damage control exercise was to simulate a breach in the hull because of a mine/torpedo strike. I was told to go to the forward mess area to watch and see how people reacted, especially the medical team. Without warning, there was what sounded like a huge *whoooommmp* from outside the hull. We were below the water line here, and the fleet team had dropped some dummy charges over the side, which went off right next to the hull where I was standing. Scared the crap out of me, but as I watched the crew reactions, I wasn't the only one. They did a great job of handling the event, especially the medical party.

The second test was quite cruel to me. I have never forgiven the fleet MAO for this. The event was to be a steering gear failure on the bridge. This can happen during battle if the bridge is hit by shells or damaged by strafing from aircraft. However, we have a very cunning plan to overcome this. Obviously, having steerage is vital, especially if you are in that position above, and you need to be able to manoeuvre. In warships, there is a compartment at the stern of the ship where the emergency steering is housed. It is usually in the last compartment near the rudder. Now even in a mild seastate, the stern of the ship moves up and down pretty violently and rolls port and starboard at the same time. This compartment does not get well ventilated other than the hatch from the previous compartment, which is closed during warlike situations to stop flooding or fire –and it stinks of oil, diesel, and other stuff! I was sent to this compartment to see how the medical team coped with an injured sailor. I was there for a while, on my own, waiting –and feeling sicker by the moment. Just as the time for the exercise was to begin, I had to start driving the porcelain bus! However, as there was no heads there, the metal garbage bin was my best friend. It was most embarrassing! Word quickly spread about the officer leaving his lunch all over the place in the aft steering compartment, but such is life.

The other event was what we call a 'safeguard' event. You plan for an exercise to occur, but something goes wrong, and life or limb could be in danger. We had planned for another medical exercise in conjunction with a fire exercise. I was positioned towards the stern two decks down with a gas mask. The plan was to drop a few smoke grenades in the compartment and see how everyone coped. I would note here that I believe they don't use these smoke canisters now as they contain some nasty stuff. Anyway, there I am, ready to don my mask and time the exercise; the smoke grenades are deployed when . . .*phhffftt*...the lights go out – a massive generator failure, a real one. All the lights go out; it is pitch dark in the belly of a warship when the lights fail. The emergency lamps came on, but the smoke was so thick, they didn't do much.

The obvious move after a few minutes' waiting, just in case this was a part of the exercise, was to get to the weather deck, outside. Now I said before I had not been to sea for a couple of years, and my knowledge of the DDG was not all that crash hot. So I had to make my way forwards in the pitch dark, hoping like hell I was going the right way. I found a ladderway up and took it. Luckily, it was only a short way to the second ladder and fresh air. We were without power for a couple of hours, and it was a tad uncomfortable as the ship tried to maintain headway, but we got through it all unscathed.

The ship, on that occasion, did not pass the pre-deployment test and had to redo the exercise. This was not uncommon and is actually a good thing. If there is even a small area where the fighting capability of the warship is not up to scratch, it is better to find out early and rectify it before you get into a shooting war.

Canberra— Directorate of Navy Health(1988)

After my short time at fleet headquarters, there was a short hiatus until my first full posting, which was to be the ASO of the MTS at HMAS *Cerberus*. So I had left the school as a trainee on the ACC at the beginning of 1988 and would return there by the end of that year. However, because of the posting cycle, I could not start there for a while, so I was sent to Canberra for about six months, to the Office of the Directorate of Naval Health. Back then, this was a department headed by a rear admiral (medical officer) and supported by doctors, nurses, medical administrators, and senior medical and/or dental sailors.

So as a fresh-faced, good-looking sub-lieutenant, I started at the Campbell Park Offices, often known as Fort Fumble, while I was living in the officer's mess at HMAS *Harman*. My wife at that time had elected to stay in Melbourne as she had a good job, and as I knew I would be moving around fairly regularly and would be back at HMAS *Cerberus* by the end of the year, we decided I would go 'married unaccompanied', which is a category of where the naval member can move away to another posting while their spouse stays put. It is a good idea and does save the navy (and you, the taxpayer) a fair bit of money.

I knew a few of the officers at the directorate, mainly by reputation, but I was warmly welcomed and thrown straight in the deep end, as I recall. The late 1980s saw the introduction of the first computers available for access to the higher headquarters. It wouldn't be for several more years that access would be possible by the naval establishments.

The system run by the medical directorate was, of course, a standalone and would not communicate with any other system in defence. Back then, the ADF as a combined, unified beast had yet to come together. It was the navy and then everyone else, which had its advantages, but over the following years, the better cohesion gained from a closer working relationship among the services would be seen and become the best driver for the defence of Australia.

Meanwhile, I was pottering around in the headquarters, learning the ropes, and seeing how policy was developed as well as a myriad other things. The admiral would hold a daily meeting for the officers in his office. We – yes, I got an invite – would discuss the news of the day and any particular messages from the CN etc. Oh, and I was the admiral's brew boy. As the newbie, I made his cuppa every morning and afternoon as required, one of the great perks of the job. However, I clearly remember the first time I stuffed up. Well, it wasn't my fault, really. Even though I had passed a computer module on my officer's course, I really had no clue to start with, so I fully blame Chief Dental Assistant Dave King!

The medical directorate had a computer system that required physical backup every day. This involved using large tape recording cassettes much like the one in your car but heaps bigger. The mainframe system was called MEDREX and was located in what you would call now the photocopier room. All the mod cons – fax, photocopier, and MEDREX. In 1988, it had been realised that static electricity can build up in carpeted office spaces, and this could cause serious damage to computer systems. As the headquarters was also located in Canberra, carpets were pretty much essential for trying to keep the place warmish in winter.

So to reduce the amount of static that could affect the MEDREX system, it was decided to put heavy-duty, non-slip plastic floor mats under the desks and MEDREX mainframe in the photocopier room. Now just a short description of MEDREX. It wasn't quite as big as it sounds. It fitted quite well under a normal office desk and was about twice as wide as a standard desktop. It contained all the current medical data gathered from around the country from sickbays and navy hospitals that arrived by snail-mail. Basically, the public service members of the directorate input the data manually. Again, towards the end of each day, the system was backed-up on tape.

On this particular day, Chief King asked for my help to place the plastic mat under the mainframe. One would have thought this shouldn't be a problem, but...It started OK. I was just there to help with the physical actions required to get the mat down. Chief King pulled the desk out from the wall so we could move the main frame and its attendant cords so we could then push the mat under. The chief was behind the desk with his back against the wall; he reached down and picked up a handful of cables and gently raised them and asked me to reach over from the front and hold them so he could clear more.

So there I am, holding a bunch of cables for about ten seconds when... *bang!* The whole system shut down. All the terminals in the directorate went down as well as the MEDREX. I could hear the senior MAO yelling from his office next door – well, swearing, actually – as he rushed into the photocopy room, where I was bent over the desk, hanging onto all the cables. Could I have looked more guilty? No.

I said I had no idea what had happened; I was just hanging on to what the chief passed to me. However, after a short investigation, it was discovered that as Chief King had moved behind the desk, he had accidentally kicked the uninterruptable power supply switch box to the off position, and the system had crashed. We lost all the morning's work by the public service staff and other work of the senior officers. Notwithstanding the fact that I hadn't actually done anything wrong, as the senior person involved, I took it in the neck. I was a bit of a pariah, in a good way, for the next couple of weeks, but now we had found a physical problem with the system, this was rectified. So I really wasn't a numpty for too long.

I only had a relatively short posting to the directorate, but I was given one job that was quite interesting. During the late 1980s, there were fiscal imperatives to make the navy, army, and airforce leaner and meaner. One way to do this was to look at training and see if there could be rationalisation of certain branches or categories of employment. One of the first branches to be looked at was the dental branch. This branch consisted of three types of ratings: dental assistant (DA), dental hygienist (DA-H), and dental technician. All three services had their own DA and DA-H, but the dental technicians were all trained by the navy. The rationalisation was to look to see if one of the services could take on the entire dental assistant training of the navy, army, and airforce as it was perceived that it was the same job anyway; why couldn't it be done?

To do this, I was given access to the manpower study group, who looked after the structure of how navy manpower was decided. They, in turn, showed me how to develop a questionnaire that would help define the actual job that the dental personnel did across the three services. Chief King and I went through this and developed a booklet of questions that would need to be filled out by every member of the dental branch in the ADF. To do this, the best way was thought to be that we visit all the major dental departments around Australia, advise each group as a whole on the whys and wherefores and how to do the review, issue the booklets, and return later that day to retrieve them.

This was agreed upon before we deployed, and both Chief King and I went on a tour. He went to Western Australia to do his section, and I went from Adelaide to Melbourne, Brisbane, Townsville, Sydney, Wagga Wagga, Puckapunyal, Singleton, and back to Canberra. The fun part from my point of view was the travel by C-130 transport plane, which took both me and Chief King to just about every state and territory except the Northern Territory. The reason we didn't go to Darwin was that at that time, the C-130 transport plane route didn't fit into our timetable.

The tour and the results we obtained were very helpful and were the basis for the future amalgamation of joint training across the defence force, including the medical branch. Today the navy health office no longer exists as it did. The three services have combined to streamline not only the provision of health care but also the training of medics. I was to be involved in medical training for quite a few years, and I helped develop the training that we now have.

By this stage, my time was up at the headquarters, and I headed to my first confirmed posting as a MAO – back to HMAS *Cerberus* and the MTS.

Recruiting

Being selected for a post in recruiting anywhere in Australia is seen as a reward for previous work well done. I had been posted to HMAS *Huon* in Hobart quite early in my career as the medic for the establishment and also the medic for the Defence Force Recruiting Centre (DFRC) in Davy Street. One thing that the navy had instilled in me was routine, and this often came in handy for all sorts of things.

Being a part of the navy also brings great mateship and a willingness to participate in sport. In Tasmania, with only a very small number of personnel, we tended to be in all the teams. In particular, in the early 1980s, we played touch football and indoor cricket.

On one particular evening, we were due to play indoor cricket over the other side of the Derwent River. As I lived in Chigwell at the time, a western suburb of Hobart, I had a bit of a drive to get to the sport centre. I was travelling along the highway, about halfway there, when I noticed something obviously quite concerning up ahead, noting that it was quite dark at the time. As I crested a slight rise in the dual carriageway, I saw on the righthand side, but in the middle of an intersection, a hatchback vehicle that was engulfed in flames!

I quickly pulled over and made my way towards the vehicle, not knowing what I was going to find. I immediately saw that another motorist had dragged the driver out, and he was lying in the middle of the highway, about five metres from the car. By now, it was fully engulfed, and flames were shooting from the rear hatch window, about ten to fifteen metres in the air. Fortunately, I was still in uniform at the time, and as I went to move the patient because of the proximity of the fire, I had to order a handful of spectators to get back as I was concerned it may explode. I helped the driver to the edge of the road and laid him down lengthways in line with a telegraph pole so that if it did explode, he had maximum protection.

Within a couple of minutes, the fire brigade arrived and had the fire out in around thirty seconds. Meanwhile, I had been working on the patient. He had a broken arm and around 10 per cent burns to the back of his head and his hands. I did the best I could at the time with the fracture; it had poked through the skin and then withdrawn back inside his arm. So I applied a World War II shell dressing to stop the bleeding. The ambulance quickly arrived, and I ended up assisting them treat the burns with gauze and sterile water, and when that was done, he was then taken to the Royal Hobart Hospital.

I reported this event to the XO of HMAS *Huon* the following day. Now for those of you who know Hobart, it is a pretty small place, and I could easily walk from HMAS *Huon* at the domain up past the hospital to the recruiting centre. This was often how I did this. The day following the accident, I ventured to the hospital to see if I could check up on how the young bloke was. I learned from the staff that he had been going a tad fast along the highway and had taken a righthand turn across the intersection and rolled the car, which then burst into flames.

I went up to the reception desk and was advised that he was in the burns unit. Now I was quite well known around Hobart for being seen out in my uniform, in particular the navy medic's whites. When I arrived at the burns unit, there was a sign over the counter that said the only visitors allowed were family. However, I did wish to see how he was doing and went to the counter to ask.

I was immediately asked, 'Are you the guy who put that weird bandage on the lad?'

I affirmed the same and had a discussion about it as no one had seen one before. Amazingly, I was allowed to visit the young fellow and did so. He vaguely remembered me and thanked me for my help. I said I was just glad I was there to assist. He did also tell me that his dad wanted to meet me, and I was given an address where he worked – the local pizza shop, about four hundred metres up the road from the hospital. I did visit the family there and was quite taken aback by their thanks for saving their son. I don't know if I saved him but was glad that I was close enough at the time to render assistance.

This incident was one of the first times of many where I was in the right place at the right time to give first aid to members of the public. One might say I became a bit of a shitmagnet, but I am happy I am.

Years later, I was posted back to recruiting in Hobart, this time as the SNRO. This situation was unusual, to say the least, as I had previously been the medic but was now the boss. Those who know me will tell you that I tend not to feel the cold – at all. So this particular day in question was in winter; there was snow on the mountain, and there was light snow falling in downtown Hobart.

My daily routine at lunchtime was to go down the street and get lunch at the local shop. As I returned towards the recruiting centre, a 4WD vehicle came through the lights and squarely cleaned up a bloke walking across the road, with the pedestrian lights being green. The bullbar caught him right in the back and threw him about five metres through the air, where he landed on his feet, but – yes, there is a 'but' – he was crouched in the road and could not move at all; he was stuck in the crouching position! The snow was falling, and I was only in my white-shirt-and-tie uniform, but I couldn't leave my patient. I organised an ambulance and stayed with him while he was loaded onto the stretcher, lying on his side, still in a crouched position. It looked quite funny at the time, and I heard he had recovered well, but it was a nasty incident that could have been much worse.

That particular corner was known for near misses and quite a few accidents. On another date, one particular gentleman was waiting at the lights, somewhat tired and emotional (pissed), and when the lights turned green for him to walk across the intersection, he didn't move. The vehicle that was turning right saw this and started to move through the righthand turn when this old fellow walked out and into the side of the car. He went down like a sack of spuds. I was only about fifteen feet from him when this happened, so I saw it all. I managed to move him off the road to a chair provided by the local chemist. As I organised an ambulance, I did my checks on him and found he had fractured his humerus, the bone in the upper arm – and no, he didn't think it was funny! The ambos arrived and took over, giving him penthrane, the 'green stick of joy', to alleviate his pain. He was loaded onto a stretcher in the half-sitting position, but unfortunately, as they were loading the stretcher onto the ambulance, the stretcher back collapsed flat, causing him severe pain with added profanity!

During this posting, I was 'unaccompanied' as my then wife had decided to remain in Victoria as she had a good job. When the boss found out she was also ill, he organised for me to return to Victoria as the deputy naval recruiting officer. I was only SNRO in Tasmania for a relatively short time, but I really enjoyed my posting there. Not many people had been posted to HMAS *Huon* twice, least of all as a leading seaman and then a lieutenant.

My time in recruiting in Victoria was to be great fun as well as hard work. On arrival at the recruiting centre in St Kilda Road in Melbourne in 1993, I was tasked to be the deputy naval recruiting officer (second in charge) and to be a part of the operations team. This was located in a fishbowl office – all windows, so we were seen by all the staff – where a junior officer from the navy, army, and airforce worked. It was our job to organise advertisements for careers days and manpower requirements and to attend schools as required to promote the ADF and, in particular, the advantages for young people if they joined via the ADFA. This academy is located in Canberra and is co-run by the University of New South Wales.

On selection for officer training, appropriate young people join the navy, army, or airforce as a certain category of officer, for example an engineering officer. They first join the academy, and while studying for their engineering degree, they are also trained to be a military officer. It is not an easy road, but defence needs not only quick thinkers but also analytical minds and those who can lead. This does take some time, of course, but the benefits to both the member and the ADF are worth it.

To get the required number of people applying takes advertising. One of the ways to do this was to award selected Year 12 students from around the state a prize of $1,000. There was no pressure to join, but the presentation was done at a school assembly so as many other people who may be interested now or in the future would see the event.

During my time at recruiting in Victoria, we had some excellent ideas to do this, and one of my favourites was to use a helicopter to make a big show of it. Now before anyone jumps up and down about wasting resources like helicopters and pilots etc., we did not just make it up. Aircrew are required to maintain certain levels of practice at different things, and flying around HMAS *Albatross* in New South Wales does not always allow that. We would bid for a certain number of helicopter flying hours and then plan against that. The idea was for me or one of my counterparts from the army or the RAAF to fly into a school, land on the oval, with the entire school watching, go to an appropriate place, and make the presentation, after which the kids could go and look at the aircraft.

We managed to do this on many occasions, and I really enjoyed being able to do so. The value we got from these exercises was incalculable. A couple of these were very memorable for me. In one day, I did seven sorties around Melbourne, where we had two helicopters available that had been on a separate mission flying to Tasmania for overwater navigation training.

The first school I landed at was St Kevin's near the tennis centre at Kooyong. We flew a navy Squirrel, which seats four, from Essendon Airport over the MCG to the school. The view of Melbourne was spectacular, and I took heaps of pictures. We landed within the school grounds, and I was greeted by the principal and taken to the school assembly hall. I spoke in front of around 1,500 students, which was a bit daunting, and afterwards invited them to look at the aircraft.

However – note to self – do not leave your camera in the back of a helicopter when there are school kids around. When I checked my camera later that evening, I found some pictures of students who had taken selfies in the cockpit and left them for me to find. Bloody kids!

At another school I went to, the helicopter pilot said to me he would bring me my briefcase after we landed. Sounds simple, but it made a huge impression on the students. I alighted from the aircraft, removed my flying jacket, put on my black Number 5s jacket, and walked towards the principal. The co-pilot then came after me and handed me my briefcase, so it made the whole experience very exciting for the students, especially at the end of the event, when the pilot said he would take off without me, hover, and then winch me up. I was like a school kid myself, and a follow-up call to the principal later that week advised that it had been a huge hit with the kids. Job done!

The final school I visited on this week was in Warragul, about an hour and a half drive from Melbourne in Gippsland. On this occasion, I was to drive to Warragul and wait for the helicopters to land on their return from a mission over water to Tasmania.

At the appointed time, no helos! We waited and waited, and of course, I was getting worried something may have happened. The school was about to be dismissed for the day, so I had to do the presentation without the visual effects of a helicopter backdrop. About fifteen minutes later, we heard from the pilot. They had encountered severe headwinds on their return from Tasmania which had not been forecast. This made it impossible to get to us as they had to land with low fuel. This was very disappointing from the school's point of view and mine too, but as they say, stuff happens.

This story does not end here though. The pilot was really keen to do something for the school, so before the squadron returned to HMAS *Albatross*, he organised for two helicopters to fly to the school as part of their return mission. I got to fly from Melbourne to Warragul and show off our toys. I was asked by the headmaster prior to the flight if I could take some aerial photos of the school and surrounds so they could use them for their future planning of new school buildings. The aircrew were great and allowed me to take pictures with the door open to get the best angles. I passed on the photos in due course, and I was later told by the school that they had indeed used them for the planning of their new buildings and facilities.

We then landed at the school, and the students had about half an hour to have a look at the two helos and chat with the aircrew. If you are wondering how I got home, one of my recruiting staff from Dandenong came and picked me up by car. This particular mission using a number of Squirrel helicopters was very fruitful from a recruiting point of view and also for the aircrew, who got to practice something different.

In recruiting, we would often get requests to attend events as we were seen as a good drawcard for the public. Such was the case with the commencement of night NASCAR and AUSCAR racing and also as a pre–ANZAC Day event at Calder Park Raceway to the northwest of Melbourne. Calder Park was owned by Bob Jane of Bob Jane T-Mart (tyres) fame. The track is an oval banked raceway and caters for many kinds of motor sport. I was 'King Ops' at the time, and so I was the lead officer in providing representation of the ADF to get as much PR as we could and speak to as many young people who might attend this event and show them we (the ADF) were an option for a career. As you would imagine, this type of thing takes a fair bit of organising to get some defence assets to attend. Recruiting was to have its three service-specific recruiting caravans present, up on the rim of the racetrack where they could be seen. I tried to get some navy helicopters to come in and land, but the overhead power lines nearby made this too dangerous.

So I tried the RAAF, and they gave us the RAAF balloon, which is a full-size hot-air balloon that would be tethered to one of our 4WD vehicles in the centre of the track, covered in RAAF logos, and I managed to entice 1 Armoured Regiment to loan us a Leopard tank and crew for a couple of days. The idea would be before the race started, the lights would be dimmed, the tank would come out onto the arena from the underground tunnel, V12 motor roaring, and it would stop and switch on its one-million candle-power search light, bathing the recruiting caravans in bright light, giving us a huge PR push. This was also to be televised on SBS – non-stop, advert free – for three hours, in addition to which each car would have either RAAF, NAVY, or ARMY in bright yellow reflective tape down one side of the windscreen.

This was a real coupe for us as to buy this much advertising would be astronomical. I had had several meetings with the promoters out at Calder Park and taken a few of my staff so they could see the setup. On the visit day prior to the actual race, we were given a chance to go for a ride in one of the cars, either AUSCAR or NASCAR. I chose a NASCAR. I was in my white uniform, but I still squeezed into the passenger seat and was taken around the track three times, at a top speed of around three hundred kilometres per hour! It was amazing, to say the least, and I do have a picture taken by one of my staff when we got back to the pits. You couldn't wipe the grin off my face!

We did have one drama though which spoiled the overall effect of our preparation somewhat. The Leopard tank had to travel from Puckapunyal to the raceway on a low-loader. It arrived safely and was put on display in the centre of the track. This was the day before the race, and there were a few people in having a look at the setup we had and admiring the cars etc. Unfortunately, the guys who were in charge of the tank didn't pay enough attention to some of the kids who were climbing on and in the tank. One of the little buggers grabbed the handle for the fire extinguisher unit and set it off. The main section of the fire safety system of this is in the engine bay, for obvious reasons, so no one in the tank was hurt. However, once these extinguishers have been used, the tank is not allowed to be moved or be driven anywhere until the extinguishers are replaced. So our plan of a triumphal entrance to the stadium, lighting up the recruiting vans, was thusly stuffed.

However, on the night, we were a big hit along with the races, of course. It was one of the most successful recruiting events we had been able to put together and one I remember well. Yes, three hundred kilometres per hour is bloody fast that close to the wall!

As I have noted, being in recruiting is a privilege, and I was wrapped that I had had two stints at it. In the early nineties, we were able to use a lot of different equipment to advertise different types of jobs in the ADF. Not only that, but also, we had a wide cross-section of personnel from different categories who were able to speak to different career prospects. As you might also assume, being in the ADF allows you to make many, many lifelong friends. We do move around a lot, but that is all part of the job.

In 1995, I think it was, I was still at recruiting in Melbourne, located in an office building onSt Kilda Road. I was in operations and had two new guys come in for the ADFA tour. The ADFA is located in Canberra and trains young people to be officers in the army, navy, or RAAF. The process to get suitable candidates is quite long but necessary. One way to let young people know that ADFA even exists is to go on the university tour. This is conducted during the year and involves many different tertiary education programs, e.g. Monash University, Victoria University, Catholic University, to name a few, and us.

One particular trip was awesome. One of the new guys was also a tank commander from 1 Armoured Regiment. We were to drive to a country town in Central Victoria to attend the tour, but on the way, he stopped at the Puckapunyal army base near Seymour, Victoria, to visit some of his mates at the regiment. While there, he organised for me to have a drive of a Leopard tank – the Bridge Layer version! I was taken out to the driving range, given instructions, and plonked into the driver's seat, and off I went! It was bloody fantastic. Those things fair fly with a V12 diesel engine and a small steering wheel shaped like a bowtie. They have automatic transmission and can literally 'stop on a dime'. I had a great time, and I know there aren't too many MAOs who have been lucky enough to drive one except me– and I've done it twice!

There are many careers in the ADF, from cooks to medics, from infantry to aviation. These are spread across both the officer corps and the lower ranks. I really enjoyed talking to young people, and when the boss was away, I also interviewed people to decide whether they were a good fit for the ADF. As I have noted above, ADFA is a key part of officer training, and one of the benefits for the applicants who do well during the selection process is they may be chosen to attend a graduation ceremony at ADFA in Canberra so they can see firsthand what it will be like if they decide to and are selected to join.

I initiated a trip from Melbourne to Canberra by mini-bus of twelve very good young applicants who had shown an interest in becoming naval officers. As I held a licence for the bus and had all the parental approvals (noting that most of the kids were under 18), I was given 'inloco parentis' status for the trip, basically meaning I was in charge of them and had the ability to make decisions on their behalf if necessary, such as in an emergency.

We were to leave Melbourne on a Friday morning and arrive at a motel complex often used by defence for courses such as recruiter induction training and others, which was located on the outskirts of Canberra. Before we left on this particular day, I gathered all the applicants in our waiting area in the St Kilda centre and advised them about their behaviour. I was not expecting anything untoward, but I had to cross the t's and dot the i's. I told them they were now under observation until they returned to their parents in a couple of days. Little did I know how this would end up, but off we went.

The first hurdle was before I even started the bus. As you would expect, we check everything. Lots! So I did a head count –and I did it again. I had one too many young people on board the bus. So I asked a simple question:'Who here is not going to the ADFA?' One sheepish hand goes up from a young fellow near the back of the bus. I ascertained that he was an army applicant who was being tested that day for a job in the infantry. When I had called my guys together and to go downstairs to the bus, he had just followed on and ended up on the bus.

After I sorted that out, we headed off. I had with me from my staff the navy medic attached to Melbourne recruiting – just in case. We had a few pitstops on the way to Canberra, and we arrived at the accommodation in good time. Note that there were females and males; they had already been allocated roommates, and we settled in on a warm evening, sitting by the pool and having pizza for dinner. Then a fairly minor incident occurred which would unluckily get worse.

As young blokes do, even when being supervised for maintaining officer-like-behaviour, a couple of them were roughhousing around the pool, chasing one another. Literally before I could say anything, one of the lads vaulted the pool fence but clipped the top with his foot, and he thusly fell quite heavily onto the concrete surrounds, landing on his elbow. Both I and my medic had a look at the injury, which looked quite OK. He had full range of movement of the arm but was understandably somewhat tender. I had my medic ice the elbow, and she would keep an eye on it overnight. I also said to the young bloke, if he had any problems with it during the night, to get someone to wake me, and we would deal with it. I did inform his parents of the incident and, at that time, allayed their fears.

Around 0600 the next day, my medic came to chat to me about this young man's injury. He could no longer move the joint, and his arm was stuck in an L shape, which was where he was most comfortable. Also, it was swollen and a very dark colour from bruising. It was obvious that even though he had been able to move his arm really well at the time of the injury, overnight, the trauma had really become noticeable.

I had to quickly come up with a plan to make sure he was OK and also to get everyone to the ceremony at ADFA as this was the reason we were here. Everyone changed into their suits/suitable dresses and boarded the bus, including the injured young man. We arrived at ADFA early, and I left my charges with the medic and another member of my staff who had joined us from the recruiting centre in Albury. I took the young bloke to the Duntroon Military Hospital, which is literally across the road from ADFA. As it was a weekend, the hospital was at minimum staffing, and there was not much they could do. They did suggest that I take him to Woden Valley Hospital as they had the nearest emergency and X-ray facilities. I had a discussion with him, and he asked if we could still go to the ceremony first so he could still get some benefit from the trip. I advised we could, but we would need to go to the hospital straight after that. He would not be able to undertake the full tour of the academy. So now he had to get changed into his suit, and – you guessed it – he couldn't manage it himself, so I had to dress him. Poor kid was mortified, but it had to be done.

Straight after the main ceremony, I spoke with my staff member from Albury who had come to ADFA in his navy vehicle. I advised him that I needed it to go to the hospital, and as he had a bus licence, he could take the others back to the motel. All good –not so much.

I took the young fellow to the hospital, and we managed to get him seen rather quickly, including an X-ray. I had spoken to his mum again, and she gave me her Medicare number to use. The X-ray showed one of the worst fractures I had seen from such a fall. How he had been able to move it just after the incident was incredible, but now the swelling and the rigidity were quite obvious. He was given two options. First, they could just plaster it up, and he could ride back to Melbourne as such, but it would be most likely quite a painful trip –or he could have it plated and pinned now.

I again spoke to his mum and also with him, and it was decided that he should have it pinned immediately. This left me in somewhat of a quandary, but pretty soon, we worked it out. I would stay in Canberra while his surgery was conducted, and when he was fit to go home, I would use the navy car to drive him back to Frankston. My chief would drive the bus with the other applicants back to Melbourne and wait until I arrived to take his car back to Albury. Luckily, my dad lives in Canberra, so I was able to stay with him.

There was only one small hiccough when the young man was due for surgery, which was to be the next day. There had been a huge smash on one of the main roads in Canberra, and there were multiple trauma patients who jumped the queue. However, no dramas. He eventually had surgery and was discharged, and I drove him home. Of course, I had to write a report on the whole thing, and I was applauded for my quick thinking. The only downside was after all that and his recuperation and subsequent return to full fitness, he joined the bloody air force!

My several postings in recruiting were ingrained on me, as it tends to be for most who undertake this. So even when I wasn't in recruiting, I was always happy to chat to young people about joining any of the services and would spin the odd warrie like I am doing in this book. If they were not interested, fair enough, but I always tried to leave them with a seed in the back of their mind about a career with us.

This would be enhanced when in 2006, the ADF introduced a new set of awards in which schools could participate. These were the 'Long Tan Youth Leadership and Teamwork Awards'. They were to gain the interest of young people who may have or may not have thought of the ADF as a career. The awards were named this in light of the leadership and teamwork that was shown during the Battle of Long Tan during the Vietnam War, where a relatively small group of Australian soldiers held off a VietCong attack force of some 2,500 soldiers. Australia won that battle and has been remembered thus.

The awards are offered to any school that wishes to participate, at no cost to them. Two awards are given, along with a cash prize, to a Year 12 and a Year 10 student, picked by the school as showing excellent leadership and teamwork skills, along with community participation, mateship, and willingness to help others, among other things. Each school that would like a military member to present the awards on the school's presentation night applied for a volunteer.

I was deployed quite a few times in 2005–2006 and 2008–2009 and didn't really become aware of the award until 2010, when I posted back to HMAS *Cerberus*. Once I learned of it, I volunteered straight away as I thought this would be a great way for me to be able to encourage those who received the awards. Initially, I picked two schools to attend, but as there were often not enough volunteers as military presenters, I increased the number of schools until I reached the number I now visit, ten, usually over a two-week period at the end of the year. The awards ceremony entailed turning up on the appointed day, looking resplendent in uniform, reading a speech, and staying and chatting to the winners and usually their parents afterwards.

In 2010, I participated with two schools, and by my retirement, I was attending ten secondary schools in a two-week period. I didn't stop there though. The program is on a volunteer basis for ADF personnel, and there are never enough, which is why I increased my workload, but I still do these to this day. The schools have enjoyed having me there, so I will keep going as long as I can. I would urge any naval personnel who think they might like this to volunteer.

In a small addendum, last year, 2020, and so far this year, 2021, as we all know, were pretty grim with the COVID-19 pandemic. This affected a lot of schools here in Victoria, where we underwent the toughest restrictions in the world for now over 248 days. This stopped the face-to-face awards ceremonies that were to be held at the end of the school year. However, with technology and Mr Google, I was able to make a video presentation for the schools to use, and the feedback I have at this time is that it went well. I aim to be at 'my' schools again as soon as restrictions allow.

Why have I mentioned this? I am not trying to big-note myself, but along with writing this book, I have tried to highlight what a great career I have had in the navy and what could be possible for new generations of young people from all walks of life in Australia.

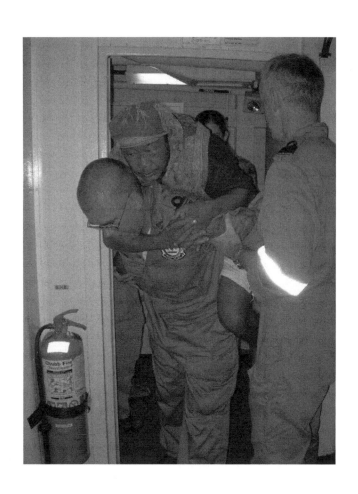

Shit Magnet

Why did I name this chapter 'shit magnet?' This moniker was given to me by one of my civilian mates many years ago now. It referred to my uncanny ability to be in the right place at the right time – not for myself but for the person or people I was able to help.

For some reason, the universe would allow incidents to occur literally in front of or very near to me. I will describe a few here, but there were quite a lot of these over the years, and interestingly, all occurred in 'Civvie Street', as we call it, out in the broader community.

In 1988, I was promoted to the officer corps. At that time, the biggest non-military incident I had attended had been the car rollover and fire on the main highway in Hobart during my first stint at recruiting.

Tyabb–Victoria— 1988

I had just completed my officer training at HMAS *Creswell* in Jervis Bay, ACT, and posted to my next job, located at Garden Island Dockyard in Darlinghurst, Sydney. As part of my continued training, I had to understudy the FMAO for three months. Before I started this, I decided to fly home for the weekend and went out for dinner with my best mate, Petty Officer Steve Pullman, his girlfriend, and my wife and stepson. We had been to Frankston for the occasion and had had a great time.

Then we started out for home. It was a pretty dismal night. It was raining very heavily, and it was quite cool as well. Many sailors from HMAS *Cerberus* will know the road we were on, the Hastings–Tyabb road. We were coming from Somerville, heading south, and were approaching the righthand sweeping bend about a kilometre from Tyabb. The rain was at a downpour; I could only see about twenty to thirty metres when what I thought was one of the stupidest bits of driving I have ever had the misfortune to see happened.

I was second last in a line of four cars. As we started to move around the bend, the last car decided to overtake...all of us! He flew past us and the other cars, but there was another car heading in the opposite direction. The driver overtaking tried to avoid the oncoming car, and as he reefed on the wheel, he clipped the back of the front car and started to spin. This, as they say, looked like time had stood still. It was bucketing down as his car slid across the road, facing the wrong way now, down the stormwater ditch, and into a telegraph pole. Suddenly, the whole area was lit up by huge sparks as the pole came down on top of his car, electrical wires sparking everywhere.

I had managed to avoid the carnage and travelled a small distance past the crash, turned around, and driven back to where the wreck was. I told my wife and son and Steve's girlfriend to stay put, and Steve and I jumped out to go and see what we could do. Both Steve and I had been on the ACC, a twelve-month intensive paramedical course, before I had been promoted, so we were both up to date in emergency care. The old but good mantra came flooding back – DRABC, as it was back then. Danger to me first and then the casualty.

I was very aware of the electric wires which were down across the road. The car was down in the ditch but sitting fairly level. However, the telegraph pole had fallen across the bonnet from the left-hand corner across to the right-hand number one pillar, thus making it impossible to open the driver's side door. After a quick look, I ascertained that the car was not electrified, but the driver was in imminent danger as he was unconscious and had fallen forward, possibly blocking his airway. I told Steve to stay back a bit while I tested to see if the car was live by touching it with the back of my hand. If it was OK, great. If not, I would be thrown backwards, and Steve could look after me.

I touched the car and found it was safe. I reefed open the passenger door to get access to the driver. The windscreen was smashed, so the rain was pouring in. Steve had made his way around the rear of the vehicle and was able to access the patient's head through the window. We checked for vital signs. He was alive, and as he was unconscious, we had to straighten his head and neck to maintain his airway. This done and with the patient breathing, Steve maintained his airway as I checked him over for other injuries, especially bleeding. It was a very difficult environment to work in, as you might imagine; it was dark and pouring with rain, and I was in a suit, as was Steve.

I quickly found he had no other apparent injuries. It was then that I noticed that there was a child seat in the back seat but no child! I frantically searched the back of the car, which was a jumbled mess, but didn't find anything. Thank god. However, the car was strewn with beer cans and other alcohol, and there was an open can wedged on the dashboard. He was a drunk driver.

Steve had been maintaining the patient's airway and tried to rouse him, which he did. We talked to him to relax him and explained what had happened when the police and the ambulance arrived. As part of our advanced medical course, there was a practical period that was spent with the Victorian Ambulance Service. Navy medics joined these crews to learn and assist with the emergency treatment of patients so that when we are at sea, we can put those skills into action where needed. Steve had recently completed the practical phase and knew the two ambulance officers who had arrived at the scene. We decided he should go and give them a situation report (SITREP) before they came over to the wreck.

By this time, the driver had started to come around and was getting somewhat belligerent, thrashing around and carrying on in a drunken rage. I was trying to calm him when a rather big ambo stuck his head up next to mine, said 'gidday', and asked me how things were going. I told him what I assume Steve had also relayed about the patient's condition, and it was obvious that the patient was really starting to get stroppy. I moved out from the car so that the ambo could ascertain the best way to remove the patient. After undoing the seatbelt, he tried to pull the patient out via the passenger door. It was quite obvious that there were no other injuries as he was thrashing around and calling us every name under the sun. This is where I saw the funniest thing for this whole episode.

The ambo said to the patient, 'OK, we won't touch you,' and as the driver relaxed, the ambo grabbed him and pulled him quickly across the passenger seat, out the door, and onto the ground. Now this may sound a bit rough, but you had to be there, and remember, it was pouring, so when he made it to the ground, it was about six inches of water!

We then helped him up the embankment to the stretcher, which was beside the ambulance. This type of ambulance door had the hinges on top, so the door opened up and gave us a bit of cover from the rain. The patient was put on the stretcher, and as he was still fighting us, he was strapped well in so his arms could not move. We left him there next to the ambulance while we spoke with the police and ambos under the door. We found out later that he had had a blood alcohol level three times the legal limit. He lost his licence for twelve months and had a community-based order placed against him.

It had been a pretty exhausting and harrowing event but one of many to happen to me. Notwithstanding this driver had been a total idiot by drinking and driving and had driven in such a manner as to possibly have killed about eight people that night, we saved his life using the skills we had been trained in during our time as navy medics. I was very proud of our efforts that night and very proud I can call Steve Pullman my friend and shipmate.

CPR at the Dog Show

As I have mentioned, my other passion apart from the navy has been purebred dogs. I started with bearded collies back in 1983, first undertaking obedience trials and later dog showing. I am also and have been, for some time, a qualified show judge. This may seem to be a strange hobby for someone in the navy, but I have found it to be fun, and it also promotes good mental health as well as letting people know about defence and their people – that is, 'we are normal and do normal things'. Well, OK, maybe not normal, but you get the idea. I mention this again as my story steps up to the first time I did cardio-pulmonary resuscitation or CPR.

After twenty-one years in the navy, I had been trained in and trained others in CPR. I was quite proficient at the practice but had never had to use it. That was to change very swiftly. I remember the date very well, 7 August 1999 or 7/8/99. I was attending a dog show at the Royal Melbourne Showgrounds, where most of our city showing was conducted at that time. It was a pretty old ground in the suburb of Ascotvale, Melbourne.

Dog showing is conducted in Australia in seven distinct groups. Each recognised breed is allotted to a group depending on what their function is. Group One is the toy dog group. This has dogs like chihuahuas, pugs, and papillons. I have always preferred larger breeds and have bred a few champions and grand champions over the years of the breed called bearded collies, which are beautiful dogs with long coats. I won't try to describe them other than to suggest you Google them. Dogs are also judged in alphabetical order; in Group Five, working dogs, we start with Australian cattle dogs, Australian kelpies, and then bearded collies. When showing, you have to be ready for your call; otherwise, if you miss it, it's all over, Red Rover. So I habitually am at least five minutes early, ready at ringside, wearing my best suit and runners! This is so I don't slip over on the grass as I run around the showring.

So at around 0920 on 07/08/99, I was outside the Group Five ring, awaiting my call. My dog, Dexter, was on lead, standing next to me. I wasn't paying particular attention to anything when I heard a quite loud thump. I looked into the ring to see a lady on the ground. My immediate thought was that she had slipped and fallen, so in the three to four seconds it took me to reach her, I was covering every possibility in my head. I had dropped my dog's lead as I ran to help, but that was OK as I knew other exhibitors would look after him.

I reached the lady to find she was already turning blue and was not breathing. I quickly did my checks and, noting she was clinically dead, commenced CPR. The adrenalin, as one would expect, was flooding my body, and this helped me immensely. I had been doing CPR for about a minute when I was joined by a nurse. She maintained compressions while I controlled the breathing.

I was told later that I had taken control of the whole area, ordered an ambulance, cleared the rings, had sentries at the gate to direct the ambulance, and organised some people to get some blankets to surround us for a bit of modesty and to protect the children who were at the show from unnecessarily seeing this traumatic event. The ambulance arrived after about five minutes, which seemed like five hours. CPR can be very tiring but is worth the effort.

I continued CPR as the ambos inserted cannulas and prepared the LifePak 5, the predecessor to today's automatic external defibrillators. The patient was shocked several times before a sinus or normal rhythm was resumed. I helped the ambulance officers to prepare her for transport, and after about a total of forty-five minutes from start to finish, she departed for the hospital. It wasn't until that moment that the adrenalin started to wear off and the enormity of what had just happened hit me. I was hopeful I had done enough and done it correctly to save the patient.

The next day, I was informed she had survived and she went on to live for another few years before she passed away at home. I have not forgotten nor will forget this incident. It proved to me that my training was excellent and that I had been able to perform well under pressure. I was also awarded a CO's commendation for my actions in aiding the civil community.

More CPR

I had several other times I did CPR, not in defence but out in the big, wide world. In 2003, I had finished my rotation at northern command in Darwin and was posted back to HMAS *Cerberus*. I counted Victoria as my home by now, and I was thrilled to be returning. However, as usual, I was in for a bit of a surprise this day.

I arrived at Melbourne Airport and was picked up by my wife at the time. On the way home, we were going to pass the Kennel Control Council of Victoria's show arena at Skye. As it was a Saturday, there was a dog show underway. So we stopped and went to have a look, although it was more to catch up with all my friends. I was only going to stay about half an hour and then go home, but that was not to be.

I was standing near the secretary's office, which is in the centre of the ground, when I heard some yelling for medical help. As I tend to react first rather than debating the matter, I was on the run pretty quickly. The call for help came from the gundog ring, which is in one of the far corners of the ground. I bolted to the ring to find an older gentleman flat on his back near the ring entrance, with a number of people standing about. No one else was doing anything. I ran through the ring to the patient and found a man who was non-responsive. I immediately started CPR and, at the same time, was barking orders to everyone around me. I remember calling for someone to call the ambulance, and what stood out to me was that I was yelling at someone to get the kids back, who were standing right near me, watching.

I kept going with the CPR, and after what felt like an eternity, the ambulance arrived. As happens with this sort of thing, once the ambos arrive, you should still continue the CPR as they need to set up their equipment. The heart-start machine was charging, the intravenous lines were prepped and inserted, and I kept going.

When they were ready, I was relieved of the duty, and they took over. Mind you, my adrenalin was going off, and I stayed close in case they needed any help, like holding IV bags or whatever, and they did. After only one or two sets of compressions, the ambo was stuffed, so I took over and kept doing CPR until they had the patient ready to transport. They managed to get his heart back to a reasonable rhythm before he was taken to the ambulance.

The gentleman later passed away in hospital, which was a bit shattering, but what happened about two weeks later was really lovely. I received a card in the mail from this gentleman's family. It read in part that they thanked me sincerely for my efforts in trying to revive their husband/dad/grandfather and especially for my efforts even after the ambos arrived. 'I wouldn't give up.' The fact that they were there and saw what I did and thanked me even though he passed away was very special to me.

HMAS *Penguin*

In 2005, I was posted to HMAS *Penguin* as the administration officer for Balmoral Naval Hospital. This hospital had been around for a very long time and was also the area from which Navy medical staff would be drawn to go to sea in the case of international emergencies where a combined medical response was required. As usual, my ability to be in a place at the right time (for the patient) followed me.

I was a keen walker, especially when I lived about fifty metres from Balmoral Beach. Every morning and afternoon I would do some exercise on the beach or on a walk from the beach access gate around the block through the suburb of Mosman, to the main gate of HMAS *Penguin*. I was on a walk one sunny afternoon, and I had managed to get up Cardiac Hill and was walking along the main street through Mosman. I was approaching the end of the shopping precinct, where the road split; one way went to the base, the other down towards Sydney Harbour, in a roundabout way.

As I was about to turn towards home, I heard a loud 'crack'. I quickly looked around and saw across the road a body on the ground. I ran through the traffic, and by the time I got to the patient, a woman was kneeling with her. I said I was a navy medic and asked if I could help.

The woman said,'Thank god. I don't know what I'm doing.'

So I took control and sent the lady for a blanket and to ensure that an ambulance was called. The lady on the ground was 87 years old, and she had tripped over a brick in the pavement that had lifted a little and caused an uneven surface. She had an obvious head injury, possible neck injury, and scraped knees. I ensured she stayed still and chatted to her while we waited. A check of the rest of her body for injuries was negative. When the ambulance arrived, I did a handover to them, and after saying goodbye to the patient, I continued on my walk home. As is usual for me, I dissect every step I took during the event so that if I found I could improve in any way, I would make sure to do so. Sounds a bit daft to some, but it is a part of any ADF mission to do this review, and that has been carried with me my whole career.

If possible, I try to follow up with any of the people I deal with. Most I have helped are in the dog showing world and are fairly easy to catch up with. The elderly lady was a little different. I called the hospital where the ambos were taking her, but they had no record of her. I thought the worst and that she may have passed away. This was upsetting to me, but I wanted to make sure of the outcome, so after a few phone calls, I found out that the hospital had been on bypass, and she had been taken to another one, reviewed, and then discharged to home. I later visited her at home in Mosman to find her hale and hearty, which was a big relief.

Disaster Management

Anyone in the ADF will tell you that we do a little bit of training throughout our careers –well, a lot, actually. Some training is compulsory and renewed annually, such as first aid, weapons training, equity training, and a few others. Some is employment training, such as damage control training before going to sea. This deals with fighting fires or dealing with floods in a shipboard scenario, both of which you never want to have occur. Other training is for professional development. This is not mandatory but is training that may enhance a member's skills and abilities in the performance of their duties. The funding for this training is bid for at budget time, and if there is a budget squeeze, which there is quite often, the first training to be cancelled is this. However, my next story only came about because I had managed to get approval and budgeting for a course for my professional development.

I was posted to HMAS *Penguin* still and had enrolled in a weeklong course/conference on disaster management. This was to be especially useful to me in my role as either OIC or Deputy OIC of the primary casualty reception facility (PCRF) aboard either HMAS *Kanimbla* or HMAS *Manoora*. The course was to be held at the Queensland University of Technology (QUT), so I wasn't complaining! The course was aimed mainly at personnel from the Australian Emergency Services, who are responsible for disaster management within our country. As we deploy in most cases of natural disaster in an overseas environment, this training would help me and the ADF in our missions to such areas.

I would like to add though that over the past twelve months as I've written this book, the ADF has been used extensively within Australia to support our emergency services in the terrible bushfires in Victoria and New South Wales last Christmas (2019–2020) and, as I write this, assistance during the COVID-19 pandemic, in particular in Victoria during our second wave. Again, I digress, as sailors do.

Back to the disaster management course. The night before I was due to fly out, I stayed at a friend's place as she lived closer to the Sydney airport. The next morning, which was a Saturday, I packed my bags and went out to wait on the footpath for my taxi. My friend, with her baby in arms, came out to wait with me. I would note here that my friend was a long-serving member of the army, and she was well aware of my 'shit magnet' status. We were chatting away when a gentleman approached from the direction of the local corner shop. He was dressed in a full tracksuit on what was a quite warm and humid Saturday morning.

He passed by us, and about five seconds later, my friend yelled, 'Dave!'

I spun around to find the gentleman unconscious on the ground, blood running from his head. I quickly got to him and checked for vital signs —all good. I asked my friend to call for an ambulance, which she had already done. I went through my protocols —danger, response, airway, breathing, circulation – and found he was OK and just starting to come around. I had stopped the head bleed and placed him in the recovery position as I was concerned about his conscious state.

The ambulance took forever to get to us. In the meantime, the taxi arrived, but I wouldn't leave my patient, and the taxi driver was great and said he would stay and wait for me, and he turned the meter off! As I usually do, I take notes on any event I am involved in. It's become a habit over the years and proved most beneficial to me in the first instance and also to the ambos or police as may be. The ambulance arrived after about thirty minutes. I had my friend just stay near the patient while I briefed the ambulance crew. I handed them my notes, including my ongoing medical stats.

They were pretty impressed, and jokingly, one of them said, 'Well, you've done everything else. Can you put him on the stretcher and put him in the ambulance?'

I had to go then as my flight time was getting closer, and as is my usual routine, I had left plenty of time. I found out during my questioning of the gentleman that he had been on the turps the night before, hadn't had any breakfast or other fluids to rehydrate, and had taken his anti-hypertensive drugs about twenty minutes before he went to get the morning paper. So a combination of heat, alcohol, and prescription drugs led to a rapid drop in blood pressure just as he walked past me... Then he kissed the pavement. I understand from follow-up, which is something I try to do in all these instances, that he was OK and was a bit more aware of how combining the above can lead to possible disaster.

The Park

I posted to the headquarters joint operations command (HQJOC), which was located at RAAF Base Fairbairn in early 2008. Here, I was involved in the strategic medical side of the ADF's operations. During this time, I was sent to the Middle East twice but also managed to maintain my 'shit magnet' status at home. Because of my love of dogs and dog showing, I have made many friends around Australia, and before you think it, yes, it costs me a fortune in friendship tax! One of my mates and his family had moved from Melbourne, where I first met them, to acreage near Gunghalin in the ACT. As I was on my own during this posting, I would often visit them.

On the day in question, they had decided to walk a couple of their dogs around Gunghalin Lake. It was a few kilometres around, and it was a beautiful day. As we made our way along, I was looking ahead and noticed in the distance, about 150 metres away, what looked like a commotion near a large granite rock which was in the middle of the park area. Without a word, I bolted ahead of my friends and quickly made my way to the area to find a young fella, of 9 years, lying face down on the ground. His parents were there, and I told them who I was and asked if I could help. They accepted my help, and I examined young Jack. He had been playing on the large boulder, slipped, and fell on his outstretched arm, snapping his radius and probably his ulna, both bones of the lower arm. He was crying a bit and was obviously in pain.

Now these situations have two distinct levels: first, the patient, who was my concern; and second, the parents, who could really not help if they panic. However, once I had introduced myself, they were relieved that I was there. I checked that an ambulance had been called as I examined Jack. He had no obvious head injuries; nor did he complain of hitting his head. He was lying on his belly with the broken left arm out to the side, but he was looking away, which was a good thing.

As an ambulance was on its way and I did not have any need to move him as he was not in danger, I let him lie still. I actually got down on my stomach with my head close to him and just chatted. This has two effects. One, it keeps me in check, and two, it reassures the patient (and his mum and dad) that someone is looking after him. In a short time, the ambulance arrived, and I told Jack I was going to speak to them and that I was not just leaving. I handed over to the ambos that I believed he had a fractured radius and that I had not moved his arm but let it lie beside his body, where it felt more comfortable. Jack was soon sucking on the magic green stick (penthrane) to alleviate his pain, and his arm was splinted before transfer to hospital. As I left, I gave my details to his parents so that, if they wished, they could advise me how he went.

I managed to stay in contact with the family for a few years and visited them at home once. Jack sent me some great drawings and a thank-you card, which really made my day. I have been out of touch with them for a while, but I often wonder how they are doing.

In 2010, I posted from HQJOC near Bungendore to my favourite naval base, HMAS *Cerberus*. As usual, one has to 'up sticks' and move from one end of the country to another —and so it was on this occasion but with yet another drama.

I was to drive down to Victoria and was also towing my dog trailer. I had the dogs in the car with most of my ready-use stuff in the trailer, and I left Bungendore, where I had lived for nearly two years, at around 0300. I love nightdriving and was well rested, so off I went. I made my way from Bungendore to Murrumbateman and then on to Yass. Once past Yass, I merged onto the Hume Highway for the pretty much straight run to Melbourne. However, as you may surmise, I was about to get a bit of a surprise.

About two or three kilometres onto the highway, I was travelling up a slight rise on a left-hand bend. It was all pretty smooth, and then I saw it: a B-double semi-trailer had rolled and was lying on its side, taking up one and a half lanes. I was the first on scene, and it was a mess. The truck had been carrying paint and cardboard, which now littered the road and the median strip which divided the highway. I managed to pull over just in front of the truck on the left shoulder. The truck's headlights were still working, and the reflection onto the road enhanced the chaos. I ran to the driver's cabin and found the driver was conscious but disoriented. Another car pulled up, and that driver rang the police and ambulance.

The truck driver was reasonably OK, with no spinal injuries, but he did have a deep gash on his arm after being cut by window glass. As the situation was still fairly dangerous, we moved the patient through the smashed windscreen onto the edge of the road. Then the police arrived. The police officer came over to me and asked what had happened, and I advised him. He asked if the car with the dog trailer was mine and then asked if he could move it onto the other side of the road to open up the lane to traffic. I told him that was fine, and off he went. However, I hadn't told him about the dogs in the car! Bearded collies are awesome dogs and are well known for their calm and quiet temperament – well, pretty much – but they can bark. The police officer got into the car and was immediately covered by licks from the two beardies. Apparently, they fair scared the crap out of him.

Anyway, the car was moved. I had taken my first aid kit when I arrived at the incident and had treated all the driver's obvious wounds, but as anyone who knows the area along the Hume Highway near Yass, it can be a bit cool at night. So I needed to get the driver a blanket to stave off the shock he would no doubt go through. I asked the other car driver to sit with him as I went to the back of my car and got a blanket which I carry for such occasions.

I was in for a bit of a shock when I headed back to the patient. It was literally only twenty-five feet away, but as I went back, the driver was not there. The other driver said he had gone back into the truck and was rummaging around in the cabin, which, as you are aware, was on its side. I went up to the truck driver and made him leave the cabin immediately, and it would be some time later that I found out what he had been up to.

I maintained a watch on the patient until the ambulance arrived. Once I had handed over to them, I spoke to the police and asked if I could go. They said OK but asked if I would mind sending them a statement after I had made it to Melbourne. Of course, that was OK, and I left my card with the officers and departed.

About a week later, I received an email from the Yass Police, where they provided me with the correct paperwork to fill out. They also told me about what had happened after I had left the scene. Apparently, the driver had been weaving all over the road for many kilometres before he came to grief. The police had ascertained that he was supposed to be travelling from Sydney to Canberra but had missed the turnoff some fifty kilometers down the road and just kept going when he rolled the truck. It turned out he was high on amphetamines at the time of the crash. Now I am pretty naive when it comes to illegal drugs. I've never taken any illicit substances and had not even thought that the driver may have been drug affected when I saw him. Rather, I was more concerned he had hit his head.

However, this comes to the next interesting bit. The reason he had gone back inside the cabin of the truck was to remove any trace of his drug stash! The police found it when they searched the truck... When I had gone back to the cabin to remove him, he had not found his stash! To end the story, the truck driver was gaoled for repeated drug-driving offences. Oh, and I made it safely back to HMAS *Cerberus* to start the next chapter of my career.

The First Bali Bombing
(12 October 2002), Headquarters
Northern Command (HQNORCOM),
and Other Adventures

On 11 September 2001, the USA was attacked by terrorists in what was to become known simply as 9/11. This was to change the face of the world as we all knew it and, particularly for defence, ushered in a time of ramped-up security and a heightened awareness of security matters.

I had, up until this time in my career, spent most of my time in the training environment as ASO for the medical school at HMAS *Cerberus* and also as the administrator of the RAN Hospital, also at *Cerberus*. However, a change was coming. There was now a requirement for personnel to widen their prospects and become more operationally focussed. This was to be a real eye-opener for many, in particular myself, but it was to be also life changing. I was given a choice of posting to an operational headquarters in Sydney or Darwin. I chose Darwin as I had never been there, and what I knew of this posting was that it could be very interesting. This, of course, as you will see, is a bit of an understatement!

I posted to Larrakeyah Barracks, an army base in Darwin, and at that time, the Darwin Naval Base was located within these environs. Headquarters Northern Command (HQNORCOM) was a lodger unit here as well. Now a lodger unit is where several different defence units are co-located in one place. Larrakeyah Barracks was an army base with a naval base and a higher headquarters all together. This was my posting.

The North Atlantic Treaty Organisation or NATO terminology uses a specific numbering system allocated to each job within a military headquarters. This was adopted by the ADF as well as it enables all members of related defence forces to understand to whom they are talking when an integrated response is required for any particular incidents or exercises. This may sound like common sense, and it is, but before this was introduced to the ADF vernacular, it could be hard to understand the roles of military personnel, especially when conducting mass exercises or missions across international borders.

So now I had to learn this nomenclature. I will try not to bore the reader with too much detail, but a little information here is a good thing. I was posted as the J073, HQNORCOM. The J stands for 'joint', so the incumbent could be from any service, but there was a preference here for navy as the operational environment was significantly at sea, thus requiring someone with a good understanding of how navy handles medical situations at sea. The 07 is for health, and the 3 is for operations. A 5 is for plans. So I was the joint health operations officer. My boss was the J07, and my partner in crime was the J075 or joint health plans, who, at this time, was an army major from the army health branch, Maj Shaun Fletcher. I hope this doesn't confuse you as it did me for a while, but it is a very good system as you get the hang of it.

So I've moved into the officer's quarters at the rear of the officer's mess, about 150 metres from the actual headquarters building. Now some more information for those who have never been to Darwin: it's *hot*, bloody hot, and *humid*, especially in the wet season. Also, when it rains, it buckets down. However, as all defence personnel who are posted to the region know, after a while, you do become acclimatised, and this is a very important part of the initial stages of a posting to Darwin. You can't be expected to be ready to go on Day 1. It takes time to get used to it. Did I mention it was *hot* and *humid*?

Luckily, I was posted to Darwin at the end of the wet season in what is locally called 'the dry-season', still bloody hot but not quite as humid.

It was a pretty big difference from what I was used to on several planes. The first was the weather, which I have mentioned. The second was the vibe of the Northern Territory. It is a totally different place to the southern States of Australia where I have previously been posted. The third difference was this was the first time I had worked in a headquarters. Within this environment, the majority of personnel are officers. There are some from the lower ranks, but about 90 per cent are officers. The reason for this is the operational imperative. Decisions made at the headquarters level may well have larger implications in the political arena of the Federal Government and affect Australia's national interest. Therefore, the people at the coalface need to be at the officer level, and, I would add here, this in no way disrespects those of the ADF from the lower deck – as we call them, the actual workers. It also means that when the bumkicking starts, they know exactly where to go!

I was in awe of this place. I'm sure you've all seen the movies that show the inner workings of an operational headquarters: lots of big-screen TVs, computers, maps, etc. Well, it's pretty much on the money. I admit, I was a tad overwhelmed at first. Usually, one does not necessarily have daily, even hourly contact with quite senior officers. At HQNORCOM, the senior officer while I was there was a brigadier general, with his deputy being a naval captain.

Without giving up national secrets, I can say that the health operations desk was located right at the front of the operations room, just behind the duty watchkeeper's desk. The watchkeeper was the first point of contact (POC) for the outside world. Signals, telephone calls, and radio contact are all directed to this station. The information is then disseminated internally as appropriate. The reason the health desk was right behind the watchkeeper was so that close contact could be maintained whenever a medical problem arose. As the reader may well know, time is often of the essence in medical emergencies.

So after a few weeks at the desk, I felt confident enough to request certain things to help during any such times. My first idea was to get an actual health resource map that could be projected onto the main screen so I could have almost instant access to health support for personnel as required. It sounds a bit dull, I suppose, but I was pretty chuffed with the outcome. The J07, my boss, had the entire north of Australia to monitor. This went from roughly Broome around to Cairns. That's a bloody lot of coastline and also apparently empty country. In conjunction with my colleague (oppo), the J075 and the boss, we were the monitors of health requirements for all defence personnel within that zone. The J075, as the planner, reviewed all the health support plans for each operation as required. This involved keeping in contact with local civilian hospitals, the Royal Flying Doctor Service, the Northern Territory Aero-Medical Evacuation Service, and Royal Darwin Hospital (RDH), to name a few. These health plans are integral to the success of every mission that the ADF undertakes. Of course, we are not the only input. All sections within the headquarters have an input into plans. Discussions regarding these plans are vital, as one would expect, and it helps every person understand how all the sections work together and, in particular, what limitations, if any, there are.

Often, when non-military people hear of a mission, the first thing that comes to mind is that it all happens *now*. Well, it doesn't. Ships can't instantly traverse an ocean, aircraft can only go so fast, and it takes time to get the myriad other resources going. We can do things pretty quickly though, and thorough pre-planning, revised planning, training, and exercise practice help to achieve the best results. So now you have a very rough idea of what my job was like at HQNORCOM. It could often be stressful but always interesting. Now to expand on some of the things I was directly involved in.

As previously alluded to, the J073 position was pretty much 'watch-on, stop-on'. I was basically on call 24/7. I had a couple of very memorable events occur during my time at the headquarters. As noted, we had a huge area to cover with regard to providing healthcare to defence personnel, who were within our area of operations or AO. This particular occasion, a Saturday evening, I was called in at about 1945 hours. I was told by the duty watchkeeper that one of the patrol boats out in the Timor Sea had a sailor on board who was in a bad way. There are no medics on patrol boats, but the coxswain (the guy who steers the boat) has extra medical training to be able to sort out minor maladies, and there is also a direct line to a medical officer via radio, in Sydney. The symptoms that were relayed indicated that the sailor had acute appendicitis. This usually requires surgery to remedy, as the reader would know, so we had to get him back to Darwin in the quickest possible time. This is where I came in.

Using our plans for retrieving patients from sea, I had to organise one of the longest medevacs that had been undertaken in many years. First, the boat had already turned about and was heading back towards Darwin at best speed –a good start –but the patient's condition was not all that good, so I had to do a little tapdancing. The quickest way to get him back would be by air, but there were no helicopters within range. The plan was to send the patrol boat to an Australian oilrig that was located a few hours away. At the same time as this, a helicopter from Troughton Island which was used to service the oilrig was sent to the oilrig. At the same time, a fixed-wing Northern Territory aeromedical service or NTAMS aircraft was sent to Troughton Island, and RDH was alerted.

By this time, I was aware that I would be up all night coordinating and reporting on this emergency mission, and I had my awesome map up on the big screens. Also, I was in the ear of the duty watchkeeper at the same time. This was the main reason my desk was located up the front. The ADF relationship with NTAMS came to the fore here, as one can imagine. So the patrol boat was enroute to the oilrig. They made good time, but the sea state meant that they had to use the oilrig's crane on the lee side (away from the ocean swell) to winch the patient up. Then the helicopter landed and transferred the patient onboard and then flew back to Troughton Island. Once landed there, the patient again transferred, this time to the fixed-wing aircraft, which departed for Darwin. About now, I lost contact with the mission as we did not have direct radio liaison, so I was flying blind – pardon the pun.

By now, it is dawn, and I'm hoping that the plane should have arrived. I briefed my boss and the brigadier and then headed off to Darwin Hospital to see if I could find my patient. I went directly to the emergency department to see if he had arrived. As in any major hospital, Saturday nights/Sunday mornings are usually pretty busy, and the number of walking wounded and crook people was amazing. Remnants of a brawl from the main street in Darwin were strewn about the waiting area – bloodied head wounds, broken limbs, and the usual overwhelming stink of alcohol –but I digress.

I went up to the counter and spoke with the triage nurse and asked if my patient had been admitted. He hadn't. He was not there. Of course, I'm thinking I've stuffed up somewhere and lost this bloke. Just as I was about to ring the boss with the great news, in through the door walks an able seaman, walking, not rushed in on a stretcher, lights flashing... He just walked in. I went up to see if he was my patient... and he was. Apparently, as the transit time was so long, his condition improved so much that he was able to make his way into emergency from the ambulance. I was stunned, but these things happen. He was checked out and diagnosed with grumbling appendicitis. He made a full recovery and was slated for surgery at a later date.

The Area of Operations

One of the most important aspects to get your head around in any new posting is the very nature and size of your AO. In a headquarters posting, the area under the control of the senior officer will be quite large and diverse. This was so at HQNORCOM. If the reader could imagine a line similar to the Tropic of Capricorn drawn across the map of Australia from roughly Townsville across to Broome, it covered all land north of this, out to the two-hundred-mile limit, and Ashmore Island. It is continuously patrolled by naval vessels and customs vessels and overflown by RAAF long-range P3-C aircraft. In other words, it's bloody huge.

When I joined HQNORCOM, I was given an option to travel the western AO or the eastern AO as a part of the induction program for the headquarters, and this is very important as it gives you a better idea of just how vast Australia is. I chose the western AO as I had never been there before. As one would gather, the areas are designated either east or west of Darwin. There were six members booked on an army flight, a small eight-seater aircraft which would take us from Darwin, down the coast of Western Australia. We stopped for fuel at Kununurra, Broome, and also visited one of the RAAF bases which is located some fifty kilometers inland from Derby. This was an amazing trip and gave me a very good grounding in just how big Australia is and the region we looked after.

To top this trip off, we had landed in Broome and were there overnight and due to fly back to Darwin the next morning. However, we were advised the next day that the plane had to leave immediately for East Timor and did not have time to refuel, so they could only take one passenger back to Darwin and then immediately go to East Timor. This left us stranded in Broome. Oh, it was terrible –not! We were booked on a civilian flight late that afternoon and so had some time to kill, as often happens in defence. So we went to Cable Beach for the day and went for a swim in the Indian Ocean. It was a small blip on our schedule but was very memorable.

One additional trip I was able to undertake was aboard a P3-C Orion. These aircraft conduct long-range surveillance as required and often are used in tandem with the navy patrol boats or customs vessels in searching for illegal fishing vessels or illegal entry vessels which are used by people smugglers. The patrol normally takes ten hours and covers vast areas of the Indian Ocean, including out to Ashmore Island. It was an amazing sight to see the island from the air but was even better as seen from a patrol craft.

During the course of my posting to HQNORCOM, I was involved in many operations, both land and sea, and some of those were particularly interesting. At this time, the Howard Government was in power, and one of the biggest issues was the influx of boat people from Indonesia and the subcontinent. I should add here that during my posting, no illegal immigrants came ashore; however, we were prepared for these possible eventualities. HQNORCOM was the overseer of this operation by using naval assets, primarily Fremantle-class patrol boats and/or customs vessels. Either one of these types of vessels was stationed at Ashmore Island, a very small Australian territory, four hundred kilometres due west of Darwin, and were to monitor and intercept possible illegal immigrant boats before they landed on Ashmore Island. Each one stayed about a week and was relieved by another boat.

To ensure safety of life at sea (SOLAS), each patrol boat was allocated a medical sailor. This is not a normal thing for a patrol boat. The usual medical cover is provided by the coxswain, who has done an advanced medical course. However, as most would know, these particular times were very politically tense, especially with relationships between Australia and Indonesia. So to help with maintaining SOLAS where necessary, a medic was sent to HQNORCOM, briefed by the J07 cell, and then transported out to Ashmore. The rotation for each medic was about one month, whereas the patrol boats would often return to Darwin, leaving the medic on the relief boat. It sounds exciting and would be for several days, but as usual, waiting is often the game we are part of.

I was the main POC for the medical sailors, and as such, I needed to be up to speed on what their duties were and what it was like out at Ashmore. So off I toddled. I was taken out to the island by the customs vessel *Dame Roma Mitchell*. These are state-of-the-art coastal patrol boats used by Australian customs, now border force. The trip takes around twenty-four hours depending on sea state, but it was quite enjoyable when I went. There were many interesting things around this mission. First, when I awoke the next morning and went on deck, there were twenty or so flying fish dead down aft on the fantail. During the night, they had been doing their thing, and as they leapt from the water, some landed on deck and could not get back into the sea.

As we approached Ashmore, the skipper showed me how the fishermen from Indonesia find their way from Roti in Indonesia all the way directly to Ashmore Island, often without GPS. As you approach Ashmore from over the horizon, the clouds which are ever present have a definite green hue. This is caused by the reflection of sunlight through the pristine water at the island, hitting the sand in the lagoon and bouncing back up into the atmosphere. It was amazing to see, huge cumulus clouds with a definite green tinge.

On this particular day, one of the customs crew was an indigenous man from the Tiwi Islands. He was a lovely bloke, and we chatted about all sorts of things. As we approached the island, he told me he would be transporting me from the *Dame Roma Mitchell* to the other boat that was already in position in the lagoon. There, I would see the medic, get a good handle on how things went on a daily basis, and therefore be able to convey this to the incoming medics. However, before we transferred, the customs crewman asked if I wanted to see the island close up, which, of course, I did. Now it should be noted here that it is not normally allowed for people to step onto the island at all. However, because the customs crewman was indigenous, he was allowed to take me there.

So I was launched from the Customs patrol boat in their rigid-hull inflatable boat or RHIB. This had eight seats forward of the steering and a very large outboard motor behind. This is capable of transferring personnel very quickly and can reach forty knots without trying too hard. We made our way towards the island and slowed for the final traverse of perhaps five hundred metres. The water was crystal clear, warm to the touch, and full of things that could kill you! I saw turtles, fish of all sorts, and sea snakes – heaps of them. They were just swimming along with their heads above the surface, some banging into the boat. It was a little unnerving. After about five minutes, we were close enough to get out and walk the last few metres. It was *hot* –and *humid*. As was the uniform of the day, I was in grey overalls, known as RAWLS. These are not comfortable and heat up quickly, so before long, I was gasping, but as this was the opportunity of a lifetime, I was not going to miss out.

Ashmore Island is not big. The reef area is quite extensive, but the main part of the island above the high water mark was around four hundred metres in diameter. There are two palm trees, a couple of graves (of Indonesian fishermen), and, at that time, a contaminated water well. It really is a gorgeous part of the world. One thing I did note though was when we walked across the island to the western shore, it was covered in garbage that the prevailing currents had pushed onto the beach. It was pretty bad, as I recall, and I hope in the intervening years that a concerted effort has been made to clean it up.

The First Bali Bombing

In 2002, 12 October was to be a day that changed our lives in Australia and was to play a huge part in the rest of my life.

As I have mentioned, my job at HQNORCOM was just about 24/7. On the odd occasions, I was able to get away from the base but had to be contactable at all times. On Sunday, 13 October 2002, as I did almost every day, I called into the headquarters to check if anything requiring a medical input was on the boil. I found that my boss, LTCOL Wiltshire, was in the operations room. I asked what was going on, and he said that a bomb had gone off in Bali last night. I was actually going to a BBQ lunch, and the boss said to go, and if he needed me, he would call.

I went with friends to Howard Springs, reasonably near to the base, where there was swimming and BBQ facilities and lots of critters for kids to see, in the wild! The goannas up there were big and would often come around when people were about to eat any food that was given to them. Feeding them is not a good idea and is actually banned as they can become very aggressive. After about half an hour, I became a bit worried about the bombing, so I excused myself and went into work. I'm glad I did. By this time, the picture had become clearer, and it was realised that the ADF would have to deploy assets to assist Australians caught up in the horror of that night.

Maj Shaun Fletcher, the J075, was called in to assist, as was the staff from the navy sickbay, which is across the road from the HQ. I was tasked with resourcing as many army stretchers as I could find within the local army units that are located at Robertson Barracks, the sickbay at Larrakeyah, basically anywhere I could find them. We were advised that Headquarters Australian Theatre, located at the Fairbairn RAAF base in Canberra, was despatching two C-130 Hercules aircraft with aero-medical evacuation teams to Darwin, where they would refuel, get

173

stores, and deploy to Bali. Time, of course, was of the essence. A huge team effort came into motion. I will tell this story from my perspective, but it should be noted that the operation, which was to be the biggest medevac conducted since the Vietnam War, went exceedingly well. From the outside, it would look so, but behind the scenes, we were like the duck on the pond: all calm on top but paddling furiously underwater.

But first, another small diversion. The RAAF base itself in Darwin is co-located at Darwin International Airport. One side of the runways is civilian; the other is RAAF. For command and control, there is a bunker located on the RAAF side where contact can be made with the defence aircraft and teams as required. For this operation, it was decided to allow the C-130 aircraft to use the civilian side of the airport for landing and storing and would be the egress area for the patients when they arrived. The most important reason for this was that RDH, which was to be the stalwart medical centre for this evacuation, was ten kilometres closer than the RAAF side of the airport as the ambulances would have to drive around the outside of the base to get to the aircraft.

With that in mind, after I managed to gather around fifty stretchers, as I recall, I delivered them to the RAAF side in the first instance before we moved everything across the airfield. We also had to get stores that the medical teams would need to load quickly on their arrival. Maj Shaun Fletcher deployed to the command post to set up and liaise with the RAAF personnel. I was tasked with going to RDH and picking up some blood to be taken to Bali for the injured. This all took time, and by about 1900 or so, we were set for the arrival of the Hercules from the south.

I had managed to obtain the stretchers, some oxygen, some intravenous fluids, and other items. When the planes landed, they were fuelled, stored, and ready to fly to Bali. I had introduced myself to the AME teams and exchanged phone numbers etc. so we could gain a better idea of what was happening on the ground when they arrived. After they left, I made my way to the bunker on the RAAF side of Darwin airport. The area had been set up by the J075, and he handed over the control to me. There was a wing commander from the RAAF in overall command of the bunker, but he was not always there as he was liaising with other commands, so as the senior officer present, it fell to me. This was my first major task and one that was to have a profound effect on me in the future–but more of that later.

As you could imagine, the most important thing we needed to get was information from the team on the ground. It was only a couple of hours' flight to Bali, so all the behind-the-scenes stuff that had to be done at our end was on the boil. Trying to pre-empt the requirements was a bit of a job but would stand us in good stead. One of the big considerations was keeping all the right people in the loop. These included RDH, the boss at HQNORCOM, and my boss, the J07 and liaison with the sickbay at Larrakeyah Barracks.

Of course, there was the waiting. This can be one of the hardest things to bear at times, but I was so busy, time just flew. I remember when the first plane had landed in Bali as I received a call from the team as they were making their way from the airport in Denpasar to the hospital. As I recall, some ADF medicos had gone ahead, while others were preparing to receive patients at the airport. As I spoke with the team in the car, one of them took a photo of them all crammed into the car, with one of them on the phone. We came to realise later that I was on the other end of the line at the time, giving them a 'headsup' on how we saw things going. Media information was also flooding out of Bali, so it was all over the news, as I'm sure those who were around at the time will remember.

While the teams in Bali were doing their stuff, I was about to receive two more Hercules aircraft with their AME teams on board. I had managed to also obtain extra oxygen from the sickbay and a pallet of intravenous fluids, which were quickly loaded as soon as practicable. I remember there had been a bit of a problem with crew flight hours, but the RAAF sorted this out very quickly.

As soon as I was informed the first Hercules was returning from Bali heading to Darwin, I informed RDH and also the police and ambulance services. In Darwin, like most capital cities in Australia, there is a combined headquarters for the emergency services. The direct liaison between them and HQNORCOM was Captain Overton, RAN, who was the second-in-command of HQNORCOM at the time. He had positioned himself at the emergency services HQ, so they had face-to-face contact, which made things much easier.

About an hour before the rescue flight landed, the ambulances had arrived on the civilian side of the airport. They were marshalled into a long line down the fence line, waiting their turn to pull up to the rear of the aircraft. When the C-130 landed, it taxied to the prepared staging area. By this time, around 0930, it was starting to get quite warm, as Darwin does. This was to prove a bit of a problem for patient comfort, but the feeling I got from the patients was that they were just glad to be back on Australian soil.

Immediately on landing, the aircraft shut down, and the rear ramp lowered. I made my way on board to do a head count and name check of all on board as I was to be the link directly to the emergency services personnel. It was one of the most eerie sights walking up the ramp. I had been on Hercules aircraft many times and knew they were designed not only to carry troops but also to carry wounded personnel. *The place looks like a bomb had gone off inside* was my immediate thought, but the chaos was well organised. The most critical patients had been loaded last so that they were first off, straight onto an ambulance, and then off to RDH.

I have a picture taken by one of the newspaper photographers who was covering this story on my wall at home. It shows a patient on a stretcher just off the plane, surrounded by medical staff, both military and civilian, including myself. Also in the photo is a RAAF sergeant, Sgt Wendy Jones. I had made good friends with all the staff during the mission, and Wendy was one. We served again together in 2005 during

Operation Sumatra Assist II, the ADF's humanitarian mission to the island of Nias, south of Sumatra, Indonesia. What makes the 2002 photo even more precious is that Sgt Wendy Jones was killed on the first day of the 2005 mission, in the SeaKing Shark 02 helicopter crash.

As already noted, the lesser injured were towards the front of the aircraft. As I made my way along the walkway, I noted one of the patients had died during the flight. It was quite a shock to see close up, but we had a job to do. As I mentioned before, the Darwin heat was becoming oppressive within the aircraft. Unfortunately, when the engines shut down, so does the airconditioning, which works an absolute treat in flight. As soon as we could, we got all the patients off the aircraft. As most were stretcher cases, we placed them on their stretchers under the wings to get the shade. The ambulances were shuttling to the rear of the plane, where I would confirm the name of the patient, ensure medical documentation was at hand, and generally keep the line moving. However, it was quite a laborious job, so I went around to check on everyone of the patients to see how they were doing.

Now, as I noted, this was a huge team effort, and we all pitched in as required. One memory that has haunted me a little was one of the young blokes who was quite badly injured. He was on a stretcher under the wing and was waiting for his turn to be transported. I rechecked him on my list and, as I do, decided to have a quick chat.

Of course, the first thing I say is 'How are you doing?'

He replied he was OK, but as I looked down, I noticed that both his feet were gone. It just felt like I said the wrong thing at that moment, but he didn't seem to worry.

It was mentioned later in the press, I believe, that some had wondered why we hadn't put all the critical patients on the first flight. The answer to this is that we don't have the personnel to look after sixty or so critical patients at one time in the air. It takes a team of four to handle each critical patient, so it is just not practicable from a personnel point and the amount of equipment required would have been enormous. So the decision on the ground in Bali was to triage the patients as best they could and allot spaces for a selection of conditions encountered. Most had burns or traumatic blast damage, so the choices for the onsite medical team would have been difficult.

We had several flights bringing patients back to Darwin. One interesting one was a young Australian guy who had been surfing in Bali. He was relatively uninjured but had made it onto one of the flights. Why interesting? Well, he managed to get his surfboard on the plane as well. When he arrived in Darwin, he was taken to the hospital to be checked out and left his surfboard on the plane. When it was discovered, the flight crew brought it to me for safekeeping. I had it placed in the bunker where we had been working and promptly forgot about it; well, I did have some other things on my mind! After the mission was completed and we were returning to our separate units, my understanding was that it was still there. The surfer had returned to the south without it. I still don't know to this day where it might now be.

Anyway, I digress yet again. I hope you will forgive this as there is so much going on in my mind as I write this, trying to recall, often vividly, everything that went on in those few days. We had moved a large number of people safely back to Australia using our excellent RAAF medevac aircraft and teams, along with army reserve and senior disaster management medical staff from South Australia. It was amazing.

Once all the patients had been transferred to the RDH, the next phase of the operation was to stabilise them all and then transfer them to other capital cities in Australia, depending on where the patients came from mainly or where the best treatment would be available for their particular injuries. I'm pretty sure that most went to the States where they lived. This, of course, was a complex undertaking and was to take place within a twenty-four-hour period. Several of the extremely critical patients were taken by air ambulance (Learjets), but the remainder were flown by the RAAF again. The Hercules crews had been rested, medical stores for use during the flights replenished, and aircraft cleaned and reset for this next leg.

After I had managed a few hours' sleep – not many, I might add – I was off to the RDH to see how things were going and advise them, from the ADF standpoint, how we would carry out this next phase. Obviously, the doctors would liaise with their counterparts in Brisbane, Sydney, Perth, Adelaide, and Melbourne regarding the transfer.

Now one piece of kit that I had only seen on the TV show *M*A*S*H* was available to us from the RAAF. It was an ambulance bus or AMBUS. As the name would indicate, it is a bus that has been gutted and fitted with the ability to hold a large number of stretchers with patients for transfer. This was invaluable and allowed us to move more people safely and with due care than trying to use all the ambulances in Darwin and the surrounding areas. So about twenty-four hours later, we were scheduled to start the flights south. I arrived at the hospital after organising ambulances and the AMBUS to transfer patients to the aircraft.

I recall we used the RAAF side of the airport this time to try to make it more comfortable from the point of view of media scrums that might occur. Each aircraft was loaded at the appropriate time for each destination. When they had arrived, the racks were four high with patients, but the outgoing trips were a lot fewer, no more than two high, as the patient load was spread out among the destination hospitals.

By this time, I had been running on adrenalin for a couple of days with minimal sleep, but the feeling of being able to help my fellow Australians as part of an extraordinary team of ADF, reserve, and civilian medical staff and aircrew was just amazing. It was also to change my life literally in the future, but of course, I wasn't to realise just how profoundly at that time.

We successfully moved all the patients to destinations south within a twenty-four-hour period. It was a brilliant effort by all involved, from the initial medical team deployed to those on the ground in Darwin and also the RAAF airmen who had no experience with anything like this who helped load patients on the AMBUS. I commend them all.

Still, it wasn't over for me quite yet. After we had moved as many patients as could be done – I believe one or two were too sick to move at that time – we had to close the bunker, and I had to write the after-action report. I was also badly in need of some sleep, and by now, it was almost the following weekend, so I was able to get some rest. Notwithstanding this, I was still on edge for a few days as I tried to return to normal.

On the Monday morning, as we attended the morning brief at HQNORCOM, our medical team – the J07, J073, and J075 – were all thanked by the brigadier in front of our colleagues for our efforts during this national crisis. As I mentioned at the start of my writings, these are my memoirs of what I went through during some pretty horrendous times in the ADF, but I didn't do any of this in isolation; it takes a great team to make great things happen. Again, this was not quite the end for my involvement with this. The day after the last patients were flown out of Darwin, the J07 tasked me with getting ready to deploy via civil aircraft to Bali to conduct a search of the hospitals for any possible remaining Australians who may have been missed. I prepared to deploy, having bought an Indonesian/English dictionary just in case. I was on standby for twenty-four hours before I was stood down. It had been decided to request the Red Cross to do this undertaking.

I will just note here that I had copies of everything I did during this time, including a list of names, destinations, etc. These do come in handy when asked to recall things at a later date, for instance during BOIs, but my list was to be of great assistance to me personally in the future.

About a week after all had calmed down, we were invited to a BBQ at RDH to thank all the emergency service workers, hospital staff, and ADF members who had been a part of the team. It was a great event in that we all got to talk about it, have a drink, and try to let the event mellow somewhat in our minds.

Within a short time after this mission, all ADF personnel who had been involved were required to attend a debriefing by the psychologist unit out at RAAF Base Darwin. This was the first time in my career that the ADF had done this and wouldn't be the last. It was a fairly rudimentary post-trauma discussion about how this made you feel etc. I had already noted some change in my thoughts, but of course, being a big tough naval officer, I would harden up and get over it —not to be, of course, but that was a little way off and a few more missions down the track.

So we all returned to work to prepare for the next mission, whatever that might be. For me, I didn't have to wait too long. Not many people are aware of or remember the follow-up C-130 flight taking, I recall, two quite ill young Balinese children from Bali to Perth for burns treatment. They had been injured during the bombing and were being treated in Bali, but their conditions had become worse, so the Australian Government organised their transfer. Now how did I get involved with this? Well, as they were flying from Bali to Perth, one of the patients' condition deteriorated badly, so they changed course for Darwin. As I was on call as usual, I was informed at around 2300 this night of the need to assist. The flight would be landing at the civilian side of the airport, which was quite busy at that time as there is usually a midnight flight from Darwin to either Melbourne or Sydney that leaves then.

I had to organise an ambulance for the transfer and inform RDH that they would be receiving another Bali victim. Also, the family was travelling with the patient this time. I also have some pictures of this, although I wasn't aware of the media being there. They were a fair way off, and their photos show the ambulance, aircraft stretchers, etc. and me standing out in my white uniform. We loaded the patient into the ambulance with their family members as well.

The aircraft needed to refuel before continuing to Perth, so the other patient had to be taken off the aircraft to allow this to occur. By this time, it was around 0030 (12:30 a.m.) or later, and as we had nowhere to go to, the family and I sat on the tarmac some twenty metres away from the aircraft with the patient. They were quite well spoken in English, and we chatted for a while as the refuelling occurred. After the plane was ready to resume its flight to Perth, we were informed from the hospital that the other patient had passed away. It was a very sad moment for all present, but we needed to get this other young patient to Perth, where they would undergo life-changing surgery at the burns unit.

I would like to note here that RDH did an amazing job during the first Bali Bombing, noting they did not have a dedicated burns unit. Today there is a state-of-the-art burns unit at RDH, provided by the Australian Government to service Darwin and the Northern Territory and also in case of future disasters such as the Bali bombing in 2002.

By 2004, I had been reposted to HMAS *Cerberus* to the position of staff officer supply, health training policy. Don't try saying that with a mouth full of marbles. By now, I was starting to struggle a bit with my mental health with regard to what I had seen and been through with the Bali bombing. To alleviate some of this, I would give presentations to the medical trainees who were located in the building where my office was. This was cathartic for me, but it was still quite raw. I remember on one occasion during a presentation, one of the students made a comment that I looked as though it still affected me. I hadn't realised until then that I was showing that and that this was leading to my eventual diagnosis of post-traumatic stress syndrome in 2011.

I soon found myself filled with a desire to touch base with some of the survivors if I could find some in Melbourne. I attended an AFL match in Melbourne where the Kangaroos were playing my team, Richmond. A large number of survivors attended, and I was thrilled that more than a few recognised me, remembering my white uniform. I enjoyed that day immensely, and it started to help me get through what I had seen, but I wanted more. I had my list – remember! So I went about trying to track down some who lived nearby and managed to do so. I found Natalie Goold and her friend Nicole McLean. Natalie had pulled Nicole from the Sari Club, and they were the last to get out alive. I also located the Woodgate sisters, Leanne and Samantha. I found Natalie's parents and asked them first if they thought it would be OK if I touched base with their daughter. They were thrilled to hear from me, and I was invited to attend their house the following weekend. I arrived there and was taken aback. Not only Natalie but also her friend Nicole McLean as well as their families were there –and what a feast! They put on a huge spread for me, although I did say to them it just wasn't me. They understood that but also understood that I had to see them again.

To top this off, I invited the girls and their families to attend the next divisional parade at HMAS *Cerberus* – in winter! This parade was attended by the navy's most senior officer, the CN. I had organised the visit through the CO and gave the survivors a tour of the base and the wardroom (the officer's mess). I am convinced from chatting with them during and afterwards that they really enjoyed their visit and now had a better understanding of the navy and the ADF.

To this day, I still keep in touch, although I haven't seen them for a while. They have all moved on and had families and are doing pretty well. I hope, after the COVID-19 crisis eases, that I will be able to catch up in person. Through a most horrendous event, we became friends, and it means a lot to me to be able to see how well they have all done.

HMAS *Penguin*— 2005–2007

In my early career, I was one of only a few medics who never posted to the RAN Hospital at HMAS *Penguin*. This facility is located on Middle Head in Sydney and was the primary medical facility for the fleet, which is based at Garden Island. I was posted there as the MAO, which was the second-in-command position. My job was to basically run the hospital for the surgeon commander and also be 'shadow posted' to either HMAS *Kanimbla* or HMAS *Manoora* when there was need of a large medical team to deploy to disaster areas, mainly in the near Pacific or Indian Oceans, or to conduct training with other nations for the above mentioned disasters.

In the year 2000, I had attended HMAS *Penguin* to undertake the RAN staff course. This course ran for six months and was one of the most intense courses in the navy at the time. We had to cram eighteen months of university-level work into six months, and at the end, we graduated with a diploma in management from the QUT and had the opportunity to complete a master's degree with a correspondence bridging course. I decided against that as at that time, I had already been in the navy for twenty-two years, I was a lieutenant commander, and I wanted to do other things.

HMAS *Penguin* is an interesting base, located on the water on the north side of Middle Head in Sydney. We had a wharf, which was used during World War II to berth Australian submarines; the School of Underwater Medicine is located adjacent to the wharf along with a decompression chamber for training the underwater medics and is used for navy divers who may have 'the bends' and can be used, on request, for civilian divers who have suffered 'the bends'. The base is also home to RANHP, the Royal Australian Naval Hospital Penguin. I was to be posted here as the ASO in 2005. It was a great posting and one which widened my experience in the roles I was to undertake both ashore and at sea. I did have one close call though which still sticks in my mind.

The accommodation for long-term live-in officers was out the back of the wardroom proper. There were double units where the heads and showers were shared, but each room had a small lounge room and a separate bedroom. It was my daily routine, which I stuck to almost obsessively, which, on this particular day, I did not follow and may well have saved my life.

Each morning after breakfast, I would return to my cabin, clean my teeth, and then watch the news at 0630. When the news was done, I would leave my cabin, walk towards the lower hospital, and then climb the stairs up a winding path, passing the diving school building, and go around a tight bend and then up a steep hill which terminated in the road adjacent to the upper hospital. At the top of these stairs, just to the right, stood an enormous ghost-gum. It had obviously been there for years and was part of the bushland in which the base sits.

The week prior to this, Sydney had had an unprecedented amount of rain, and the whole area had been well and truly soaked through. So on the morning of this incident, I had watched the news as usual and was about to leave when something caught my attention on the TV, so I lingered about sixty seconds. I truly believe these sixty seconds saved my life. I left my cabin, locked the door, and walked towards the stairs. I had almost reached the tight bend, and there was an almighty crash and thud. I increased my pace, and as I rounded the bend, I was stunned to see this huge tree had fallen over! I reckoned if I had been on time, as I was almost every day, I would have been cleaned up by this tree. It certainly shook me up for a bit, but as they say, one must 'sailor on'...I don't do the 'soldier on' thing.

As I have noted, HMAS *Penguin* is located on Middle Head in Sydney. It has awesome views to the northern part of the harbour and access directly onto Balmoral Beach, which was great for me and early morning walks and afternoon runs. However, aside from hospital duties, there were also some other jobs that arose. One in particular was for senior officer volunteers to be escort officers to foreign senior officers during the 2006 World Seapower Conference, which was to be held at Darling Harbour in early 2006.

I was volun-told that my presence was required at a briefing at fleet headquarters, located within HMAS *Kuttabul*, up the hill from Garden Island. I dutifully arrived along with a number of other officers and was given a general brief on the requirements of an escort officer, issue of epaulettes (all the gold dangly bits) to wear during the visit, and who I was escorting. My charge was Rear Admiral Al-Kayal of the Royal Saudi Navy (RSN). I was pretty chuffed at this and promptly made the necessary preparations for his arrival.

Of note, as the CN (Australia) had personally invited senior officers from many countries around the world, they would all fairly obviously arrive at different times in the several days prior to the symposium. As it turned out, Rear Admiral Al-Kayal arrived just the day before. I met him at the airport and was quite surprised at how short he was, not that there is anything wrong with that. I settled him in his hotel room and was discussing the first day of the conference and which things he wished to see. He had a list of the scheduled items and marked off those he wished to see.

Of course, on day one, there was going to be a welcome speech given by the CN. The rear admiral asked me then what time his car would pick him up in the morning. Unfortunately, this was not going to happen. His hotel was actually just outside the Darling Harbour precinct, and when I explained he would have to walk (all of four hundred metres), he was less than impressed. However, once I explained the location of the forum, he calmed down.

The next morning, I met him at the hotel, and we proceeded to walk to the forum in time for the welcome speech. However, this is where I learnt very quickly that he was not necessarily interested in the logistic side of the conference. He was more interested in what we call 'the gunrunners', the people who manufactured military hardware. The CN had been speaking for about ten minutes when Rear Admiral Al-Kayal got up and walked out, followed somewhat sheepishly by his escort officer, yours truly. I also discovered quite quickly that even though he had checked off several other presentations, his main goal was to talk to 'the gunrunners'. This term does not mean that the people were doing anything illegal. At such an event as the World Seapower Conference, a number of large and small companies that deal in warships, weapons, and other military technologies have exhibition stands where they can showcase their weaponry. This was the case here. Companies such as McDonnell Douglas, Krupp, Blohm und Voss, and many others were on show.

Rear Admiral Al-Kayal spoke quite good English, but his heavy accent made it somewhat difficult to understand. I tend to have a good ear for accents, and as the morning progressed, I would introduce him to the individual exhibitors as Rear Admiral Al-Kayal of the RSN. This, of course, got the immediate attention of the sellers. Anyone from that neck- of-the-woods would have large chequebooks to purchase their weaponry. One of the main items that the admiral was interested in was for a littoral warship, which means one that can work well both close to a coast line as well as blue water. A blue water navy is one in which the ships of the line can travel great distances across oceans in both attack or defensive positions.

As I listened to his requests, I got to know what the RSN was looking for, so I offered to do the explaining for the admiral. This might not sound like much, but to me, a lieutenant commander of the medical fraternity, to be able to have input on behalf of the admiral of a Middle Eastern ally meant a great deal, especially when I was able to present the Australian ship builders to him.

One of the jobs the admiral asked me to do was to collect handouts, booklets, and any other pertinent information from the vendors so he could review them at a later time. This, I did, and I was quite surprised at how much (and how heavy) this information was. On the third day, as we had done for the past couple of days, we had a meeting in the admiral's hotel room where I had to catalogue all the information I had gathered for him during the day. As he was leaving the next day, he then asked me to go back to the conference centre and get 'one of everything' – again! He said he wanted to mail them home but also to have spare copies to put in his luggage just to make sure the information got home.

So off I went, pretty well flat out. Luckily, the exhibitors were very happy to give me more information, and I eventually got back to the hotel with a heap of stuff. The next day, before I took him to the airport, we went through all the information, and he requested that I mail it to Saudi Arabia, and yes, he gave me US$100 for postage, and following emails later that month, he advised me that the package had arrived. This had been a totally new experience for me, but it is one that many ADF personnel have had in their careers, and these are vital for continued dialogue between countries.

As a postscript to this event, the following year, another interesting thing occurred. HMAS *Penguin* is often used to accommodate officers from other countries who undertake training with the ADF, particularly in Sydney. On this Saturday, I was having lunch in the wardroom at HMAS *Penguin*, and I started chatting to some officers who were staying there. They were intending to go to the shopping mall a few suburbs over and asked about buses. I said I was happy to run them over, so after we finished lunch, we headed out. These officers were from Saudi Arabia and were stationed in the south of the country.

Of course, I piped up and said, 'Oh, I know your boss.'

They had a laugh and said that they didn't believe me.

When I said, 'I know RADM Al-Kayal quite well as I had been his staff officer on his trip to Australia,' they changed their tune very quickly.

It was quite funny, and they were a bit sheepish after that, but we still left as friends. Now that probably sounds dreary to most, but it can be amazing how our military contacts all over the world may someday surface. I had a laugh anyway.

During my tenure as the medical ASO at RANH(P), I deployed overseas several times, including Operation Astute, Operation Quickstep, and Exercise Croix Du Sud. I will deal with the operations separately as they were both high intensity and worthy of note.

Exercise Croix Du Sud (Southern Cross)

This exercise was a biennial event involving the RAN and other navies and was aimed at improving amphibious landings and interoperability between Allied forces. This exercise was conducted in New Caledonia and would stand me in good stead for Operation Quickstep the following year. We were to embark on HMAS *Manoora* for this exercise, but there were only three of us within the PCRF: me and two nursing officers. My remit was to review all the standing orders and write or rewrite as appropriate.

It was a two-week exercise, and the nursing officers were excellent in their work on the orders. There was a fair bit of time to watch what was going on with the landing forces, which, in turn, helped update all the medical data. In naval terms, it was a bit of a 'jolly' but we did get a lot of work done as well as visiting New Caledonia on a port visit. We also attended a combined military parade to mark, if I remember correctly, Bastille Day; as I'm sure the reader is aware, New Caledonia remains a French colony to this day.

On return to Australia, I immediately went back to my normal job as the admino, dealing with all sorts of new and constantly challenging issues from civilian nurses manning the wards to having to close the operating theatre because possums had managed to get into the roof and wreck the roof space directly above the operating table. I didn't make any friends within fleet command doing that, but safety first.

During OP Quickstep in 2006, noted further in another chapter, one of the important aspects was for all personnel to maintain a certain level of fitness. During the day when medical training was not conducted, on-deck fitness classes were conducted using some of our army comrades who are trained in conducting PT. Why do I mention this here? Well, during the push-ups, sit-ups, running, and other gut-crunching exercise,

I somehow managed to injure my shoulder, but it was not evident for some time. When the operation was completed and we returned to Australia, I again returned to HMAS *Penguin* to resume my duties.

In January 2007, I awoke one morning unable to move my shoulder. The pain was excruciating, and I could not move my arm above the horizontal. I was seen by the doctor and, after tests, was diagnosed with frozen shoulder. This was to stop me deploying in 2007, and it took most of the year to come good. Eventually, an injection directly into my shoulder under an ultrasound fixed the problem within a week. I was pretty devastated in missing a large military exercise with the U.S. Navy in Queensland because of this, but as they say, 'drink a cup of concrete and harden up'. My next posting was fast approaching. I was off to the HQJOC, located at that time at RAAF Base Fairbairn, in Canberra.

Operation Sumatra Assist II— The Loss of a Sea King: Call Sign Shark02

I started this chapter on the fourteenth anniversary of the loss of Sea King 02 (SK02). I have had many thoughts of the people we lost on that fateful day as we, the ADF, returned to another part of Indonesia. The operation was codenamed Sumatra Assist II. The first mission (OP Sumatra Assist) had been in response to the tsunami on Boxing Day 2004 that destroyed Banda Aceh and affected many countries in that region. On completion of this mission, HMAS *Kanimbla* was returning to Australia via Singapore for some much-needed rest and recreation for the crew. Some of the crew would fly back to Australia from Singapore, and a large part of the medical team did so, in March 2005.

In late March, another earthquake devastated the island of Nias, which is to the south of the Indonesian island of Sumatra. There were reports of extreme damage and deaths among the island's people, and Australia was, I believe, the first country in the region to offer help. The obvious response from the ADF was to re-deploy HMAS *Kanimbla* from Singapore to Nias. As most of the medical team had returned home, another team was stood up. I was selected to deploy as the second-in-command (2IC) under Commander (CMDR) Wallace as the leader of the detachment. I was posted to HMAS *Penguin* at this time; I had only been there for a short while when the earthquake occurred.

We were informed of the notice to move (NTM) and duly arrived at RAAF Base Richmond. My navy team from Sydney was myself, Petty Officer Medical Steve Slattery, and two other young medics. We were flown from Richmond to RAAF Base Amberley, where we boarded the RAAF 707 refuelling plane and took on extra medical personnel from the RAAF. This flight took us to Djakarta, where we were billeted overnight in a hotel.

The next day, we were flown by C-130 cargo/troop transport aircraft to Sabang Island, off the coast of Banda Aceh, and this is where things became somewhat interesting. The ADF had been on this island some few weeks prior as a staging point for assisting with the post-tsunami rebuild of Banda Aceh. The problem with our mission occurred when a fax did not arrive at the island airport from Djakarta advising them that we were coming!

The C-130 landed at the airport and taxied to a hard-standing or parking area. As the rear door dropped, we were greeted by a team of Indonesian security and army personnel with weapons trained on us. CMDR Wallace was asked by the leader of this team if we were invading Indonesia; the fax about our arrival had not been received from Djakarta, so the local garrison had no idea we were coming. After a short period, we were allowed to disembark the aircraft but were kept in an area near a hangar until confirmation arrived.

Within a very short period, two RAN Sea King helicopters arrived at the airfield. My main priority at this stage was to get all of our team onboard the *Kanimbla*, which was now off the south coast of Sumatra, heading for Nias Island. At about this time, a senior Indonesian officer arrived. As Commander Wallace had departed along with the other specialist medical personnel, I was the senior Australian naval officer present at the air base. I – along with Major Flint, who was the senior army officer for the Australian army personnel – was summoned to a small office in the hangar, where the colonel (as I believed him to be) had positioned himself. After some very snappy salutes from me and my army colleague, the colonel read me the riot act with regard to our presence. He was waving his swagger stick at me, and I was apologising for an obvious clerical error – on their side. The main aim was to continue to get all the medical and diving team from the island out to HMAS *Kanimbla* in the shortest possible time, safely.

The two Sea Kings did their relay flights to the ship, while I kept the colonel in the picture. Just prior to the last transfer, which consisted of me and two other personnel and the last of the equipment and baggage, I went and saw the colonel to thank him for his assistance. He gave one last wave of his swagger stick and sent me on my way with a warning not to do it again! I boarded the helicopter, and we departed for the ship. Little did I know at that time that within twenty-four hours, the aircraft I was in would crash, killing nine of the eleven personnel on board.

On reaching the ship that day, we were all excited to be a part of this mission. There were a few medical staff that had remained on *Kanimbla* and were a great help to us newbies. I would like to particularly thank Lt Cmdr Annette Lambert, RAN (Ret), who assisted me greatly by organising every new medical staff member before I got on board.

After introductions to the CO and XO, accommodation sorted, and SCRAN eaten, which was actually very good, plans were made for the next day. Two helicopters were to deploy, one with an Indonesian official and RAN scout team, the other with a medical team to do the first sweep for casualties. The teams were put together and briefed about the sorties and were obviously keen to get started.

The following morning, the ship was ready to deploy the two teams. Final briefings were conducted in the main hangar, gear checked, and preparations made for takeoff. My role after we launched the helicopters was to go to the operations room, located just behind the bridge. Just like in the movies, it was dark and full of equipment that I did not understand. I was there so that I could advise the medical teams that remained on board of any incoming patients prior to their embarkation on *Kanimbla*.

All appeared to be going normally when a sudden burst of radio chatter came from one of the helicopters. It did not sound good to my ear, and it took a couple of moments to grasp what had possibly happened. One of the helicopters, Shark 02, appeared to have crashed! The other helicopter had moved to the vicinity and reported that they could see wreckage burning in the middle of a field near the village of

Amandraya (Ahh-mun-dray-ya). It was Shark 02, and it had crashed onto a soccer field just above the village. At this time in the operations room, only four people knew what had happened, and it really did feel like I had been punched in the stomach. This just couldn't be happening, but it was.

Certain things have to happen in these situations. Obviously, we needed to assist any survivors and transport them back to the ship ASAP. The second helicopter landed and found that there were two survivors, an able seaman (I believe he was a navy communications sailor) and a leading aircraftsman medic from the airforce. They were quickly loaded into the helicopter and departed for HMAS *Kanimbla*.

Once I had been made aware of this situation, we piped over the ship's communications system for the PCRF to close up. This meant that all resuscitation teams and medics were to immediately muster in the hangar and prepare to receive casualties. I made my way from the operations room to the hangar deck to advise the staff of the situation because at this time, no one else knew what had happened. It is one of the hardest things to do, informing personnel that shipmates were injured and a number had been killed.

After the initial shock, all members quickly went into action mode. All stretchers were made ready, resuscitation kits brought to standby, and the triage area made ready. Once the helicopter landed, the two injured personnel were brought into the hangar by one of the side hatches and taken to the forward bulkhead area in the hangar which was the resuscitation bay. Think of it like the emergency department of any hospital but with no curtains.

The assigned teams, which had really not had any time to train together, started their work as soon as the patients arrived. My job as the second-in-command of the PCRF was to take an overview of the event, noting as much as I could of the action as it occurred. This information was then relayed to the OIC and could then brief the CO of HMAS

Kanimbla, who had overall operational control. It is worthy of note here for those unfamiliar with life at sea and especially life in the navy that the CO is the overruling power on the ship. What he or she says goes. This is particularly important during warfare as the safety of the ship and crew is the CO's prime responsibility.

One of the very important aspects of this type of incident is to make sure we correctly identify the personnel. Manifest lists are required to be checked and identity verified. At this time, both members were conscious and were able to verbally identify themselves. Their injuries were not life threatening, but one had a badly broken leg, the other a head wound. Both were obviously in shock. I was extremely proud of the entire PCRF team that day. They went about their work in a professional manner while having to come to terms with the loss of nine shipmates, which included six medical staff, our colleagues and friends.

Once triage and initial treatment were carried out, both members were transferred to the ward. The airman with the broken leg had a complicated fracture of the tibia, the big bone at the front of the lower leg, which required surgery to realign and stabilisation with external fixateurs. These are the metal rods drilled into place through the bone and connected externally with metal joints. These are adjustable to keep the bones in alignment as it heals and is a much better treatment than the old plaster of Paris. Unfortunately, we did not have any external fixateurs onboard the ship, so his leg was realigned under sedation and plastered while we waited for a fixateur set to arrive from Australia. These did arrive within twenty-four hours and is a testament to the logistic system which worked very well during this deployment. When we obtained the surgical fixateurs, the member was sent to surgery again and had his injury repaired. Within a couple of days after the crash, both members were returned to Australia to undergo further assessment.

In the meantime, a team from HMAS *Kanimbla* was despatched to the crash site and, along with a team from Australia, went about the task of body recovery and identification with subsequent repatriation to Australia. A team of air crash experts was also deployed to Amandraya to conduct the investigation into the crash.

This incident was tragic and did affect every member of the crew, but we still had a mission to complete, and it would not be right to 'up sticks' and return to Australia as this would be seen to lessen their sacrifice. As Amandraya was a small village in the highland area of Nias Island, it was decided to conduct a medical clinic in the town. This was duly organised, and teams were selected to travel to the site. *Kanimbla* anchored off the coast in the north of the island, and medical staff and others were transferred by the ship's boat to the nearest town.

From there, it took about an hour to get to the village in the back of a truck, much like a cattle truck. It was quite a difficult trip as there was some road (if you could call it a road) damage caused by the earthquake some days before. At one point, the road was so badly damaged, we had to get off the truck while several trees were used to patch the area of road that had dislodged and slipped down the hill to get the truck through as there was a foot-and-a-half difference in height from one section of the road as well as subsidence.

After an eventful journey, we arrived at the village of Amandraya. It was not a large place but did have a soccer field just above the town, which is where the helicopter had crashed. Directly adjacent to the soccer field was the police station, and next to this was the only public toilet, if you could call it that. I will get back to this as I was to spend some not-so-joyful time in it.

There were a number of houses on the main street, which was dirt. However, they were made of concrete and surprisingly sturdy. This was where we set up the medical clinic. It did not take long for the team to set up and start seeing patients. We were limited in what we could do overall, but the locals were very happy to see us. It was my understanding that many had never seen a doctor, and those who had said it was some long time ago. As usual, the climate was against us pretty much the whole time. The daytime temperature got up around thirty-five degrees, with the humidity around 80 per cent. To say it was stifling was an understatement, but the team performed admirably. As my role was mainly liaison with the local mayor and police, I was doing a fair bit of moving around between the medical clinic and the police station. As I dislike hot weather, I was suffering a bit and was drinking copious amounts of water. This now takes me back to the public dunny.

Imagine, if you will, a room about ten metres by ten metres. The walls are concrete and about four metres high. There is no roof. The sun is beating down upon you. It does not smell terribly good at all. There are no stalls... In this large area, there is one long-drop hole. That's it! Add to this a somewhat dehydrated but good-looking lieutenant commander (me), a very rumbly tummy, and being dressed in the navy's overalls, which take a bit of getting out of, along with the above conditions...I did not have a pleasant day, but this was an aside. I cannot express my absolute awe at the job the medical and support staff did for this village, in the highlands of a remote Indonesian island, now inextricably bound to the ADF.

We saw many patients over the two days we had a clinic here. I know that I and all my team gained a lot and were able to feel totally involved in this endeavour, and this helped us grieve the loss of our comrades. Several members of the ship's company designed and created a memorial, which included part of a helicopter tail rotor placed vertically in a hole and cemented in, with soft-rank insignia of those who perished attached to the blade. It was a simple yet very striking cenotaph.

Over the couple of days we were at Amandraya, our medical teams helped a lot of people. Unfortunately, there were some whom we could only help a little. Those people had attended our clinic with diseases or illnesses that were long-term, and we could not provide continuous care. One young lass who was, we thought, about 16 years old had been carried for two days to get to Amandraya from another small village.

She had been born with deformed limbs and could not walk or look after herself. There was nothing we could do other than provide some antibiotics for bed sores and clean her open wounds. However, the family who had brought her there were really thankful to us for what we could do. It was very moving to be a part of the team, but it was still quite distressing at times.

Lahewa

We left Amandraya, returned to the ship, and weighed anchor to sail to the north coast area of the island as no one had heard from any of the villages in this area since the earthquake. Our destination was Lahewa (La-hay-waa). This village lies at the southern part of a small bay on the north coast. The earthquake had severely damaged the area as a whole, and this made bringing the *Kanimbla* alongside impossible. The entire cement wharf had collapsed into the sea, and its position was only visible by the electric streetlight poles that stuck up out of the water, some distance from shore. Nearer the shore, the concrete mess that was once this pier was obvious. The destruction of this town was almost complete. Not many buildings had survived the earthquake at all. Many had pancaked – crushing people, cars, everything. It did look like Armageddon had come to this little place.

As it had been about eight days since the earthquake, unfortunately, those who had been severely injured had already perished. However, there were those who had survivable injuries but had not been treated as well as a lot of people who had long-term illness or disease who had heard of our presence and had travelled long distances to see a doctor. This is quite a common occurrence in these types of situations, but we were ready for them.

We set up a medical area at the local convent/orphanage, which was located about one kilometre along the main street. It was stiflingly hot and humid, but the team did extremely well under the circumstances, and it wasn't just the medical teams that pitched in. We were still grieving the loss of our shipmates and colleagues, and everyone wished to add something to the mission in their memory. We had communications specialists to keep contact with the CO on *Kanimbla*, stores personnel who provided food to the medics and the people, security personnel to keep an eye on us, and engineers who repaired the local pumps to get the water supply up and running. It was a great team effort across the board, but there were a couple of things to come which held my teams up as being outstanding.

We had been offered a small room at the edge of the convent to hold our medical clinics. One should remember that in Australia, we have rules about medical-in-confidence – only the patient and the medic know what goes on. However, in some countries, they have no idea about this. So there we were, treating patients on a table in the middle of this small concrete room, no airconditioning, windows open, and crowds of people being triaged at the door, with every window packed with people and kids looking in at what was going on. The medics, doctors, and nurses of my team did an outstanding job treating each patient with care and respect and treating their conditions as best we could. It was an extremely uplifting and fulfilling time, one that I am sure none of us will forget –and then an aftershock hit!

I happened to be outside the clinic, standing under a tree, taking photos of the area and, in particular, the chapel area of the convent. It consisted of a large still-standing outdoor area covered by a sloping roof with open sides. It sat on a concrete slab with pew-like areas for chapel services. On the roof was a Christian cross; however, during the main quake, it had been dislodged and now hung upside down, barely hanging onto its position. It looked quite bizarre, but I digress slightly. Suddenly, there was a loud noise, and the ground started to move. There were a number of locals sheltering from the sun under the chapel roof, but I have never seen people move so fast as when the aftershock hit. Luckily, the clinic survived the shock, as did the chapel, but it did raise the feeling of apprehension just a tad!

Over the few days we were in Lahewa, we transferred a couple of locals to the ship for further medical treatment: X-rays, blood tests, etc. Some of the crew who were non-medical also wanted to help in some way, and when they were allowed ashore, they started up games for the kids in the large park-like area next to the convent. Some cricket and kicking of an Aussie rules football were well received by the kids.

As one might expect, the loss of our shipmates in the helicopter crash made world news and had shocked the people of Australia. To support us in our mission, it was decided that the MinDef, the chief of defence (CDF), and the CN would pay the ship a visit in Lahewa. This was organised, and the minister, CDF, and CN arrived by UN helicopter a few days before the mission was completed.

On this particular day, I had gone ashore as the overall medical supervisor, and I was to greet and brief them when they arrived at the clinic. Their arrival was somewhat unceremonious as resources were limited, so when the cattle truck pulled up with them in the back, it was quite a sight, also noting that the CDF and CN were both very tall and their heads stuck out the top of the canvas roof.

They visited and spoke with the entire medical team after being briefed by myself. Sometimes you would think that this sort of thing was a bit over the top, but to us, it gave a sense that people back home cared about what had happened to us and supported our efforts. After a relatively short visit, the dignitaries returned by truck to the 'town square', where they were to wait for the UN helicopter to pick them up. The CO of the *Kanimbla* was also present with them during this visit, and as we waited, we chatted about the mission and how I thought it was progressing. Suddenly, a loud crack was heard, with the sound of a building collapsing.

Just opposite the town square park area, there were several houses, some quite badly damaged in the initial quake. I had just taken a picture of this house literally minutes before the main wall that had been left standing suddenly fell.

The CO just looked straight at me and said, 'Go.'

I ran the two hundred metres or so, in navy coveralls, in stifling heat and humidity, in world record time – or maybe a bit slower. We had seen that when the collapse had occurred, several locals nearby had rushed in to drag someone out. When I and one of my medics arrived, the injured man was gone! I quickly found out that he had been dragged out, unconscious, placed on a motor bike, sandwiched between two locals, and taken the one kilometre to our clinic. So we commandeered two motor bikes, with drivers, and they whisked us to the clinic also. It was a hair-raising ride which I did not think I was going to survive! On arriving at the clinic, the man had regained consciousness, but it appeared he had a badly broken leg which needed to be X-rayed. So I found a local truck nearby and had the driver take the injured man with some medics back to the wharf and subsequently to the ship.

As the clinic had already packed up for the day, I returned to the park area on foot, lugging a large medical pack. When I arrived there, the CO, MinDef, CDF, and CN were still waiting for the UN helicopter. I walked up to the group, saluted, and reported to the CO about the actions we had carried out. From the time the wall collapsed until the patient was on the wharf, ready to make it out to the ship, it had taken only twenty-five minutes!

I was extremely proud of our efforts with this, and it was also noted by the senior personnel. Two little things regarding the end of this story... The next day, as I was at the clinic again, I was greatly pleased to see the patient walk into the convent. His leg had not been broken, just badly bruised, and his care was transferred to the nuns, who were doing a fantastic job. The other thing was the reason the guy had been in the rubble in the first place. Apparently, he had gone into the house and had been trying to remove the taps from the sink, and he had been yanking on them quite hard when the wall collapsed –a very lucky man.

We finally left Lahewa and made our way to Singapore, leaving the area in a bit better shape than we had found it. I know this had a profound effect on me and many others – the loss of friends and colleagues but also the feeling that we had accomplished the mission we had set out to do and thus honoured their memory.

Epilogue

The ship sailed from Singapore to return to Australia. This would be via the Arafura Sea and down the Queensland coast, inside the Great Barrier Reef. Of course, the mission and the loss of nine personnel was headline news in Australia, and as we got closer to Townsville, this became evident.

One of the main army regions located in Northern Australia is located in Townsville. Here, a large number of army aircraft are located. To welcome the ship home and to memorialise the passing of so many ADF personnel, a flypast of all the types of helicopters the army had occurred over the ship. It was an amazing spectacle as they overflew the *Kanimbla*, yet there was to be one more, a flyover by an F-1-11 fighter bomber from Amberley AirForce Base. They flew north to coincide with the helicopters. It flew over the ship and down the starboard side at very low altitude...only a few metres above the level of the upper bridge of the ship. The noise was incredibly loud, but the whole event was a great boost to the crew's morale, having so many others doing this for our crew.

Two further things occurred on our trip home. First, the CO anchored the *Kanimbla* adjacent to the Percy Island group, on the landward side. The reason here was so that we could prepare the ship to enter harbour in Sydney, so it was all hands to cleaning stations. Everyone mucked in, and this was done relatively quickly. On completion, we remained at anchor overnight before leaving in the early hours the next day. In the interim, the CO allowed personnel to go ashore to one of the larger islands for a wander around if they wished. I jumped at the chance. It's not often you get these chances, so I took it. Only three others from the crew took up the invitation, much to my surprise.

The ship launched a RHIB, and off we went, in our mufti clothes (shorts and T-shirts). As we approached the beach, the RHIB driver would not beach the craft as it was not clear how deep the water was. So he said to jump off. Let me just say this – it was a tad deeper than I thought, and I lost my glasses as I was submerged. Luckily, I got them back, and we landed on the beach. The island was pretty big and quite rugged, and we explored it for an hour or so. We found what appeared to be a rear door from a large cargo plane fairly high up a ridge. We could only guess how it got there and how long ago, but the estimation was it was World War II wreckage.

We returned to the ship well exhausted from the climb, but it was worth it. Later that night, we weighed anchor and headed for Sydney, where we understood the PM was going to meet the ship, along with the Indonesian consul general and senior military staff. As we turned into Sydney Heads, we were confronted by an awesome scene. Hundreds of small craft had come out to welcome us, including large tugboats with their fire hoses going full bore. It was quite emotional, really, and even more so when we came alongside in Garden Island.

The crowd to greet us was huge. There were banners all over the place: wives, kids, sailors, and the PM and the senior military staff. It really was amazing. I didn't have anyone particular waiting for me, so I did not get off the ship straight away until I noticed a great friend of mine, Warrant Officer Karen Edwards, had come to the wharf. I had served with Karen at HQNORCOM in Darwin, and we had become lifelong friends. I made it down to the wharf and got hugs, as one does. Then she said to me to go and get a picture with the PM. This, I did. So I have a picture of me and PM John Howard on the wharf in Sydney. About a month later, all members who had been on Operation Sumatra Assist II were invited to a morning tea with the PM and MinDef held at Parliament House in Canberra, where I managed to get another picture with the PM but in a different uniform.

It was a pretty dark time in the ADF. We live and work in a very dangerous environment. However, we don't go to work thinking we may not come home that night. We serve our nation for many and varied reasons, and I certainly hope I have served my country well.

On a final note, apart from that fact that we lost nine of our ADF brothers and sisters, two in particular still haunt me. The first was the loss of Petty Officer Medical Steve Slattery. When the team for this mission was put together, four came from Sydney: me, Steve, and two others. We returned home without Steve.

The second was the loss of FLTSGT Wendy Jones. Those of you have read the chapter on the Bali bombings will note that she was one of the ADF medics who worked with me on the repatriation of Australian citizens injured during that heinous terrorist attack. When I got to *Kanimbla*, I ran into her, and we had a good chat and were going to catch up again after the first day of the mission. Unfortunately, she died the next day, and we never did get to chat.

Operation Quickstep and Black Hawk Down

As you've probably noticed, 2005 and 2006 were very busy for the ADF and our operations within Australia's area of interest. Such was OP Quickstep, the Australian response to a military coup in Fiji. This was to send HMAS *Kanimbla* and HMAS *Newcastle* towards Fiji in case there was a need to evacuate Australian citizens. In doing so, we needed to standup the PCRF. This is a mobile unit of medical personnel that deployed to either HMAS *Kanimbla* or HMAS *Manoora* in the 2000s. Both these ships were fitted out with operating theatres, X-ray and laboratory facilities, several wards (including a high dependency unit), and a three-space emergency triage area in the aircraft hangar which is directly outside the PCRF access doors.

Because of early signs that Australia may need to be on standby to help in the evacuation if required, HMAS *Kanimbla* was ordered to steam to Townsville, where she would take on stores, army personnel trained in mass evacuation, and a Level Three PCRF. The PCRF is not normally borne on the ship but is a lodger unit as required. The makeup of the medical staff is from across the three services and also relies on specialist medical staff from the army reserves. These are usually doctors from some of the biggest emergency hospitals in Australia, such as Royal North Shore and St Vincent's in Sydney.

I was given command of the PCRF for this deployment, one where I was outranked by several of the senior specialists, including a brigadier general. To make sure all went smoothly, I called them either sir or ma'am, and they called me boss. It is not a usual thing to have an officer junior in rank to be put in charge, but in the medical branch, this can occur in such situations where the senior personnel have a clinical role, whereas I didn't; I was the administrator and the POC between the ship's CO and the PCRF.

So off we go. The army team arrived in bits and pieces on the wharf in Townsville and were taken onboard *Kanimbla* and went through the usual checks. It is vitally important to ensure that every member is accounted for and allocated not only bunk space but also life raft space. So in the event of a 'man-overboard' or 'abandon ship' situation, every person onboard must know where their 'leaving-ship' station is. This was even more important as there were a lot more personnel on board for this mission. The *Kanimbla* can support a crew of 601 persons, including army members. As most have little or no experience on ships, their safety is paramount.

After all stores and personnel were embarked, HMAS *Kanimbla* sailed for the Fiji Islands area. HMAS *Newcastle* was in New Zealand, which is where I and the specialist medical team met up with the ship. We sailed about eight hours after we boarded for the AO adjacent to the islands of Fiji. As you may be aware, a coup had occurred in Fiji, and there were concerns that Australians may be targeted, so the Australian Government enacted a plan to deploy our military closer to Fiji. This was the start of a very long forty-five days at sea, without seeing land. On board were the PCRF, members of the army evacuation unit, and some commandos.

As the *Newcastle* came close enough to the *Kanimbla*, a helicopter was sent to pick us up and fly us back to the *Kanimbla* to join the rest of the PCRF team. Now I will just pause here for a moment. The helicopter type sent to pick us up was a SeaKing. As you will recall from an earlier chapter, this was the type of helicopter that had crashed less than twelve months before, and here I was, in another one! I was a little nervous, as you might expect, but I managed to keep calm. When we landed on the ship, we were quickly briefed on the plan for the rest of the day, i.e. accommodation, wardroom etiquette for the officers, etc. I mention the etiquette because there are usually only a relatively small number of officers on the ship, but this time, there were about three times the norm, with all the SAS and medical specialists.

The major in charge of the army health team was Maj Brett Dick, a great bloke and someone with whom I got on very well. He had already started his troops' training during the voyage from Townsville, so I was free to liaise with the CO and the operations staff when I arrived. This mission was to be long and somewhat tedious, but that is usually the way in defence –hurry up and wait. Still, it was also a chance for members of the three services to train together, understand how things work on a ship from a manpower aspect, and be the best we can if the need arises. Unfortunately, that need would arise nearer the end of the deployment.

The first three or four days were spent honing our medical skills and working in different areas of the PCRF. There were teams formed for the emergency treatment area, and their time was used practicing for a variety of medical presentations, such as airway management, serious bleeding, head injuries, etc. Each team would stay together at their particular stations so that they could work as cohesively as possible. There were operating theatre teams manned by specialist medical personnel, from surgeons to anaesthetists and theatre nurses. We had ward staff, laboratory technicians, X-ray technicians, and medics from the navy and the army.

The teams were quickly up-to-speed, and then we waited, which, as noted above, is a usual function of defence –plan, hurry up, wait, train, wait. I guess you get the drift. The ship was, for the duration of the mission, constantly moving inside what we call 'the box'. This is an area on a chart that the ship moves within to remain fairly close to a point where it can quickly move towards as the situation requires. In total, we sailed within the box for forty-five days. That is a long time, especially when you don't sight land, but that's what we were there for –to remain on station to assist with the evacuation of Australian nationals from Fiji should that be required.

I would like to mention here that although all members of the ADF are highly trained, we also must exercise this training so that when it is needed, things go as well as can be expected. Therefore, the specialist training got underway quite soon after we sailed. On the medical side, we had stretcher drills, operating theatre drills, patient movement drills, emergency care drills in the triage area, suturing drills, chest tube insertions, and first aid. Everywhere, there were personnel training in one form or other. We had daily emergency exercises in the triage zone within the hangar. We also have to keep fit, so physical exercise must also happen.

Assisting us with this task were a large number of army personnel and a couple of their BlackHawk helicopters. These aircraft are the quick transport and deployment helicopters. Army personnel use the 'fast rope' system to get from the aircraft to the ground or the deck of a ship in quick time. They carry a number of large coiled ropes that are dropped from inside the helicopters and out the side doors, and then the soldiers rappel down them. I'm sure the reader will have seen this on any number of American military television shows. To ensure training levels were maintained, the army personnel practiced deck drops fairly regularly. It was pretty awesome to watch, and on one occasion, I was allowed to watch the evolution from the helicopter control room.

On HMAS *Kanimbla*, this is located on the port side aft (lefthand side down the back), about three decks above the flight deck. Large windows allow close surveillance of each aircraft movement in and around the ship. To say the display of flying skills and rapid evacuation of the helicopter were spectacular is an understatement. The helicopter would approach from either the port or starboard side at a fair speed when the pilot would pull hard back on the control stick, and the helicopter would go nose up, tail down and then level out, all within a pretty short time. The ropes would be unfurled from within the aircraft on either side, and then the soldiers would rapidly slide down the ropes and take up defensive positions while the helicopter left the flight deck area. Being that close to the action from my point of view was quite exciting.

Even though I have flown in numerous helicopter sorties over the years, this evolution was awesome to watch. Later that same evening, I did have a chat with one of the pilots, Captain Bingley, in the wardroom, and he explained how he did this manoeuvre. It was very interesting, and we had a great chat about his flying career. Little was I to know that this would be the last time I would see him.

Before I go further with the events of the next day, I will give a little background on where the medical contingent was accommodated within the ship. HMAS *Kanimbla* and HMAS *Manoora* were a similar layout as both were the navy's amphibious warfare ships. They have a crew of 230 or so and can also carry 400 embarked forces. This refers to either an army unit or a medical unit. The accommodation for this many personnel is spread over a number of large messes, which have bunks three levels high.

When we embarked for this operation, as there were a large number of soldiers and fifty-four medical staff, the accommodation quickly filled. As such, even though I should have been in the officer's mess or wardroom, I was down aft below the waterline in a large mess holding around forty-five medical personnel. I had no worries about this as that's how things go sometimes. Noting that this mess was down aft, the reader can surmise that it is directly below the flight deck but two decks below. Now back to the following day.

The day started, as usual, with a muster of all the medical personnel in the PCRF with training aspects noted for the day. As I recall, after lunch, there were to be helicopter serials or practice runs for the SAS troops to practice fast roping. During flying stations (i.e. when they are flying), the main hangar doors are closed. Inside the hangar were a SeaKing helicopter and, I recall, another BlackHawk. To the front of the helicopters was a rack holding a number of flak jackets, and directly in front of these was the triage area for the PCRF. We didn't have much room at all in this area, which was fitted with three army litter-style stretchers with just enough room for each trauma team to move around their respective casualties.

The practice serials were underway, and every now and again, you would hear the Black Hawk come in, either port or starboard, come to a hover, wait a few seconds or so, and then move off while the soldiers landed on the deck and came into the hangar via the starboard-side gangway. Up until this point, the mission had been very quiet, with the main medical focus being on training and, of course, the usual accidents that can happen aboard the ship. One such accident occurred when a sailor was moving through a doorway and slipped, shinning himself on the combing. The combing is the area that sits proud of the deck into which a watertight door or hatch fits. You will have seen in any movie with a warship in it where, as a sailor moves through a doorway, he or she has to step through and over the combing. Now if you mistime your movement, you can shin yourself. This hurts —a lot! This poor bloke had a dog-eared laceration around ten centimeters long right to the bone. Luckily for him, we had a huge team of surgeons and operating techs who looked after him. He couldn't have done it in a better place, but I digress again.

As the mission had been pretty quiet and we had been rotating the reserve personnel back to Australia as they needed to get back to their normal workplaces, I was discussing the next rotation with my chief medic, standing in the resuscitation bay behind the flak jackets. We discussed whether he should also return to Australia as it appeared we may not have to be in the AO much longer. He had just left the hangar, and I was writing some points in my notebook when it happened. I could hear the next Black Hawk approaching from the port side. As he came to the flight deck, he was too low, and as he stood the machine on its tail, the rear rotor hit the outer side of the flight deck, right on a ladder. This tore the entire tail off the aircraft. The emergency klaxon sounded, a terrible sound which I had heard before on the aircraft carrier HMAS *Melbourne.* As my head snapped up from what I was doing, I saw the entire hangar door vibrate, and I ducked down right behind the Kevlar vests. I then heard another crash and the klaxon still blaring. Remember, the door to the hangar was closed, and I had not seen the crash, but I was certainly aware of what had happened.

The helicopter had spun around, hit the starboard side of the deck, and then rolled straight off the deck into the ocean. Note that as this aircraft was doing fast-roping practice, both the main body doors were locked open, so as it hit the water, it sank straight away. Most of the personnel managed to escape and made it back to the surface. Sadly, the pilot, Captain Bingley, was dragged unconscious from the water, and though my medical teams worked on him for over half an hour, he could not be revived. Additionally, one young soldier was caught up in the ropes and other pieces of broken aircraft, and his body sank with the aircraft. The area in which the incident occurred was nearly three kilometres deep, and it wasn't until three months later that the helicopter and the remains of the young soldier were recovered.

Now as you might imagine, there was organised chaos occurring. However, training takes over pretty quickly, and rescue efforts began. Life rings were thrown into the water, and even a couple of soldiers who were on the flag deck jumped over the side to give assistance. This is not the done thing as it can complicate the entire rescue, but it is understandable. Additionally, we had divers in the water at the time of the crash, and as such, the stern door was in the down position. This then made things even more complex as there was a large number of people in the water: rescuers, divers, and survivors of the crash. A RHIB was already in the water for just this sort of emergency and was deployed to pick up survivors, while others made their way onto the rear door and were helped up to the hangar deck to undergo medical assessment.

One problem that became immediately apparent was that half my medical staff was below at the time of the crash, in the medical accommodation and were locked in. As the mess was below the flight deck, all the hatches were closed in case of just this type of accident. Fortuitously, near the ladderway out of the mess, there was a CCTV setup which showed a live picture of the flightdeck. The personnel in the mess realised that there was no fire involved, so they quickly opened the hatch and got out, closing the hatch behind them. This quickly bolstered the number of medics both in the hangar and in the PCRF, and we were at full Level Three capability within minutes.

In the meantime, patients were coming into the hangar and being assessed. The most badly injured were looked after first, as expected. Captain Bingley was brought into the resuscitation bay after being dragged from the water and rushed back to the ship. The crew of the RHIB were conducting CPR on him the entire time, and they transferred his care to the medical staff as soon as he was brought into the hangar. The PCRF resuscitation team immediately continued CPR and applied the necessary protocols to try to save his life. Unfortunately, after half-an-hour, nothing more could be done, and Captain Bingley was pronounced dead.

However, the remaining teams were still sorting through the other survivors. To make sure I was across everything, I had taken up a position just in the breezeway in an area next to the PCRF doorway, and I stood on some pallets which were luckily stacked there. This gave me a great overview of the situation, especially as I needed to keep the CO apprised of the situation. We still did not have a final number of patients and injuries, and I was making sure we had all the right names as I knew that if I got it wrong, then the ADF may have informed someone of the loss of a loved one, and that may not have been the case.

At the end of the emergency, we had accounted for all but one person, whom we kept searching for, for another twenty-four hours. His remains were located and returned to Australia some three months later when the helicopter was recovered from the sea floor, some three kilometres deep.

As I have previously mentioned, I always carry around with me an army field notebook. During every emergency I have been involved with, be it within the navy/ADF or in civilian street, I make notes immediately after I have finished the first aid treatment. So it was on this day as I stood above the scene, watching my navy and army medical teams doing everything to save lives and treat the injured. I made copious notes of times and the main parts of the scenes, and these would later be most helpful.

The following day, Captain Bingley's body was carefully and, with full military courtesy, taken from HMAS *Kanimbla* and transferred to HMAS *Newcastle*, which would take him to New Caledonia for further repatriation to Australia via RAAF Hercules, along with several other members of the army helicopter crew and SAS men who could not continue because of their injuries.

HMAS *Kanimbla* held a memorial service in the hangar a day or so later, and the navy sent a critical incident team with several psychologists out to the ship to speak to the crew. This was the first time, I believe, that this had been done, but at the time, I felt it was a little too soon (my personal opinion only). The crew really needed a day or so to grieve before having to fill out forms about how we felt, so the CISM team were not heralded when they arrived. There is a superhuman bond among members of defence, especially when there is a tragedy such as this. However, it was a sign that the ADF had a better appreciation of the need to provide a quick and thoughtful process to managing ADF personnel's mental health.

The ship remained on station until early December, when we returned to Townsville, and most of the PCRF staff disembarked and flew back to our different navy, army, or RAAF bases from all over the country. It had been a long and sometimes boring deployment but will be remembered for the loss of two lives, men serving their country and sadly paying the ultimate price.

Epilogue

After I returned to HMAS *Penguin*, I resumed my role as the MAO, and in due course, I was ordered to attend a BOI for the helicopter crash on Operation Quickstep. This was to be conducted at Randwick Army Barracks in Sydney and would run for several days to a week or so. On the day required, I attended the base and, in turn, was brought before the court to answer questions about that day. I have never been so nervous in my entire career.

I entered the courtroom and was seated in the dock while I recited the oath. There were, on my left, several senior officers and lawyers presiding over the inquiry. The room was packed with people, including the families of the deceased ADF personnel. I would state here that I had been briefed by the ADF lawyers that the reason I had been called to testify was that the PCRF had done an outstanding job and the court needed to hear our side of the events of that day. I was questioned at length about our protocols and how I thought we handled everything, and as I had been asked to provide a copy of my army field notes, I was asked about that, in particular why I, as a naval officer, was using it, not that there was anything wrong with it but just to clarify why to the inquiry. As I've previously stated, I have used and still do use the notebook to write down everything I do or, as in this case, everything I could see my staff doing. I had been around long enough to know that when we are in full working mode in an emergency, the adrenalin keeps you going and assists in making sure you make the right decisions. When the emergency is over and the adrenalin slows, the ability to recall details can be impaired. So writing things down at the time helps me to write the after action report, which can then be used in a variety of situations.

After an hour or so on the stand, I was dismissed with thanks from the inquiry. I was sweating pretty badly and must admit I was glad to be finished; however, it must have been terrible for the parents and relatives who were in the court for the entire enquiry. As I left the room, I was followed out the door by one of the junior legal officers with whom I was acquainted from all the pre-inquiry work we did. She caught me before I left the building to ask about a couple of the acronyms and shorthand notes I had submitted. At the same time, I was aware of a gentleman standing behind her, waiting to speak to me.

When she had finished, the man came towards me and offered his hand, which I shook. He immediately said he wanted to thank me and my PCRF personnel for trying so hard to save the pilot's life. To be honest, I was taken aback and could not speak for some moments, having a dry throat and feeling pretty down after this experience. I did manage to reply with a thank you, and then he turned and walked back to the courtroom. The man: Captain Bingley's father.

Operation Astute— 2006

Operation Astute was an ADF operation to assist the people of East Timor in 2006 following a second uprising of local militias that were threatening the local population. From an ADF standpoint, the mission was to deploy personnel to Dili to secure the airport and allow aid from Australia to get to the people. A deployment of army personnel was taken via navy catamaran from Darwin to Dili, where they would deploy to secure the airport. The navy would then follow up with HMAS *Kanimbla*.

The navy was to provide HMAS *Kanimbla* with a Level Two-Enhanced medical team aboard to provide medical support to army personnel. Again, at this time, I was still posted to HMAS *Penguin* and thus was to deploy to the ship with a mainly navy medical contingent with several RAAF specialist officers, with X-ray and pathology personnel and a couple of army operating theatre staff. The senior medical officer deploying was a commander, but he delegated the overall medical mission command to me as the second-in-command as he was dealing with the clinical issues.

I was flown to Darwin to join *Kanimbla*, which had made her way there from Townsville, as I recall, where she had been conducting exercises. I arrived at the ship and immediately found we had a few problems. Unfortunately, as the deployment had been a little rushed, certain things from a medical point of view had been missed. One particularly important one was that all of our surgical operations equipment's sterility status was about to expire and would do so before we reached Dili. The steriliser on board was not able to redo the entire equipment list, so a quick fix had to be prepared. The reader will remember that I had been heavily involved with the Bali bombing evacuations in 2002, and I was quite well known at RDH.

My plan was to take all of our surgical instruments to RDH and get them to sterilise the whole lot in one go if they could. I arranged to get access to the sterilisers, and as *Kanimbla* was moored at an ammunitioning buoy in Darwin Harbour, a young corporal who was a part of the operating theatre staff on board and I loaded our gear into a boat to head to the wharf. I had been ordered by the XO that we had to wear civilian clothes and take our passports just in case it took longer to get the gear sterilised and the ship had to leave without us! We would then have to make our way to RAAF Base Darwin and organise a flight to Dili. Thankfully, we were able to get all the gear re-sterilised and back to the ship before she sailed.

It took us, as I recall, about a day or so to reach Dili. It was quite distressing to see a large portion of the capital burning – well, it appeared that way. HMAS *Kanimbla* stayed out at sea but well within sight of Dili. This was so that the army could ensure the ship's safety by occupying the wharf area once they had secured the airport. As we sailed up and down the coast, we could see fires burning all over the city. We also could hear gunshots ringing out sporadically.

When the Australian Army took control of the port, HMAS *Kanimbla* came alongside. From this point, the CO told us we were to be a form of floating hotel for the army, where they could get hot meals, have showers, and get some down time. We also provided medical support as required and, in general,'showed the flag'. This refers to the actual presence of the ship and how that projects power so that any of the local militias would be less likely to continue the disruptions. At first, we did not venture ashore as there were some people taking the odd potshots at the ship. It wasn't too long though that they were routed and the violence decreased markedly.

During the remainder of our stay alongside, my medical team made good use of the ship's ability to use the landing craft that we had on board to travel the coastline around Dili. We went to see the second largest statue of Jesus (in the world), which is on the hill directly adjacent to Dili, and also ventured the other direction towards the airport. One funny moment was when the CO took me aside just before we went to take some supplies to the army members who were still protecting the airport. He told me (and the LCH coxswain) that neither I or any of my medical team were to get off the LCH when we reached the beach as 'he did not want the second invasion of East Timor since WWII to be a herd of medics'.

This operation was initially quite quick, but the results were good. After two weeks, the city had returned to almost normal, and the requirement for a full medical team to remain deployed had been reviewed, and it was decided that the majority of us would return to Australia. So the commander and I discussed the details and chose a couple of the medics to remain with the army first aid post located at the airport while we flew back to Darwin. Commander Donavan was the medical officer. Now anyone who knows him realises he is slightly vertically challenged –not that that is a crime, but the funny side of our departure will become evident.

The departure was scheduled for early in the morning. We were to travel via an open truck through Dili to the airport, where we were to board a C-130 Hercules transport plane. The C-130 has been a mainstay of many of the world's defence forces and has been in the RAAF for well over fifty years.

The arrangement was for us to be woken up at zero-stupid-hundred hours – that is, around 0500 – and we would leave the ship around 0600. All was going to plan – not! We were woken up at 0400 and told we had ten minutes to get our gear on the wharf and get our body armour on. The body armour was dark blue and consisted of a bullet-resistant vest and a Kevlar helmet. Now comes the funny bit, in my opinion, and I apologise to Commander Donavan in advance. As I said, he is quite a short man and has a big bushy beard. When he got decked out in his gear, he looked very much like one of the dwarves from *Lord of the Rings*. Sorry, sir.

So we were on the wharf – duffel bags packed, Kevlar in place – and we were loaded onto the truck. As I said, it was an open-topped truck, and we all sat along the benches located at the sides. Even though we had body armour, we did feel quite exposed. Although the city had calmed right down, there were the odd sporadic spates of violence, which was one reason why the actual movement of the team to the airport time had changed, and to make matters really bad, the truck driver got lost! There we were at zero dark hundred hours in a city that had been on fire with riots and gunplay a short while ago... and not a weapon between us! Not that it is always good to give a medic a weapon.

Eventually, we arrived at the airport, and as dawn broke, we were loaded onto a C-130 for the flight back to Darwin. There were only ten or so personnel on board, which made a huge difference comfort wise. After arriving in Darwin, the medical team split up to return to our original ports of origin.

Operation Astute was relatively short, but again, Australia was seen to be supporting our regional neighbours, thus stabilising the region.

USNS *Mercy* — 2006

I start this chapter as the COVID-19 virus pandemic continues, in late March 2020. I was encouraged to start this chapter when I saw on the television news tonight the sight of the U.S. hospital ship *Mercy* docked in Los Angeles to act as the largest hospital in that city. I am hoping that this will be seen as a beacon to all our friends in the United States at this particularly grim time in our history.

In 2006, I remained posted to HMAS *Penguin*, which is located on Middle Head in Sydney, New South Wales. I was the MAO at the Balmoral Naval Hospital, and as such, I was also shadow-posted to a deployable billet. This means that when Australia needs to deploy medical staff to assist in disaster relief anywhere in our region, I would automatically be chosen as either the OIC or the deputy OIC of this medical contingent. At the time, either HMAS *Kanimbla* or HMAS *Manoora* was declared to be the responding Australian naval unit to any particular crisis, mainly because of the logistics and the onboard hospital in support of operations. I had previously deployed on HMAS *Kanimbla* as part of Australia's response to the Indonesian earthquake which occurred on the island of Nias in March 2005, but I digress.

In June 2006, I received a message from the fleet commander that I was to report to his office at fleet headquarters, which is located at HMAS *Kuttabul*, just above Garden Island Dockyard in Sydney. On arrival, I was ushered into his office, admittedly with some trepidation as I was not entirely sure why I was there. I was absolutely thrilled to find that I had been chosen to lead an Australian navy medical contingent that was deploying to the USNS *Mercy*. The *Mercy* was to undertake its first ever humanitarian mission to the South Pacific and the subcontinent, and Australia was assisting by the deployment of a small nine-person medical specialist team.

As I said, I was exceedingly pleased to be given command of this team. Apart from myself, all the members were from the Australian Naval Reserve and included two gynaecologists, a psychiatrist, a psychologist, a paediatric nurse, an operating theatre nurse, and two medics. The first time we all came together was at the airport when we boarded a plane to Djakarta, Indonesia. I was a lieutenant commander at the time and realised that the situation we were in was quite unusual as I was given command of this deployment with the powers of a CO, and half my team were senior to me in rank. This can, as you might imagine, be a little difficult; however, the team were great, and all called me 'boss', which solved that very minor problem. We landed in Djakarta and were taken to a hotel in the centre of the city. This was a bit stressful as Djakarta had a lot of military on the streets and the hotel was blast-proofed with sand bags because of recent terrorist attacks.

After a good night's sleep, we continued our journey and flew to Medan, on the island of Sumatra. As the boss, I was, of course, trying to look out for my team and ensuring a smooth transfer between picking up our luggage prior to transferring to yet another plane. Unfortunately, it was not to be.

The Medan airport was quite small, and the baggage collection area consisted of one carousel. It was very busy and noisy. My team's baggage slowly started to appear, along with one of my duffel bags. Before I left Australia, I bought an extra bag as we had a fair bit of kit to take. After a little while, all baggage was retrieved except my new bag. Of course, I was a little perplexed but not as much as when it finally appeared. I had started with a brand-new navy duffel bag, but the bag that came out on the carousel looked very unlike it. It had been covered in bag wrap, similar to that which some people put on their luggage to prevent access by anyone else. My bag's zipper was broken, and all the contents were being held in by this plastic. I was shocked but more worried that someone may have planted some contraband or stolen some of my gear. As we had to get our next flight, I had no time to undo it and check.

So we transferred to another, smaller plane which then flew us to a town called Gunungsitoli, (Gun-ung-sit-oli), located on the north of the island of Nias. Nias lies to the south of Sumatra and was the island that the HMAS *Kanimbla* had deployed to following the horrendous earthquake twelve months before, where Australia lost nine military personnel in a helicopter crash. One of the reasons that we joined the *Mercy* was that they were visiting this island as part of their mission.

The next part of our deployment was very interesting indeed. We landed at the airport. Now it would have to be the most un-airport-looking airport anywhere. The terminal was about the same size as a lounge room; the carousel was nonexistent, and the cooling system was a tad outdated. It was an airconditioner, high up in the wall, which had a large bird's nest in the filter. To make matters somewhat more difficult, there was no one there to greet us. Now back in 2006, I didn't have a mobile phone and had not really anticipated requiring one for this mission. Fortunately, one of my team had one with international roaming, and I managed to get a call back to fleet headquarters requesting advice.

So it's about thirty-five degrees and humid, and we are standing in this tiny airport, waiting. I might add we were all in civilian clothes at this time. Within about twenty minutes, a small minivan arrives, driven by a local lady. She was our transport. Something I had not been aware of at the time was that the USN has many contracts in place around the world for local people to provide services to visiting warships. This includes transport, garbage collection, and other essential requirements that have to be provided but are not permanent to an area.

So all nine of us cram into the minivan that has seats for nine and only a small amount of room for luggage. This began the first hair-raising part of this mission. The pickup point to join the ship was at the wharf in the township. We headed in that direction at speed and with no seat belts! As the boss, I was in the front with one of the team and the driver. The roads on Nias are not the best, anyway – only one vehicle wide, paved but fairly lumpy.

As we passed through the countryside, we noticed many of the locals farmed rice. So that they could dry the rice after it was harvested, they lay blue tarps right on the edge of the roads, on both sides, and spread the rice out to dry in the sun. Several times, we came a bit close as we sped along, and tarps went flapping and rice went flying. As I recall, it took about twenty minutes to cover the distance to town. I vividly recall the near miss we had as the driver approached a more built-up area and had to slam on the brakes to avoid hitting the back of a truck. My view of this event was especially close, but we all survived.

I was advised by the driver that the *Mercy* was out at sea, being replenished, so I decided we should go directly to the local hospital. We arrived at a fairly chaotic scene, with U.S. sailors and officers conducting the second pre-operation checks on local people who had been chosen to have surgery onboard the ship. Initially, about a week before the *Mercy* arrives in any port to commence humanitarian assistance, a team is deployed to do pre-operative checks. They choose the people who can be helped and with less likelihood of requiring extensive aftercare. This is necessary as the ship will only be in each town for about a week, so the patients have to be screened, join the ship, undergo surgery, and be discharged to shore in that time. This may sound a little weird, but it is necessary and, I might add, really does get the most people help in the shortest time.

So here we are at the local hospital. It is a pretty unassuming-looking building. The street outside is packed with people wanting to get a look at what was going on. The people who had been previously selected were again checked to make sure they were still fit to undergo surgery. As well, there were clinics being held inside the hospital, including inoculations, medications, and general health checks.

My overall leadership strategy at this time was to get my team to start helping straight away. We found a small room where we could change into our uniforms, and as soon as that was done, I told everyone to spread out and go help. My team were brilliant from the start. We availed ourselves to the USN personnel and were soon administering inoculations, helping with administration, and various other jobs. I knew we were only there for two weeks, so the quicker we got stuck in, the better. This work ethic was noticed from the start and was commented on many times by the captain of the medical department. I should note here that there were other nations supplementing the *Mercy* team – India and Malaysia, to name two.

After about an hour, one of the American sailors approached and asked if we wanted something to eat. There was a local stall that was selling food, and even though I was a bit concerned about this, he said that the food was good, and they had not had any problems with it. About ten minutes later, some food arrived, and we went up onto the roof to keep out of the way while we ate. One very important thing to note about how the locals build in Indonesia, especially in the more remote places–when they build something like a hospital, they plan for at least two storeys but almost inevitably only manage one. So the roof of this hospital was flat, but we were standing literally in a mantrap. All the supporting reinforcing steel stuck up through the concrete to about three feet in height –an absolute 'work, health, and safety' nightmare –but we survived.

About another hour or so went by, and the clinics and pre-operation checks finished, and we all made our way to the wharf so we could join the ship. We were on the wharf for a little while, chatting to other crew members, and the USNS *Mercy* came into sight. This ship is huge. It is a converted oil tanker of seventy thousand tons displacement. It is painted all white with huge red crosses in several areas to denote it is a hospital ship. It is a little hard to explain just how big it is, but when it was repurposed, it had all the mod cons.

However, we had to get out there first. The ship was so big that there was no way it could come alongside Gunungsitoli, so we obviously needed to transfer to her by sea. The ship has on its deck two forty-foot transport boats, also painted white with red crosses on them, and these were called Band-Aids! They were to be one of the two ways we got patients and crew onboard, the other being the Sea Hawk medevac helicopter.

The ship also has its own wharf, so to speak. There is a large door in the port side that swings out to allow entry at just above the waterline. To make life a little easier, the floating pontoon (wharf) is lowered from the main deck and sits in the water, so when the Band-Aids come alongside, the patients or crew are offloaded onto it and then make their way up a short gangway into the ship. Here, we were checked in, and then we had to walk up the six ramps to the main hospital deck. Imagine a walkway in the largest Westfield shopping town, but it doesn't move and is six levels. That is how we got into the ship. At the top of the ramps, we came onto the resuscitation deck. This is where the injured/ill are brought for initial triage and treatment. To give you a feeling of just how big this area is in, most Australian hospital emergency areas have around twenty beds or cubicles. On the *Mercy*, there were fifty. The area was called the 'fishbowl' as the main observation office was all glassed in.

Another thing that caught the eye was the presence of an armed marine –a very-large armed marine. He was there to assist with possible unruly patients that were brought to the ship; remember, the two hospital ships that the USN has, *Mercy* and *Comfort*, were built for war service. I did make friends with this lad, who was six-foot-six tall and solid build and, of all things, was Scottish! He had emigrated to the USA when he was young and had become a citizen and joined the marines. His brogue accent was quite funny to hear when you expected to hear a U.S. accent.

We were soon mustered and shown to our quarters. Talk about luxury! Well, lots of space anyway. On smaller Australian warships, even in the officer's mess, the room was very limited –three bunks with a very small clearance so you could just turn over without belting your shoulders. I took a picture of one of the racks, as we call them, noting you could fit a manila folder upright and have another inch or so room. However, on *Mercy*, you could actually sit up in bed!

After we were settled in, we were advised that we had a briefing at 1900 in the main café or eating area. We attended this and were given the plans for the next day and advised that we (the newcomers) were required to undertake an orientation program and would not be allowed ashore the next day. This was to give us some time to work out our way around the ship and was indeed an important requirement. It wasn't to everyone's liking, of course, as we wanted to get stuck in, but we had already done some good work when we first arrived, so it wasn't too much of a burden.

Part of the orientation involved what was called a blind evacuation. Those who have served on a warship will know that if there is a power failure, emergency lights come on to assist you with an evacuation. However, in case this doesn't happen, being in a large ship with no lights, below decks is pitch *black*! You cannot see anything at all. So we were broken into two groups, one group blindfolded, the other being the helpers. One big difference to note here is that your standard warship has ladderways, not stairs. Ladderways are steep and require some care to navigate. The *Mercy*, however, had staircases, which did make the job of making your way around much easier.

A few statistics about the ship: she is big. I mean *huge*! Originally an oil tanker, she was converted to a hospital ship and weighs in at seventy thousand tons. She is fitted with 1,000 hospital beds, 12 operating theatres, a CAT scanner, multiple X-ray systems, a huge laboratory, enough accommodation, for 1,250 medical staff, and a large administration centre. By the way, did I mention she is huge?

One interesting thing onboard is how the USN run the ship. As it is a hospital ship, she is painted white with large red crosses on just about every external bulkhead. She is 'driven' by a civilian captain, and the crew to run the ship, such as engineers and seamanship, are all civilian. The head of the medical section is also a captain, and the planning and safety of the medical staff and our MEDCAPs ashore are his responsibility. There is also a senior captain, a war-fighter, who is overall in charge of the mission. Even though the USN does not have the rank of commodore, this officer was given the title of commodore to show he was the guy in charge.

The first evening onboard was spent training and lectures on safety such as fire drills, leaving ship stations (lifeboat drills), blind evacuation training, and generally getting to know the environment. It is easy to get lost – did I mention she is *huge*? The next day was somewhat stressful as we were not allowed ashore, but several of my staff were allowed to go to their specific departments, including the operating theatre nurse and the medics, who went to the sickbay, which provided medical assistance for the ship's medical staff only.

That evening, after all personnel had returned to the ship, we attended the next briefing at 1900. This time, several of the team were placed on the MEDCAPs. Now this acronym stands for medical capability. Basically, we would put ashore up to seven MEDCAPs a day to different areas where we were working. *Mercy* remained at sea, and each tranch of personnel were moved ashore via the Band-Aids. These ran back and forth all day, moving patients to and from the ship and staff to and from shore.

As I was the CO of the detachment, I had a number of administrative roles to conduct, so I spent the first couple of days onboard working with the USN administrative staff. I was warmly welcomed by the crew and was able to help them quite a bit. An interesting note here: one of the civilian positions was filled by a young lady whose role was 'entertainments officer'. Now normally, on a warship, we don't have this, but on a large hospital ship, keeping the staff's spirits up is vitally important. Medical staff can see many upsetting things on such deployments, and having an outlet for staff is essential. Her job was to organise game nights etc., and also, when the ship went to a port such as Singapore, she would organise tours to the zoo or theatres or whatever. I worked quite closely with her as she also maintained the staffing list of personnel borne, and we had to ensure no one went missing during the mission. Here, you must remember that we were on an American mission, and not everyone likes Americans, even when they are helping the poor and infirm.

We did have many conversations about all sorts of things, one being where the ship was going after the next port, Banda Aceh. The plan at that time was for the ship to head to East Timor and then to Guam, where there is a U.S. military installation, and fly the medical crew home while the ship made her way back to San Diego with a skeleton medical staff and the civilian mariners. I joked that we should start a rumour that *Mercy* was going to go to Darwin and that the crew would fly home from there. Well, we did start a rumour, and with some encouragement from me, the CO changed the route of the *Mercy* so that she would go to Darwin after Dili –but more on that later.

We spent a week off Nias island and Gunungsitoli to the south. We participated in many MEDCAPs, which were very interesting in their own right. Each MEDCAP would concentrate on a number of subgroup areas. For instance, at one village, we set up under a large tin-roofed shed which was surrounded by a metal fence about four feet high. We set up areas within the confines of this fence, including a vaccination station, GP access, optical assessment, pharmacy, and dental. It was pretty rugged, but each day, hundreds of people would gather to be seen.

The first thing I noticed was that each patient could only get two different reviews – that is, you could get a dental appointment and a pharmacy appointment or optical and GP. One of the things that the U.S. staff did was to make sure any children that were present were vaccinated. If the parent would not allow this, then they themselves could not get any treatment. Most people agreed, but there were some who were scared. Still, I thought it was a good idea. If we were able to inoculate the kids, it would mean less disease and deaths in the future. The USAF provided an optometrist for these MEDCAPs, and she came with a plethora of glasses already made up to certain prescriptions. Thus, she would check their eyes with a special portable ophthalmic machine and then provide the correct glasses. This made a huge difference, and people who presented with bad eyesight walked away being able to see clearly for the first time in years.

Additionally, one of the several NGOs or non-governmental organisations that were also onboard provided things like wheelchairs for those in need. They were not your usual wheelchairs though. These were modified garden furniture – that is, those stackable plastic chairs that have had bicycle wheels and smaller castors attached. They are cheap to make and very versatile in the areas where we worked.

As the reader is aware, I am in the administrative area, but I do have an extensive clinical background, so I wanted to help if I could. I asked if I could do so at the vaccination area and was gladly accepted. I was to hang on to the kids when they got their jabs –not easy, especially if the mum was hovering and the kid was hollering all over the shop. There is a photo of me assisting in this process, and it was taken a millisecond before I copped a kick to my nether regions from the young fella who was getting his jabs. Mind you, he had five injections in one hit, so I couldn't blame him, really.

One last mention here of an area in the clinic: the dental section. When the patient requested dental treatment, they were sent to a roped-off area with several plastic chairs. Now it is probably obvious to the reader that not much could be done regarding restorative dentistry, and that's true. However, if the patient could have their pain relieved by extraction, this was the most common outcome. Several patients had most of their teeth pulled out. They were mostly elderly who had a mouth full of rotting teeth which were causing them huge problems. Also, the dentist didn't use local anaesthetic, not because they were cruel, but there just was not enough time and way too many patients to muck around. Several of the young USN medics asked if they could help and were given on-the-spot direction by the dentists, so they performed quite a few of the extractions.

The crowd behaviour waiting in line in the sun for treatment was quite good, but it was obvious that the men thought they could push to the front and knock the women out of the way. They were in for another think! Each of the MEDCAPs had at least two heavily armed marines to protect us. Some of the places we went to in Indonesia and other countries would quite happily kidnap people, especially Americans, and hold them for ransom. The marines detailed to protect us were awesome and did not allow the men to push the women around. Amazing what just holding an M16 can do.

At our first port, Gunungsitoli, all went well for my team. They were really enthusiastic, and this was noticed by the medical CO. My team excelled in any job they were given, and this led to a higher level of trust and responsibility being given to us.

One special mention here. On the first day when we arrived at the Gunungsitoli Hospital and I directed my team to get stuck in and help where we could, two of the team were outside the hospital buildings, getting a feel for the area. Commander Slader and Leading Seaman Medical Luke Trevathen came across a young lad who was having trouble breathing. Actually, he was having an extremely bad asthma attack. Both of my team worked on resuscitating him and managed his care until we could get him on the ship. He was in a very bad way such that he remained on *Mercy* until after we sailed for Banda Aceh. This was highly unusual as patients were normally seen and returned ashore before sailing. The young fella's mother accompanied him, and when we reached Banda Aceh, he had recovered very well and was medevaced ashore, taken to the airport, and transferred back to Gunungsitoli by USAF aircraft that had been flown in especially for him.

Before the ship deployed towards our next stop, Banda Aceh, we had to return all the patients to the island, where they would come under the follow-up care of the local hospital. However, as soon as that was completed, there was a closing ceremony. We had had an opening ceremony ashore when the ship first came to the region (we were onboard that day). The USN has found that conducting the closing ceremony allows closure and allows the team to provide better expectations management. This basically means that you leave the area and that the people won't be expecting the ship to be there indefinitely and that they would be back sometime in the future but not locking in a date. Of course, the ship cannot be everywhere at once or for necessarily long periods, but having definite dates for starting and finishing helped the locals cope with this.

So the closing ceremony is conducted onboard at a lunch attended by senior staff, all the captains, and a large number of local council members, including the mayor. Additionally, the U.S. ambassador to Indonesia and the surgeon general of the United States attended this quite historic function. Both my staff and I chatted to these senior people and also the local Indonesian military commander, helping to fulfil my role in furthering cooperation between Australia and Indonesia as well as continuing the alliance with the USA.

Now many would know that the USN are very aware of their role in the big picture of the world, so they manage to document everything, especially during the'hearts and minds' phase of any mission. Thus, they have a full combat cameraman unit onboard the USNS *Mercy* when she deploys. This unit has a huge office/laboratory area, and they can make just about anything for promotional reasons. On this mission, the camera team were busy taking photos of everyone doing everything. They could then transfer photos to a large one-and-a-half-by-one-metre picture board with pictures of the *Mercy* and a collage of people helping the locals. This was to be presented to the mayor of each village or town that the *Mercy* assisted. It was a very well-received gift, and the townspeople would also present the ship with a memento. Once the ceremony was complete, the ship then departed for the overnight transit to Banda Aceh. Of course, just over a year before, the 2004 tsunami wiped out most of this town, and we were returning to conduct further assistance with the *Mercy*.

During my time with the 'fun director', we had also discussed the crash of the SeaKing helicopter 'Shark 02' the year before, and this event was also one of the reasons the Australian contingent had been tasked to join *Mercy*. After this chat, the young lass asked me to stay in the office, and she disappeared. She had gone and approached the commodore and told him the story of the helicopter crash. He had then approved for my team to fly to the Amandraya township using the *Mercy*'s medical helicopter to pay our respects to our fallen colleagues. My team was very enthused to hear this as it was not something we had expected. The transit was to take place as the *Mercy* made way to Banda Aceh, as we passed the northern tip of Nias Island.

The following morning, as were preparing for the flight, I was called to the commodore's cabin. He advised me that unfortunately, he had had to withdraw his offer of the flight. He apologised and indicated a mission priority had changed and the helicopter was elsewhere, but I did state that we were there for the main mission and that while being able to visit the crash site and memorial would have been nice, we understood the change and would continue as planned. Although this was disappointing, my team took the news well and went about preparations for the next port, Banda Aceh.

Again, the *Mercy* was too large to come alongside, so she remained at sea while we deployed over the days to different areas ashore, mainly by boat and then bus or sometimes by helicopter. As usual, the pre-medical support team had already made it to Banda Aceh and were reviewing those who had been checked and who would receive the most benefit from treatment or surgery onboard.

The first sight of Banda Aceh was pretty sobering. The devastation from twelve months before was still very evident, as you would expect. Solitary houses stood alone in the middle of huge debris fields, although the roads had been cleared somewhat. We had buses arranged to pick us up on what was left of the dock, and they took us to several locations.

It was a bit different in Banda Aceh from Gunungsitoli. Banda Aceh was a much bigger town originally, but most of the first few kilometres had been washed into the ocean, and how we managed the MEDCAPs was a little different. One that I went to with the psychiatrist and psychologist was a teaching session for local nurses on how to deal with the vast number of PTSD patients, noting that a large number of the nurses also suffered from it as they too had lost everything in the tsunami of Christmas 2004.

We were also accompanied by a USN psychiatrist who, in conjunction with the ADF psychiatrist and psychologist, had arranged the session before we left Australia. We were greeted by the local staff in the hospital, which had miraculously survived, and were warmly welcomed. About twenty minutes into the presentation, another earthquake was felt. I was standing in the doorway of the meeting room and was less than impressed! Again, the locals were quick to move as they were used to such earth movement. After a few minutes, everyone had settled down, and we continued the session. It was my second brush with an earthquake, the other being on Nias Island. They are not fun.

As usual, every evening a briefing on the next day's MEDCAPs was held onboard *Mercy*. Not all personnel went ashore every day; some were required for the operating theatres and other departments, and also, having a rest day was imperative. The Australian contingent was only on board two weeks, but I was going to make sure we made the most of it. Getting my team enthused was not necessary. From the word 'go', they were quick to dig in with the U.S. and foreign medical staff and performed to the highest standards. To this day, I still have contact through social media with some of the USN staff. It is true to say that you make lifelong friends in the military no matter which country you are from.

After the first few days on board, my main administrative jobs had been completed, so I volunteered for any other things that might arise. I was despatched to the patient return area, where those who had been operated on and were about to leave the ship were gathered. The nursing OIC gave me the 'dangerous drug' keys and had me organise all the medications for those who needed them. It was a bit of a change for me, but I relished the opportunity to help. It is amazing how a team like we had, from many nations and specialities, can gel quickly and act together to help people.

One other task I was given was to be the helicopter medic for patient transfers. I was really chuffed at being given this and enjoyed being able to undertake a number of flights to and from Banda Aceh. I was there specifically to provide immediate first aid if required by the patients as they were transferred either to the ship or back ashore. I was fortunate not to have to do any emergency resuscitation during these flights. A later part of this job is returning patients to their homes, and I took it upon myself to attend to this thoroughly and make it as normal a procedure as possible but one which my USN counterparts were happy to let me do.

Adjacent to the helicopter pad on the *Mercy* is the access from the large lifts from the lower decks. This was the obvious route for patients to take when their treatment onboard had been completed. As each patient was retrieved from the ward, I took them to the flight deck and prepared them to depart. This included placing life jackets on each patient and the classic egg-shell helmet which protects their head and ears. I would take the time to explain to them what would be happening. You have to remember these people had been through an absolutely horrendous time during the tsunami and may not have come on board by helicopter, and if they are unsure of what is happening, the whole thing can be quite frightening, especially for kids.

One of my patients was a young lad who had been seriously burned a few weeks after the tsunami, when he fell into a fire that had been lit to provide light and warmth. He had survived the initial wave and had been near a fire one night, and he had fallen into it. He had been so badly burned, his right arm had fused to his body. He had remained that way for over twelve months until we arrived on the *Mercy*. His surgery was successful, and he was returning to Banda Aceh by helicopter. I took him up to the flight deck and prepared him for transfer. I explained what was going to happen, and he said he understood. I stayed with him until I wheeled him to the helicopter, and along with some other patients, he boarded the chopper and departed. Now I mention this in particular because as I had been standing there, the commodore had come into the flight deck preparation area. He had stood there and watched what I did, and by the time I got back from the helicopter, he had gone.

Shortly thereafter, I received a message that he wanted to see me, so I made my way up to the bridge. He took me aside into his day cabin and said that he was extremely impressed by my handling of the young lad and others who had been returned to shore. He said that they, the USN, were great at getting patients onto the ship and conducting surgery etc., but the way they returned patients was perhaps not as good. He praised me highly for this and said he would ensure this was noted. I was very chuffed at this but just thought it was the normal way to do things when looking after someone who had had surgery, most likely life-changing, and moving them back to their own medical care.

My main duties were to ensure my team were looked after, were being appropriately used with their individual skill sets, and were happy. Sounds a bit wishy-washy, perhaps, but as every military commander knows, if the troops are happy, all will be well –and it was. Every member of the team worked hard, made new friends and colleagues, and got that great sense of achievement that comes from seeing positive outcomes from what can be a pretty confronting environment.

I will note here a couple of astounding things that we saw or were a part of. The first was a young woman who was brought to the ship for abdominal surgery. She had been diagnosed with a large abdominal growth that needed to be removed. She was only a slight lass, but her initial appearance was that she was pregnant. She weighed around fifty-five kilogrammes when she came in. She left weighing approximately thirty-two kilogrammes. The twenty-three-kilgram mass was huge and was one of the most complicated surgeries undertaken during the Banda Aceh mission.

Second, when we deployed for the psychiatric seminar, we were given access to the mental health ward area of the hospital. It was horrendous. It was literally several gaol cells with a few scattered beds. It only had a few patients at that time as most had either perished during and after the tsunami or had managed to escape at a later time.

The third was a sight that I won't forget in a hurry. I had seen it both from the air and from close up on the ground. About five kilometres inland from the sea, the tsunami had weakened and deposited many items, including a huge generator ship. My guess is that it was about 1,500 tonnes and was rectangular in shape with obvious generator chimney stacks and deck equipment. It now sat squarely on several houses and vehicles and had not been moved since it had unceremoniously landed there. It had been in the harbour when the wave hit and been carried inland. What also made it unforgettable was the old gentleman selling bottles of Coke from a drinks stand nearby and charging for you to take photos, which I did. His family had been in the house when they were all killed. He had been out on higher ground at the time. It was a pretty horrible sight, let alone knowing that there were bodies still unable to be buried properly under tonnes of steel, but as they say, life goes on.

After a couple of days of surgeries, patient transfers, report writing, and liaison with officials and senior U.S. naval personnel, it was almost time for us to prepare to leave. When we had arrived initially, we had needed to pay some extra money to retrieve our baggage from Indonesian baggage handlers. Luckily, I had changed some Aussie dollars into rupiah and, along with one of my team, managed to sort that out. So before we left Banda Aceh, I thought we may have similar problems on the return journey, and I would need to get some more cash. I checked with the admin staff, and they advised that there was an ATM that

I could access in town. So I arranged to take the bus we used to the appropriate place, and I was escorted by an armed marine. I still have the receipts as I took out two lots of Rp500,000! Not that it is that much, about 150AUD at the time, but having the marine standing near me while I got the cash was great. As was always going to happen though, I did not need the cash, but I felt it better to be prepared. I had managed to write reports on all my team, and I had received two reports from the USN captain: one for the team as a whole and the other on myself. I also had to write a mission report and note any lessons learned and present this to the fleet commander and fleet medical officer on our return to Australia.

USNS *Mercy* was due to leave Banda Aceh for East Timor, and we were to fly back to Australia before she departed for East Timor. As you will remember, my team was composed of all reserve medical personnel, and as such, they needed to get back to Australia to carry on with their normal employment. As I said before, I and the entertainments officer had managed to get the ship to steam to Darwin on completion of the mission to allow R&R for their sailors and then for them to fly back to the USA. However, before that, the ship was to go to East Timor and conduct another set of MEDCAPs. The medical captain did ask that I should stay with the ship and sail to Dili and then Darwin with them as the Australian liaison officer, but we had not had a reply from the fleet commander in Sydney before I was due to lead my team home.

We re-deployed to Australia, and I made an appointment to visit the fleet commander and debrief him on the mission. I also informed him about the USNS *Mercy* visiting Australia and the program that had been devised for this. I also suggested that it might prove to be prudent to send me back to Darwin to greet the ship and be able to be a liaison for them. I was quite amazed that this was agreed to but didn't argue the toss. I arrived in Darwin the day before *Mercy* was due to arrive and visited the Larrakeyah Barracks navy sickbay. Here, I advised the staff that I may be able to organise a tour of the ship for them and any other ADF medics from the local army bases.

The next day, I was on the wharf early to greet the ship. As she came alongside, the commodore spotted me, and once the gangway was down, he made it onto the wharf and, dare I say it, greeted me like an old friend. He then conducted a TV interview with the local news teams and invited them onto the ship a little later. In the meantime, I had gathered my medics and was taking them aboard for a tour. What happened next was great from my point of view. As we waited for approval to come into the ship, I was met by the visits officer.

She obviously knew me and just said, 'It's OK, Dave. Off you go. You take them around,' which I did. I was a tad chuffed that they would allow that, but again, I didn't argue the toss.

We had a thorough tour, and the feedback from the medics was great. At one stage, I took them into the operating theatre suites. As previously mentioned, there are twelve operating theatres on board, and they work from a central hub arrangement. As we arrived in the hub, there were a number of reporters and local dignitaries doing a tour with the commodore. He started to explain where we were in relation to the ship when he spotted me. He stopped what he was doing and called out to me, much to my embarrassment, and asked me to come to the front with him. I was introduced as the Australian contingent commander, and he praised my team very highly for all our work and efforts we made during our time on the ship. I believe this was reported in the local news.

Anyway, in the end, I was extremely proud of our efforts and that the *Mercy* had come to Australia (lots of money into the economy), and it was good to see all the guys I had met on the mission before they went home. To this day, I still keep in contact with some of them. A fair few of the crew flew out almost straight away, but I did enjoy the company of some of the officers in Darwin that night before they flew home too.

I returned to Sydney the next day and resumed my role as the MAO at Balmoral Naval Hospital. Luckily, one of my best mates at the time,

Barry Fregon, was available to stand in for me while I was deployed. Barry was also a lieutenant commander and had been the previous incumbent in my job. Sadly, Barry has passed away since then, but he is well remembered by his navy brethren.

A somewhat noteworthy addendum to this chapter started when the USNS *Mercy* was bestowed with a meritorious unit commendation for its service on the mission that the Australian medical contingent had played a conspicuous part in. Whilst on board, I had been advised by the commodore that my team, as part of Team Mercy, were entitled to receive this recognition. At the time, I was requested to provide all appropriate details to the administration staff on board, and that would then culminate in my team receiving this award.

This sort of thing does not happen every day. To be awarded this prestigious accolade is quite special, noting that one of my remits for the mission was to raise the profile of the Royal Australian Navy in both Indonesia and within the USN. This, we did, but it wasn't to be as black and white as that. I kept in touch with the medical captain once he returned to Hawaii, and I obtained some new points of contact within the CinCPACFLT's office. This was in 2006, and I tried, for the next few years, to get the recognition for the outstanding work my team had done, not only in their fields of expertise but also in the liaison and firmer ties we all made with not only USN personnel but also other foreign defence personnel that were on the mission.

After seemingly countless emails and chasing up with anyone I could find, I was advised that all our information had been lost. So having kept copies of everything, I resubmitted it to CinCPACFLT in Hawaii. Eventually, I was given word that we were approved to receive the award, but we still had not received anything from the USN. I was pretty frustrated at the red tape, but as I was aware, that is often the way. Before I received the nod for this award, I had applied for recognition for my team through a then Australian awards system; however, this was denied. Needless to say, I was a tad annoyed. I had tried everything to enable my team to be able to wear an award we had been granted. In April 2016, nearly ten years after the mission, I received a letter from the navy honours and awards department while I was serving at the joint health services offices in Victoria Barracks, Melbourne. It read as follows.

USNS Mercy — Chief of Naval Operations Meritorious Unit Commendation: Recognition and Approval to Wear

> I am pleased to be able to advise you that approval has been granted for you to wear the CNO Meritorious Unit Commendation awarded to USNS *Mercy* for the period of operations 01 April 2006 to 30 September 2006.
>
> In approving the wearing of the award, it was noted that the Commanding Officer of the USNS *Mercy* stated that your 'contributions were direct, recognisable, contributed directly to the success of the high-visibility deployment, and strengthened the bond between the U.S. and other countries'.
>
> Your professional expertise and devotion to duty are in keeping with the finest traditions of the Royal Australian Navy.

This letter ended ten long years of constantly trying to get the recognition my team had earned during a short but eventful mission. This award is now permanently on our records.

Epilogue

I filed my report with both the fleet commander and the fleet medical officer and noted that I believed the mission was an outstanding success and all the goals I had set as the CO had been met. I also mentioned several recommendations for future missions conducted by Australian forces in the humanitarian sphere and that I highly recommended we continue to support the United States in future years on similar missions.

Subsequently, the USN changed the name of this annual mission to 'Pacific Partnership', which better describes it, and from the humble beginnings of nine ADF and reserve medical personnel, the Australian contingent now often numbers greater than fifty, both medical and other specialists such as engineers. I and my team take great pride in the fact that we led the way for these successful future endeavours.

Headquarters Joint Operations Command— 2008–2010

After what I saw as an extremely rewarding and eventful posting to HMAS Penguin in Sydney between 2005 and 2007, 2008 saw me posted to HQ JOC, at RAAF Base Fairbairn in Canberra. I will be fairly general in my story in this chapter; as the reader might imagine, some of the information I was privy to was extremely confidential.

As I had had some experience in working within a headquarters in Darwin, I was feeling pretty good about my upcoming adventure. I moved to Canberra, renting a five-hundred-acre farm in Murrumbateman, in the heart of New South Wales wine country. I took this measure so that I could have my dogs with me and they would have room to run. My wife left me in 2007, and I had to place our show dogs in kennels for twelve months, back in Victoria. I will take the opportunity here to thank Beaconsfield Pet Resort, owned and run by Chris and Sue Moore, who were aware of my situation and had already been great friends from my days of conformation dog showing and judging. They looked after my three bearded collies as if they were their own. Thank you so much.

So with my dogs sorted out and with a plan in place if I had to deploy, I started work at HQ JOC. It was quite different from HQNORCOM in Darwin as during my tenure, not only did I have the job of reviewing and maintaining health plans for all of Australia's operations overseas, but also, in 2008, the headquarters moved to a purpose-built, green-field location in Bungendore, New South Wales, in an area to the east of the ACT. To maintain overall mission awareness and safety for our members overseas, a quite complex plan to move into the new location was drafted. I won't bore you with the details, but when one approaches the headquarters, it seems to be miles away from anywhere and looks like a high-security prison, with the attendant secure-entry requirements. The distance from the car park to my desk was more than six different security checks.

The work conducted by HQJOC ranges from health and logistics to security and defence. As you would expect, making sure all things are thought of before we commit personnel to probable dangerous zones throughout the world is vital –so more meetings than you could poke a stick at; constant updating of documentation (in my case, health plans for overseas operations) was daunting. It really was 'playing with the big boys', and it is essential that you know your stuff.

This can be quite difficult at times, and I was thrown in the deep end somewhat. In my previous headquarters posting, I had been involved at a lower level in plans for more local operations. In the overseas desk, I was responsible for the health planning from Africa to the Sinai to Iraq and Afghanistan. It really was exciting work, even though I was more desk bound at HQJOC –but not for long. By mid-2008, plans were being made to move the main effort of Australian deployed units from Iraq to Afghanistan. This would require moving the support, logistics, and health centres for Australian defence personnel from Kuwait to the United Arab Emirates (UAE). This would shorten the supply route and thus the time needed to get personnel in or out of the AO, including any injured personnel.

This was to be a monumental task. At this time, the ADF was co-located with the United States on a U.S. AirForce base outside Kuwait City, and we were to move to a UAE air base in the desert outside Dubai. A contingent of Canadian support and medical staff were also located on the UAE base. It was well out into the desert and just a few kilometres from the local camel milk farm –truly.

How do I know this? Well, I was sent there as a member of the HQJOC team that would start the ball rolling in preparing for this move. However, before one is sent to the desert, you have to undertake preparation training. You will, of course, all realise that at that time, the entire region of the Middle East was a pretty dangerous place. So to prepare everyone to the same level, we undertook extra training. This included combat first aid, where you are required to conduct the usual basic medical assistance while wearing full combat protection – including bulletproof armour, Kevlar helmets, and battlegoggles – all whilst being fired upon (using blanks) to add realism to the exercise, and have also completed requalification on weapons, mainly the AUSTEYR rifle.

We also did cultural training, which was extremely helpful in getting to understand the locals and their traditions. I recall this preparation training went for over a week and was current for twelve months. Why I mention this will become clearer later on. This training was conducted at Randwick Army Barracks in Sydney as this was the stepping-off point for anyone attached to this operation, being OP Catalyst.

So training over, I returned to Canberra to get myself prepared to deploy. I drove my dogs down to Melbourne, where Chris and Sue Moore looked after them at their dog boarding kennels again. On the appointed date, I flew from Canberra to Sydney to join the rest of the deploying members of the project survey team (PST).

We departed Australia and headed for Kuwait City and out to a U.S. Air Force base. We staged through this base but were in-country for a couple of days. We were given accommodation that was 'bloody luxury'; it consisted of a large tent set on a concrete slab with about eight sets of bunks and, thankfully, a very large airconditioner. The doorway was like an airlock to keep the cool air inside.

So here we were, in a Middle Eastern country, only fifty kilometres or so from Iraq, on a huge USAF base. We were just getting settled into our accommodation when there was a huge explosion. We hit the deck (quite quickly, I might add) and waited for the sirens and gunfire –nothing! Slowly, I regained my dignity and stood up, and we were wondering what had happened. So I went outside and looked in the direction of the explosion. There was a huge black cloud rising into the desert sky, which is a sandy colour, by the way. Still no response from the ready reaction force or anyone else. The U.S. troops who were moving about the area were not worried, and I asked someone what the noise had been. They told me that every Tuesday, just outside the main entry point, they detonate a heap of munitions that have passed their use by date! No one had bothered to tell us. So after changing my jocks, all was well.

One thing we found perhaps a little disconcerting but totally understandable was all the U.S. troops always carried their weapons with them. The base was a staging point for troops who were going to Iraq. To get them used to depending on their weapons at every moment, they took them everywhere, including the mess hall. The mess hall on this base was huge and run by contractors from the local population. As I said, it was really 'spooky' to see men and women carrying long guns, including machineguns (no ammunition though), into breakfast!

After a couple of days in Kuwait, we flew by civilian aircraft to the UAE, and after an hour and a half in a minibus, through mountainous terrain that looked like we were on the moon, we arrived at the Australian compound on Al-Minhad Airbase. It was some twenty kilometres out into the desert from Dubai. Conditions were pretty basic. The Australian contingent had two compounds – one for work, the other for accommodation – but we ate at the Canadian-run mess hall and, as you would expect had a great, 'friendly' rivalry with our Canadian cousins.

Something that probably doesn't get much notice is that when we deploy to places like this, especially for a long time, it is to keep the troops not only physically fit but also mentally fit. Being able to do things like Skype home, watch the AFL Grand Final on a big-screen TV, and play competition sport are all integral in ensuring the best possible outcomes for all who serve in this type of environment.

Noting, of course, we were in the Middle East, where it is *hot* but not so humid, still leaves the times to conduct sport or exercise either early

in the morning or later in the evening. On one such evening, the PTIs
organised a game of beach volleyball – no, we weren't close to a beach,
but we had heaps of sand, so a game between Australia and Canada
was organised to start at 2200 or 10:00 p.m. All was going well; the
game was progressing, to and fro. It is here that I should note that part
of the Canadian team were pilots from the Royal Canadian Air Force.
These guys were super fit and were flying the new C-17 cargo jets. So as
I was saying, all was going well . . . when the Canadian spiker went up
to smash the ball over the net. Unfortunately, he landed awkwardly in
the sand, and we heard a 'crack' as he fell to the ground, clutching his
lower leg. Yep, he had fractured his fibula, as I remember. This bone is
the smaller of the two lower-leg bones but is nonetheless important for
a person to be able to walk –or fly. This mishap caused a heap of drama
as the whole contingent was now down a pilot, and at that time, they
were as rare as rocking horse poo. We did survive and actually won the
volleyball game, so the night wasn't really wasted, and to add to this, I
had competed for Australia at an international level sport...Who would
have thought?

Back at work, my job was to look at consolidating the medical support
for the Australian defence members, especially the medevac of wounded
to higher-level medical treatment areas. Now a medevac can be by land,
sea, or air. In the environment we were in, we relied quite heavily on
the United States to assist in providing the initial medevac by helicopter
to the forward aid stations or directly to the field hospitals. This was
done so quickly and efficiently that a wounded member could be under
a surgical team's care within fifteen minutes of wounding, on average.
However, while our support areas were in several different countries, we
needed, at this time, to reduce the overall number of ADF personnel as
agreed in several higher-command objectives.

So we had ADF medical staff in Kuwait, Qatar, and the UAE.
These were manned by small teams with what we call a relatively
small footprint. They had to be centralised, and this job fell to me, in
addition to overseeing the creation of a new, larger ADF health centre

in Al-Minhad. It was not an easy task, but I managed to herd all the appropriate cats into the right place. The doctors and staff at the Al-Minhad base did a great job on drafting plans for the new hospital, and somehow I managed successfully to argue with the brigadier who was in charge of the PST to leave the numbers of medics incountry as they were. As we were supposed to be downsizing the force, this was a struggle, but in the end, I even managed to get an extra person, a physiotherapist, to be deployed.

Why a physio, you ask? Well, just imagine you are in an operational warzone. Apart from the obvious injuries from small arms, roadside bombs, and other not-so-nice things, there were always those other injuries, such as back injury from carrying too much weight in packs(such as ammunition), sprained ankles from running for cover when the shooting starts, or even playing volleyball! These personnel had to be brought back to staging points and often had to move to larger medical facilities further from the AO, which was an inordinate cost in both time and manpower, so we got a physiotherapist. As well as having the physio close at hand, being able to have the member stay within the zone helped them mentally. As those who are or have been in the ADF, you want to be where your mates are. The closer, the better, so staying in the same country for minor medical treatment is a bonus.

We also retained all the personnel as we required several types of medical assistance at this point: teams to do the day-to-day sickbay work, evacuation teams which were assigned to seriously wounded patients and went with them to Germany for either surgery or repatriation to Australia. It was a very complex system but one that would serve us well. I found some very interesting things on my first trip to the Middle East. On the base in Kuwait, before I left for the UAE, I was directed to have a look around at some of the buildings to see where it might be possible to set up a medical centre. We found the command centre of the Kuwaiti Army, which was a building in what appeared to be a crater. It was actually set below ground level to avoid the Iraqi aircraft during the First Gulf War. We managed to get inside and see what it must have been like for them during that time. It was very eerie. Dust and sand covered everything, and maps were still on the walls, old computers everywhere.

Although this building had its advantages, there was no telling how badly damaged it was as many bombs had fallen on this base before it was taken over by the United States. I did see many aeroplane bunkers that had been destroyed by what must have been some seriously big bombs. It was very much an eye opener for this young fella – well, OK, not so young, maybe.

The main PST was due to stay incountry for about three months, but I had completed the medical stage in fairly quick time. I did not want to go back too soon as I wanted to really make a difference, at least in my own mind. Fortunately, the brigadier needed someone to be responsible for the manning document. Now this is produced by HQ JOC to assign the manpower levels of defence personnel on any given operation.

I had no idea what to do, but with the aid of a logistics squadron leader who was from HQ JOC as well, we managed to sort it out. We were given a ceiling level of numbers required and also the designations of those personnel – for example, how many POL(petroleum, oils, lubricants) soldiers would be needed at the forward operating bases in Afghanistan? How many medics? I did learn a lot by conducting this procedure, noting we had all the personnel from Kuwait to redistribute, although some would remain there, members in Qatar, Bahrain, and other Middle Eastern areas.

It took quite some time to do this, as you might expect, and I was most proud that not only did I manage to get the same number of medics deployed, but also, we got another position, that of a physiotherapist. I was away from Australia for around three months, as I recall. It was a real eye opener for me, and I know that the work the PST did ensured as smooth as possible a transition and consolidation of ADF personnel in the Middle East. I felt very privileged to have been able not only to serve in the warzone but also to have been able to make a difference. This extended later to my second deployment into the MEAO, the Middle East AO.

OP Slipper

Almost twelve months later to the day, I was informed I was to return to the MEAO this time to review and make recommendations to the HQ regarding in-country combat first aid. With the Australian contingent moving to the UAE as we had withdrawn from Iraq but remained in Afghanistan, the ADF needed to pivot from a support angle. We had been in Kuwait for a number of years and had been able to centrally provide support to the frontline troops from there. However, moving to the UAE allowed us to shorten the supply chain and, importantly, shorten the medevac chain.

One of the key areas that our troops had to maintain to a high standard, apart from weapons familiarity, was the ability to provide first aid to wounded personnel. In 2009, we were able to use the U.S. combat first aid complex located somewhere in the desert in Kuwait. My job was to review this and see if we could organise for the same or a similar provider to train ADF members in combat first aid on site in the UAE.

So off I go –well, not quite. A quick check of my previous pre-deployment training showed that I was out of date by one week! So I had to redo the training, but there was a hitch here. Normally, ADF members went through Randwick Barracks in Sydney for this training. There was accommodation and all the requisite training areas available such as a rifle range. However, this was the year that the Pope visited Australia... and guess where they decided to accommodate all the ADF personnel who were attending and/or working in and around the areas the Pope would be? Yes, Randwick Barracks. So my training had to be redone at Enoggera Barracks in Brisbane!

As usual, I had driven my dogs to Melbourne to be kennelled with my friends prior to this training; then I drove back to Canberra and then flew to Queensland. When I returned to HQ JOC from Queensland, I had about a week before I deployed. I was taking two army members with me, Maj Brett Dick and his warrant officer, both from the medical corp. I had served with Brett before on OP Quickstep, so we were well acquainted.

Off we went. We flew to Kuwait City and were accommodated again – for me, anyway – in the lines in the USAF base. We were to stay here for about three weeks, during which we were to review the above mentioned training. To understand a little more of how this was done, I will explain what happens. When U.S. or Allied troops come into the designated warzone, they have to become acclimatised. This can take two weeks to get used to the heat and the sand. Before they deploy to the frontlines, they move from the relative comfort of air-conditioned tentage to a less salubrious setting.

Thus we headed out into the desert...waaaaaay out. It was a real eye opener. The only road was paved and stretched out for kilometres. The sand wafted across the road, which was intermittently bordered by concrete crash barriers. This was to keep any vehicles from straying into the minefields, which still littered the area. As well, all the vehicles that had been destroyed during the First Gulf War were strewn around the landscape, some only metres from the road. They had just been left where they were destroyed. It was quite a sad sight, noting that there were a number of sand-coloured ambulances within the wreckage. After about an hour, we arrived at another U.S. military camp. We had the usual security cordon to go through until we reached the next level down as regards to creature comforts. This area was deliberately less comfortable to allow the troops to further acclimatise to their environment.

Located on this base was another firing range and also the combat first aid building. This building was built like an old quonset hut – that is, like a half-pipe. It was covered in heat-reducing layers and had a ten-thousand-litre water tank, filled with imitation blood just outside it, where pipes led into the building. Sounds a bit gory, but you must remember we were in a warzone, and realistic first aid training is vital.

There were a number of computer-controlled mannequins that had serious wounds, in particular massive amputations that caused severe blood loss. As well, the conduct of the course was done in such a way that you really got the feeling you were under fire. Speakers cracked out small arms fire and incoming RPGs and could be done in the dark as well to represent a night fighting situation. Additionally, there were helicopter sounds with associated downdraught to simulate a medevac by air.

Overall, it was pretty amazing. We spoke at length with the contractors, who were a U.S.-based organisation staffed by ex–U.S. defence medical personnel. Each of them had been under fire on many occasions. After a day of watching an entire company of U.S. soldiers pass through the training and with long discussions well under way, we decamped for the USAF base back near Kuwait City. We wrote a report on our deployment for sending to HQ JOC, where the decision would be made to contract this company to set up a CFA training area on the Al-Minhad Airbase.

I had already started to draft the contract to save time if we had an affirmative response from the general. This came in due course, but we had headed back to Australia by then. I am happy to say that the contract was awarded, and those deploying to Afghanistan and/or the small number who remained in Iraq all receive excellent combat first aid refresher training before they 'step over the line'.

Volunteering

In the ADF, there is an old saying: 'Never volunteer for anything.' I suppose that was the norm as some of the jobs may well have been not all that flash. My thoughts were that there were two good reasons to volunteer: first, it may have benefits later on; and second, it may not be that bad after all.

I did volunteer for quite a few jobs over the years, and several were very memorable. Most of these occasions were as a representative of the CO as he (or she) would receive many requests for support from civilian entities such as the Red Cross or RSLs.

Submarine Association — Speech at the Shrine

What must be about fifteen years ago, a volunteer was requested by the CO's office at HMAS *Cerberus* to attend a major memorial for the RAN Submarine Service. The memorial was to be conducted inside the Shrine of Remembrance, located on St Kilda Road in Melbourne. This shrine is where the ANZAC Day march that is conducted through the streets of Melbourne finishes and also where the dawn service is conducted.

I was advised that I had been approved by the CO to attend in his absence and went about preparing a speech. I had prepared many speeches in the past for different events, including visits to schools during my recruiting postings, but this one, I was particularly looking forward to. To be asked to give a speech within the shrine was to be an amazing event.

Those who have ever visited the shrine in Melbourne will attest to the feeling of quiet, contemplative silence in the main chamber. This is located at the top of the staircase that faces towards the city. On this particular day, I made my way to Melbourne from HMAS *Cerberus*, some eighty kilometres away. I was introduced to all the main players and, as I recall, moved to the side to await my turn to speak.

I could feel the closeness of the environment – the magnificent pictorials of navy, army, and RAAF personnel that represented all those past, present, and future members of the ADF. I was called forward and made my speech. It was almost an eerie feeling, standing there, speaking in relatively hushed tones, knowing that I was a part of quite an historic chapter in the navy's history.

Following this, we made our way to one of the many tree plots surrounding the shrine, and members of the Submarine Association planted a tree, and many stories were told, most of which I can't repeat. It was an amazing event to be a part of, and I was proud to do so.

The Red Cross

In the mid-1990s, the Cranbourne chapter of the Red Cross wrote to the CO at HMAS *Cerberus* and asked if an officer could be provided to be the guest speaker at their seventy-fifth anniversary function, to be held at the community hall in Cranbourne. At that time, I recall I was the OIC medical school, and the CO asked me if I could represent him in this matter. Although not necessarily volunteering, I jumped at the chance.

I contacted the secretary and asked if there was anything in particular she would like me to speak about, but she said it was up to me. So I had a bit of a think and decided to talk about the actual red cross that is the signature of the organisation and its relativity today. Now you may think that, of course, it's relative, but let me explain.

In modern warfare, technology has improved the effectiveness of weapons of war. During the First Gulf War, the United States had developed 'clever' bombs and missile systems that you could 'fire and forget'. When the enemy was detected, the missile could be locked on and launched, and the crew that fired it could then withdraw or concentrate on the next target. Unfortunately, the target was often not fully classified, and field ambulances and field hospitals could be hit as the Red Cross that denoted these units may not have been seen as the missiles were fired from some way away.

I discussed this and offered thoughts about how this may be avoided in future conflicts by GPS or electronic tagging that would lessen the likelihood of accidentally destroying what is, under the Geneva Convention, a non-viable target. I was surprised some months after this to receive a letter through the CO from the headquarters of the Red Cross in Geneva thanking me for my input into this issue, which had been realised, but a remedy was yet to be forthcoming. The ladies at Cranbourne Red Cross were very chuffed at this too.

The Defence Medal

A decade or so ago, the ADF decided to initiate a new medal for serving and past personnel who had completed their initial period of enlistment. Back in the 'good old days', the only medal (gong) you really ever saw was the yellow-and-blue Parramatta Medal, which was awarded for fifteen years' service. So even though you may have served a reasonable length of time – say, ten years – and then left the ADF, there was no recognition for your valued service.

The introduction of this was well received, especially by those who had completed their service many years ago. It was a monumental task to find and issue medals to all those who were entitled. So volunteers were called for to help with this. I was tasked with awarding the gongs to members of the Cranbourne RSL and did so at a quite moving ceremony held at Cranbourne. It was a great event and only took a relatively short time but was definitely worth the time to see the recipients, including many Vietnam veterans, receive their just entitlements.

Royal North Shore (RNS) Hospital

When I was posted to HMAS *Penguin* in 2005–2008, I was able to be a part of many operations overseas, but one of my voluntary duties was to speak to the staff at RNS when they requested a guest speaker. The navy and RNS had a very good relationship, and many navy medical staff had done some extra training at the operating theatres or the emergency department to maintain their skills. On this particular day, I was invited to speak about the Bali bombings and another occasion about my time on the USNS *Mercy*. Obviously, the staff at RNS were exceptionally talented in their fields, but my lectures were very well received in that it gave them all an insight to the ADF's capabilities and those of our defence brethren from the United States. It also kept them availed of our requirements for reserve specialist medical staff and the possibility that they could be a part of these types of operations.

As I have already noted, my volunteering had allowed me to do things I never dreamed of. Attendance as the RAN support to Admiral Al-Kayal from the RSN, the presentation of the ADF Long Tan Awards to schools, and many others gave me a great insight into how the navy and the ADF were an integral part of our local communities and also on the larger world stage, and it also allowed me to be a consistent part of the training of many junior personnel, not only in the medical branch but also sailors in general.

My last comment on this subject is to describe how I felt when I was given the opportunity to be the parade commander at divisions at HMAS *Cerberus*.

Parade Commander

As I have previously mentioned, HMAS *Cerberus* is the largest naval training establishment in Australia and is located at Crib Point, about eighty kilometres southeast of Melbourne. One of the rituals we would have to do is called divisions. This is where the entire base population would have a formal parade in full uniform, which was presented to a senior officer, usually an admiral but often the base CO. This occurred on the main parade ground on the base.

I would note here that this area, the parade ground, is hallowed turf. If you ever had to cross it during the day, sailors had to double (run) around the edge to get to the other side. Officers were to march smartly across it, but I always went around the edge. The parade ground is guarded by a very angry man known as the buffer. Woe betide anyone who did not obey the rules, officer or not!

Officers in the ADF are expected to lead by example, to do the right thing at all times. Now I realise that no one is perfect, and sometimes the little things slip through to the keeper, especially if 'no harm is done'. However, my thoughts are that these sorts of things should be avoided at pretty much all costs as complacency breeds contempt, and this can lead to accidents where people may get hurt or worse.

So this philosophy is what kept me on my toes to keep others on theirs. Almost every morning at HMAS *Cerberus*, at 0715 hours, all trainees would gather along Cook Road, in their squads from the different schools and prepared to march to their classes. This had two effects. First, it helped maintain the sailors' ability to march together properly, and second, it sorted out any would-be stragglers because if you missed the march down, you could face disciplinary charges.

During my time as the OIC of the medical school and also as the staff officer supply health training policy (SO SHTP), I was located in either the top deck or second deck of 'A Block', which was adjacent to Cook Road. So every morning I would make sure I was at work before the parade and would stand out on the veranda and watch. Now I'm sure some of you are thinking that I was a bit of a goose (or other inappropriate noun/adjective)) to do this, but I saw it as a part of my duty as an officer. Although the parade was supervised by our gunnery staff at ground level, they did not have the ability to see all that was going on. I did.

As I said, keeping the trainees on their toes was, in my opinion, a good thing to instil in their behaviour because you never knew when this may actually save a life in the future. So I watched. The second someone made an error or was talking to their mate or just mucking around, I would bellow from my perch three storeys above and frighten the living daylights out of them. They would immediately look up to where I was, and I would redirect their attention to their front, not look at me. Yes, I enjoyed it, I won't lie, but it had the desired effect. After only a fairly short period of a week or so, the marching improved, there was little or no misbehaviour, and the gunnery jacks (sailors) were very happy with me! I did hear one rumour sometime later, noting that my medical school trainees were also required to march, that I had acquired a nickname ...They called me 'God' as my voice came from above to keep them on their toes. True!

As I mentioned, the gunnery jacks were happy with me as it helped them, and after some time, one of my mates in the gunnery training school called and asked to see me. So I went to have a brew with him, and he asked if I would like to be the parade commander for the upcoming CO's divisions. Well, of course, I jumped at the chance. As I've said before, if you volunteer for something, you never know where it may lead, and this was the case with this.

I undertook some training in regards to what words were required for me to use to control the parade. Mind you, I had been to enough division parades over the years, so I knew them reasonably well. I would also mention here that on the day, as the parade evolves, there is a young sailor standing behind the parade commander with the wording written down, and he whispers the orders if you forget them. So my first experience went well –a lovely sunny day, not too hot, a coolish breeze keeping everything ticking along nicely. When it was over, I reported to the gunnery staff to discuss any shortcomings on my behalf, but they were happy with how it went.

Then they asked the question 'Sir, would you like to do it again?'

Again, I jumped at the chance. I believe I was the only medical administrator up to that time ever to be the parade commander at HMAS *Cerberus*.

It wasn't until sometime later that I found out who the reviewing officer was to be. My first effort had been for the CO, as I mentioned. The next one was probably the biggest divisions you could get other than if the Queen or the Governor General were in attendance. The next divisions was to be reviewed by the CN, the most senior naval officer in the RAN, and it was to be his last before he retired!

Now my civilian friends reading this may think I'm overstating the issue a bit, but this was a big deal. The top man was coming to have a squiz, and obviously, we had to get it right. We therefore had a number of practice runs so that we sharpened up our marching and ensured our dress uniforms were up to scratch. This actually involved the trainees and staff bringing these uniforms to work about a week before the parade to have them inspected by my senior chief and other officers under my command. If they were not good enough, you were sent off to buy new shirts or trousers etc. and had to re-present them.

Came the day, and all was going to plan. This was not to last too long, of course. The parade had fallen in – that is, they were in their squads and had had a pre-inspection done again for last-second straightening of lanyards, check on shoes, etc. When all was ready, the CO, who was in his office, was informed that he go into his car and prepared to move off to the parade ground. The CN was in his car and was supposed to follow a minute later. This allowed the CO to arrive and take up his position to greet the admiral; then they would walk over to the squads and inspect them. By this time, the error had been made. Instead of waiting the one minute, the admiral's car arrived directly behind the CO, at the same time. This literally buggered up the whole routine at this point as during the minute break, I was supposed to hand over control of the parade to the XO. This did not occur as I had no time to do it. So thinking quickly, I just carried on with the XO's job as well. Not a biggie – the sailor with the directions was still feeding me lines, and I played my part.

At the end of the inspection, the admiral stood on the dais and gave a speech about his career, how things had changed, and how more change was coming. At the conclusion of this, which took about half an hour, the final stages of the parade were to occur. I was called to the front to start the march past, similar to those seen on TV in Russia or China where the troops march past a senior officer or the President and salute. So I kick it off, the band is playing, and the squads are timed to move off at different times to allow an orderly movement of the sailors. My part was just about over –and then the troops let us down. The marching was appalling! They were supposed to be in straight lines as they passed the dais so the admiral could see, but every squad looked like a dog's hind leg! It was really woeful. As I was close to the dais, even with the band playing, I could hear the admiral's 'not so pleasant' comments about this. However, we got through it pretty much unscathed.

There were only a few incidents of collapse, but they had been treated quickly by the ever-present medical teams, but there were two repercussions. First, the parade was circled back to their original positions to wait. Once the admiral and CO had left, the gunnery jacks ripped into everyone for their piss-poor efforts. The other slight downer for me was I ended up being chastised by the XO for not handing over the parade to her at the appropriate time. I think I explained that well enough above, but as happens, sometimes things go a bit awry, and no matter how hard you try, you cop it in the neck.

Cousin Clare

I have had many moments during my career where I have felt proud of other members of the ADF and the job they do. I am particularly proud of my cousin's daughter, Clare Lassam, who joined the navy on 18 January 2010 as an aviation technician in avionics. Her training would enable her to work on the systems of the navy helicopter fleet. I must admit, at first, I was a bit puzzled by her choice of branch, but she would soon excel.

Of course, she had to complete the eleven-week recruit school training first and several other small courses before she was posted to RAAF Base Wagga Wagga, where she undertook her next level of training into the ADF aviation world. I was posted to HMAS *Cerberus* at the time she was in recruit school, but I didn't hover. I was a lieutenant commander at the time, and recruit training is difficult enough without having me looking over her shoulder. I did manage to see her though, with CO recruit school's permission, and found she was enjoying the first part of her career, and I was sure she was going to do well. I attended her graduation parade at *Cerberus* along with her parents and saw her off when she posted to Wagga Wagga.

Clare did very well on her courses with the RAAF, and when she was due to graduate, I drove up to the base and attended that as well. It was a great day, and I also ran into some navy types that I knew, including the navy captain who was the head of the detachment. Clare soon posted to the home of the 'birdies', all those sailors in the aviation branch of the navy, HMAS *Albatross*, where I had been a mere thirty-two years before. As expected, she did particularly well in her on-job training at the 'Tross and was soon flagged to undertake technical training on the new helicopters that the navy had purchased from the United States. These were the new variants of the SeaHawk helicopters, nicknamed 'Romeos'. To do this training, Clare was sent to the NAS in Jacksonville in Florida, USA, for twelve months! I have never been so jealous...but I got over it.

Initially, training was on the legacy S-70B-2 Sea Hawk (Bravo) before moving onto the MH-60R (Romeo). Clare did very well in the United States and, as one does, made many friends, which she still has today. On returning to Australia, she settled back into life as a technical maintainer on the helicopter line, but it wouldn't be long before she was on the move – up. She was promoted to leading seaman in March 2017, this rank acknowledged as being one of the most difficult in the navy, but Clare wanted to try something new and passed the selection board for aircrew, and in August 2017, she transferred to this branch and began more training. I must admit, when I was in the navy, I averaged about one course per year of personal and professional training.

Clare aced her training, of course, and became one of the first females (if not the first female) to become an aircrew. She sits in the rear of the helicopter and manages the systems required to hunt submarines and surface vessels in a multi-platform environment as well as be the pilot's eyes in the rear during confined area landings and utility operations on land and at sea and is trained as a rescue swimmer and wireman for search-and-rescue operations.

It was just this week before Australia Day 2021 that Clare helped make history in the RAN. She was in the first all-female crew of the MHR-90 helicopter in the navy, and I believe they conducted the fly-past carrying a huge Australian flag beneath the helicopter through Canberra on 26 January 2021.

I wish I could have been there to see this, but COVID has stuffed up a lot of things over the past year or so. Still, all my ADF brothers and sisters remain onwatch, protecting our country and helping those in need. So I salute my cousin and hope she continues for as long as she wants in the RAN because I know she is making a difference. Together with my brother Ross, we have served in the Royal Australian Navy for over fifty years, and I know we have all done our best for our country, our mates, and the Royal Australian Navy.

Post-Traumatic Stress Disorder (PTSD) andProstate Cancer

A lot has been said in recent times about post-traumatic stress disorder (PTSD) in the ADF. In my career, the earliest 'intervention', I recall, was the post–Bali bombing meeting that was held for all those who had been a part of the operation. This was conducted at RAAF Base Darwin, where a senior Parliamentarian came in and patted us on the back. That was it, really. However, since that time, things have improved markedly, but there is still a long way to go. It is a sad fact that young and older ADF members and retired members have a higher incidence of suicide during and after service than the general population.

As I said, things have improved, but there is much to do. I was diagnosed with PTSD in 2010 when I was the OIC of the medical school at HMAS *Cerberus*. This was my second time in command of the school, which I have always felt was a pinnacle of a MAO's posting.

Before I was officially diagnosed with this disorder, I had started to show signs of not being all that well. I knew something was wrong but tried my best to get on with the job. I was posted to HQ JOC in 2008, and my boss at the time, LTCOL Kim Sullivan, and my RAAF and army colleagues noticed that I did not seem all that well, and I was advised to go and seek help through our medical system. I was then provided with an appointment with a psychiatrist and trundled off to see him. On that day, I was a bit of a mess mentally, and not long after the appointment started, the psychiatrist said the weirdest thing: he asked why I hadn't killed myself yet! To say I was taken aback is an understatement, and once I got out of his office, I never went back. Funnily enough, this shocking statement made me feel a bit better, and my stress levels decreased for the next little while.

I posted to HMAS *Cerberus* yet again (I love the place), as the OIC of the medical school, but I was not well. I was OK for a little while, but it became obvious to my staff that I wasn't coping. Several of my senior staff had a chat to me, and I thank them unreservedly for their compassion and also their guts to come to a senior officer and tell him that they thought I was not well. I especially wish to thank then chief petty officer Victoria Brading, who had several 'deep and meaningful' chats with me. I went to the health centre and saw the medical officer who referred me to the base psychologist, Jackie. I had known Jackie for about twenty years and had worked closely with her during my several postings to the medical school, when she helped a number of my trainees who were struggling with their training.

After several appointments which brought to the surface the many traumatic events I had been part of, she suggested I be referred to the outpatient's facility at the Austen Hospital in Melbourne. This was a part of the old repatriation hospital which had stood in Fairfield since World War II. Ward 17 (the psych ward) was brand new, and as an outpatient, I was admitted to the three-month program. This required three days a week full time in the hospital environment on the PTSD treatment program. There were ten people on the program I attended; I was the only still-serving member. All the others were Vietnam veterans and one being a sailor who had served in Iraq.

It was quite confronting to start with, as the reader would probably guess –ten blokes sitting in a circle with psychiatrists and psychologists talking about the stuff that brought them there. Learning about the condition was a huge step, especially for those who were less inclined to understand or really want to understand why they were like we were. It was not easy for anyone, and I really felt sometimes I didn't deserve to be there. The Vietnam veterans had been pilloried for years after they returned from the war, and I can't imagine the hell they went through over there and moreso when they came home to Australia. The sessions were interspersed with one-on-one therapy, and by the end of three days, we were all exhausted. This, as I mentioned, went on for three months.

There were others in attendance at different courses, mainly police, ambulance officers, and firefighters.

I made some lifelong friends on the program and remain in contact with several of them today. We all had different levels of response, usually depending on how long we had been untreated. The Vietnam veterans found it particularly difficult. One of the follow-up programs was conducted at a different place, a children's farm in the Dandenong Ranges. It was for the same group but with partners. At that time, I did not have a partner but attended alone anyway. This program helped not only us but the wives as well, helping them gain a better understanding of what we were dealing with.

I vividly recall one moment which I'll never forget. This particularly deals with a symptom of PTSD, that being hypervigilance. I had a pretty bad case of this, and it became apparent to one of the wives. We were sitting in a circle as usual, and I was facing a large window that looked out over the farm area and up a well-wooded hill. Right through the middle of this ran a local train line. Sounds pretty tame, but to me, it was an accident waiting to happen. As the leader of the group was speaking, a train suddenly appeared from the left and sped across the hillside until it disappeared behind the tree line. I jumped –pretty high, apparently – and this was noticed by the wife of one of the other guys; she was sitting beside me.

She didn't say anything at first, and during the afternoon tea break, she asked me what had happened. I told her I was very hypervigilant and explained to her that from the second the train appeared from the left until it disappeared behind the trees was a matter of seven to eight seconds. In that time, I had already analysed what I was going to do if it had derailed. Now this might seem weird to the reader, but when someone has been in so many situations where split-second decisions have to be made with regard to saving someone's life, as I had been, there is a tendency to react immediately, thinking through the worst-case scenarios which obviously may never happen. My mate's wife was quite surprised at this, but it did help her understand a little more, as I hope you, the reader, do.

PTSD has been sometimes misused by people, but I can tell you from experience I would rather not have it at all. Even with all the medication and psychological support, it can be devastating to the sufferer and those in the immediate family/friends or colleagues. I am quite open about my diagnosis, and I am happy to talk to anyone who may be going through similar things. Just yesterday, in July 2021, I was talking to a young lady who has suffered severely from a similar affliction brought on by the lockdowns we have endured here in Victoria. I made it known to her that she could talk to me anytime about anything, and I feel that I may have helped lift the veil of darkness that hung over her. I hope this doesn't sound self-serving or self-indulgent. PTSD, especially among members of the ADF, past and present, is a scourge, and I hope that my little bit in writing this book may help others.

On the whole, I gained a lot from the program, and this helped me continue in the navy for a few more years. Fortunately, my staff back at the medical school had really supported me and had done a great job in my absence. At the end of the three months, I returned pretty much full time to work, but it was still a struggle, and I would be exhausted very quickly. Then came my annual medical.

I will digress here just a little. In August 2010, at a dog show, one of my female friends came up to me and asked, 'Do you like Glenda Cherry?'

Now I had no idea who Glenda was at that time, even though I'd apparently been talking to her only an hour before, and to make matters worse, my PTSD and my medications affected my short-term memory, so remembering people's names was a problem. After a few dates, with things progressing well, I moved into Glenda's place in Pakenham, Victoria. She has several show dogs of the papillon breed. They are small pocket rockets with huge ears that look like butterfly wings, hence the French name 'papillon'. We have been together for over eleven years now, and I owe my sanity (what's left of it) to her. Not long after I moved in with her, I was diagnosed with prostate cancer. She has supported me and looked after me whenever I had to have surgeries and procedures that really knocked me around. We both continue to be involved in the dog showing world, with Glenda showing her papillons and me as sometimes duty medic for the show or, on the odd occasion, being the judge.

Once you reach the age of 50 in the navy, you are required to have an annual medical check-up. This involves a series of tests for eyes, hearing, blood, etc. and an examination by one of our defence medical officers. At this time in the ADF, we relied heavily on civilian health practitioners to support us on our bases. Doctors in uniform were hard to find and were really reserved for frontline units and ships at sea. However, the civilian doctors that we had at *Cerberus* were awesome. I saw Dr Robert Porter, who was not only my MO but also a friend, and I had worked with him for some years. He noted during the examination that some of the tests were a bit off, so I was referred to a specialist. So about a couple of weeks after I had finished my PTSD program, I was advised I had prostate cancer.

Now – and I am being quite open here – I was initially shocked. When you are told you have the 'big C', your world dissolves very quickly, but – and here is another good thing I learned from my PTSD program – I literally said seconds after being told this news, 'Well, how do we beat this bastard?'

There were several treatment options ranging from total removal of the prostate, which has certain side effects, to brachytherapy. This was highly recommended to me by the specialist and consisted of several procedures whereby radioactive pellets were inserted into the prostate to provide a highly targeted dose of radiation that remains inside me but has a short half-life. This means it decays quite quickly and only destroys the specific cancer cells. I had ninety such pellets inserted. Now I won't sugarcoat this. I was uncomfortable for many days, but the procedure(s) were very successful, and as I write this chapter, I am ten years free of cancer! I would like to take this opportunity to thank Dr Porter for pushing me to get tested and Dr Alwyn Tan and Dr Michael Chao for their brilliant surgical skills. I believe if I had not undergone the treatment, I would most likely be dead now, and that would not be a good thing – well, from my perspective anyway. I will also take this opportunity to urge all my shipmates, past and present, to go and get tested. It can save your life.

With both these conditions, I knew that I had to get as well as possible, as quickly as possible, to remain an effective member of the Royal Australian Navy. So what to do? I was pretty crook during all this and needed to rest a lot. It was patently obvious that I could not remain as the OIC of the medical school, so I was posted out of that position and into a temporary position, located in the dental department, and then later into an office in the main administration building. Here, I was tasked with a fairly low-stress position as the accommodation officer. My main job was to improve the standards in which the trainees and those who lived on board maintained their living quarters.

Each trainee block was allocated to one of the schools in *Cerberus*, and the block had a senior sailor (usually a warrant officer) who kept an eye on things. I decided we should increase the number of 'rounds' that were conducted of each block. This, I did about once a fortnight during working hours, and the only person I told was the warrant officer a day or so beforehand, the idea being that each sailor had to maintain a reasonable standard of cleanliness at all times. I also introduced a chit system where I would leave a note in each cabin saying I and the warrant officer had been in there and that they were either doing well or they weren't. If not, I would conduct rounds at 1900 hours on a Friday night... which was designed to change their attitudes and inconvenience them. This system worked very well, and it didn't take too long before most personnel improved.

One other job I used to do, off my own back, was to pick up rubbish from around the depot on my daily walks. I would arm myself with some empty shopping bags, and during my daily exercise walks that my doctors said I had to do, I would pick up rubbish. Apparently, I was noticed by some junior officers (either sub-lieutenants and lieutenants), and at a meeting that several attended with the XO, the subject of rubbish around the establishment was discussed. This was after I had posted out to Victoria Barracks.

One of the junior guys asked the XO, 'Whatever happened to that guy who used to walk around, picking up rubbish?'

They were embarrassed to find out that I, a senior officer, had been doing my bit to keep *Cerberus* clean. I did enjoy these jobs as both my PTSD and cancer treatment had knocked me around a fair bit, but it came time to move on. I had been given a notice that they were looking at making me leave the navy on medical grounds. I must admit, I was quite shocked, and I did request a little more time to see if my condition (PTSD) would improve. So I was posted to the joint health command (JHC) department in Victoria Barracks, Melbourne. I was definitely unwell when I was at JHC, but my boss and the other staff were all aware of that and were extremely kind. I did manage to do a few things as the XO of the unit, and I visited many of our health facilities in Victoria, from RAAF Laverton to Puckapunyal and Sale.

On one occasion, I was asked to go to Sale. Now at that time, I lived at Pakenham, which is an hour and a half closer to Sale, to represent JHC when the CDF, Air Marshall Binskin, was arriving as part of a motorcycle ride from Canberra to Melbourne via Sale to highlight the level of prostate cancer in ADF personnel. I went to this event having only fairly recently been diagnosed and treated for the same thing.

I met the CDF and was standing around, gathering dust (as one does sometimes), when he asked me if I would speak on this. The bloke who was supposed to say some words had pulled out because of further illness, so I was it. It was a tad daunting as I made my way up onto the dais in front of around a thousand people and speak about my cancer and how I got through it. No doubt those who know me would have expected me to make it a funny speech, which I did, but it was quite serious as well. The event was a great success and raised a heap of money for research. It also helped me to further talk about it and also my PTSD. I have taken that attitude right from the diagnoses of both these conditions as I believe talking about them can help de-stigmatise them and possibly save lives.

My position at JHC was as the XO, and I spent about two years here before I was finally discharged on Remembrance Day 2016. My last official job was attending the ceremony at the cenotaph in Pakenham, where I live.

Glenda

I would be remiss and also flogged if I did not mention my partner, Glenda. As you are aware, I was a part of the dog showing world for many years. After my divorce in 2007, I was on my own for three years, but at that time, I was happy with that. I was posted to *Cerberus* in 2010, and I would show my dogs as regularly as I could. This was also the time that I started to develop signs of PTSD, but it was not too bad.

One day at a dog show, one of my friends came up to me and asked if I liked Glenda. I had no idea who Glenda was, but I was promptly informed I had been talking to her about ten minutes beforehand. As I was to find out later, PTSD really does play with your head, and my forgetfulness was a symptom of this. However, my friend pointed Glenda out to me, and I said she was nice. Yep, all over this! I was told to go and talk to her, and funnily enough, I did. I say that because this was not like me as I had also started to crawl into my shell from the PTSD. Anyway, that day, I approached Glenda, and after a chat, we decided to go for a meal sometime. This 'date' was soon upon us and was most memorable as I got a speeding ticket on my way to pick her up. Needless to say, we hit it off, and after six months or so, I moved in with my dogs!

Glenda had a breed of dog called papillons, and I had my bearded collies. Although we both enjoyed going to shows at this time, my mental health was crashing, and I undertook a treatment program at Ward 17 at the repatriation hospital in Fairfield, Melbourne. This lasted three months and greatly helped me, as had Glenda.

As I have mentioned previously, it wasn't long after I completed this treatment that I was diagnosed with prostate cancer. This was pretty devastating to not only me but Glenda as well. She supported me through all the dramas, surgeries, and follow-up medical procedures, and she still puts up with me today (2022). I would like to take this opportunity to thank her for all she has done for me. XXX.

ADF Long Tan Youth LeadershipandTeamwork Awards

I've deliberately left this chapter till last as five years after my retirement, I continue to provide support to these awards by attending the 'end of year' functions that 'my' schools hold. I give a speech in most cases, present the awards, and also speak afterwards to the recipients and/or any students who are interested in possible careers in the ADF. As you will have noted, I am a firm believer in supporting young people and promoting the ADF as a possible career. I had no idea, really, of what the ADF was when I was a kid. I had never met a soldier, sailor, or airman but after I joined and especially in my later career, I wanted to talk to others with the prospect of possibly joining and at least informing them that the option to join the ADF is there.

In 2006, the ADF introduced an award system into Australian schools called the 'ADF Long Tan Youth, Leadership, and Teamwork Awards'. It is an opt-in system where any school could nominate a Year 10 and Year 12 student, each year, to receive the award. This included a monetary prize as well as a certificate and would be presented at each school's presentation evening at the end of each year. The system also encouraged ADF personnel to attend the presentation, if requested, where they could conduct the award and perhaps give a short speech. As sometimes occurs, there will be a shortage of ADF personnel who volunteer to undertake these commitments. I started with three schools in the first year, and I quickly found I enjoyed the events. They are mostly conducted in the evening, but there are a couple of schools that held them during the day.

I had enjoyed the first year so much, I thought I would increase the number of schools I would volunteer to attend. Pre–COVID-19, I was attending ten schools, located mostly near where I live in Pakenham,

Victoria. I had chosen a couple of schools that were some distance away, such as Foster Secondary College, which is located in south Gippsland; Nossal High School, which has their presentations at the Melbourne town hall; and Worawa Aboriginal College, located near Healesville. All 'my' schools are different, as you would expect, from regional to city and, as mentioned, the aboriginal college.

I would just like to mention Worawa a little more as I have really enjoyed presenting there, and also, I have learned a great deal about indigenous culture as we, the ADF, support them. This school was formed in 1983 on aboriginal-owned land near Healesville, Victoria, by Hyllus Maris. The school is a full boarding school, catering for indigenous girls in their middle years of school. The current principal, Aunty Lois Peeler, is an outstanding aboriginal leader who has devoted her life to the education of indigenous girls from all over Australia. Each year, one girl is chosen from each of the different tribes with the expectation that when they have completed their final year at the school, they will return to their families and help create a better life for their people. Up until a few years ago, the school catered for Year 7 to Year 10, but recently, the school has been accredited to also teach up to Year 12. This has increased the possibilities of the students to attend university, and quite a few scholarships have been awarded to successful applicants.

The first time I attended, the presentation was conducted indoors at 1200 hours. It was very warm – well, actually, bloody hot, especially inside – but I was mesmerised by the achievements of the young ladies who attended this school. Not only does the school provide classic teaching in subjects such as mathematics and English, but also, they have a very solid indigenous arts program, including painting, dance, and other cultural subjects. In more recent times, the school built an outdoor auditorium under shade sails, which allows more people to attend, including the local police inspector and other community groups such as rotary. One of the things that I do really enjoy is the smoking ceremony that occurs before the presentation ceremony. One of the local elders, an uncle, conducts the ceremony, which is obviously very moving and a joyous time for everyone present.

Even though COVID-19 has badly disrupted these presentations in 2020 and 2021, I am hopeful that these will once again return this year. I will note here that over the last two years, I did make a video speech which all the schools could access to use in their virtual presentation ceremonies. Don't you just love technology?

As with my other schools, each year, I recognise the youngsters as they come up through the grades and watch how they have matured and excelled in their education. I have really enjoyed these opportunities, and I will continue to support the awards program, which has recently extended to include a new set of awards, the Future Innovator's Awards, so that not only the academic prowess of students but also the science, technology, and VCAL subjects are recognised.

Epilogue

Well, here we are at the end of my book. It has taken some six years to write and thirty-nine years to develop. I have procrastinated at times during the writing sometimes because I could not get motivated and other times because my PTSD and/or prostate cancer played havoc with my mind and body.

I started out writing this at the behest mainly of my civilian friends in the dog showing world; the principals and teachers of the schools I have visited and been proactive with during my career and especially those in which I have over the last ten to fifteen years have asked me to be present for their awards night. However, I would say that the main drive for me to do this has been my wish to promote the ADF, especially the good things we do, and even talk about the bad things and put them in context for my civilian friends who often only see or hear the versions that the media present.

I would also say to my defence brothers and sisters, don't be afraid to talk about your mental health if you do not feel OK. Back in the dim, dark past, the ADF did not look after us as they should have. I know it takes a lot of guts and determination to serve in the ADF and especially to admit when you may not be well. Times have changed, and the ADF is now paying more attention to this, as they should, and those who are not self-conscious about their problems, who speak about it, can help those in the future.

I would hope, as a grumpy old retired lieutenant commander who has not been concerned about how others may see me, that I have been able to help others confront their demons and get help before those demons become overpowering.

I thank you all for reading my book; I hope you enjoyed it as much as I enjoyed living it. Again, I thank all those who came before me, those who served with me, and those who will serve their country in the future. I also thank a young lady who was taken way too soon, but in the short time I knew her, she prodded and poked me into completing this autobiography.

Dedications

I have decided to make two dedications in my book.

First, I dedicate this book to all those with whom I have served during my career, be they navy, army, or air force as well as defence civilians, without whom we literally could not do our jobs. I also remember all those who have made the ultimate sacrifice for their country and their comrades. Thank you all for your service.

Second, I dedicate this to a young lady, Candis Colman. I met Candis at her work in the Priceline Pharmacy in Pakenham, Victoria. She was a published author, and she goaded me, encouraged me, and prodded me to keep writing this book. She was taken from us way too soon, and I miss her.

Glossary of Naval Terminology Used in This Book

Port or Portside	When facing forward or the 'pointy end', port is on the left. Represented by the colour red.
Starboard or Larboard	When facing forward or the 'pointy end', starboard is on the right side. Represented by the colour green.
Bow or Pointy End	The front end of the ship.
Stern or Blunt End	The back end of the ship.
Forward	Any area towards the front from your current position.
Aft	Any area towards the rear from your current position.
Sickbay	Area designated to treat the unwell. Usually midships and slightly forward.
Dogged Down	Big clips to hold a door or hatch closed and used to ensure watertight and airtight integrity within the ship.
Ship's Boat	A small vessel carried by a ship.
Admiral's Barge	A smallish boat used by the admiral as required, very flash.
Gangway	Usually a separate structure to the ship which allows access to the ship via the quarterdeck.
	It is lashed to the deck on the ship, and the other end has rollers so that as the ship moves up and down with the tide, the gangway can easily roll as required.
Very Flash	Really well maintained and looks perfect.

Volun-told	Sort of volunteering, but you don't have an option.
Specky	All cleaned, brass polished, couldn't look better.
Gaiters	Used nowadays by any guard forming on parade. They are white leather and fit around ankles/boots.
Kellick	A sailor rank. Leading seaman. Probably the hardest rank in the navy. Moving from the lower ranks but not quite to the senior sailor level.
Victualler	Pronounced 'vit-ler'. This branch were the providers of the navy (got the food in).
Signals	A special form of communications sent on a defence system.
Oppo	Any other sailor you step ashore with.
Watch On, Stop On	A particularly lengthy time at work.
AO	Area of operations.
Coxswain	Helmsman on a ship/service police.
Medevac	Medical evacuation, which can be by sea, land, or air.
Sea State	The level of roughness of the ocean at a particular time. An international scale.
Triage	Sorting medical injuries for assistance.
Naval Establishment	Any land base supporting navy. Also called a ship and has the prenominals HMAS.
HMAS	Her Majesty's Australian Ship.
Mid-ships	Along the centre line of a ship or a rudder position.
Patch	Term used to describe the quarters set aside for married personnel posted to an establishment.

Working Title

Lieutenant Commander Dave Lassam, RAN — The Man for the Job

An Autobiography of My Thirty-Nine Years in the Royal Australian Navy

Index